Nigel McCarthy

Economic and Business News on Television

Nigel McCarthy

Economic and Business News on Television

How Political and Business Leaders Connect
with Journalists and why Television News is
Addicted to Leaders for Material

VDM Verlag Dr. Müller

Imprint

Bibliographic information by the German National Library: The German National Library lists this publication at the German National Bibliography; detailed bibliographic information is available on the Internet at http://dnb.d-nb.de.

Cover image: www.purestockx.com

Publisher:
VDM Verlag Dr. Müller Aktiengesellschaft & Co. KG, Dudweiler Landstr. 125 a, 66123 Saarbrücken, Germany,
Phone +49 681 9100-698, Fax +49 681 9100-988,
Email: info@vdm-verlag.de

Produced in USA and UK by:
Lightning Source Inc., La Vergne, Tennessee, USA
Lightning Source UK Ltd., Milton Keynes, UK
BookSurge LLC, 5341 Dorchester Road, Suite 16, North Charleston, SC 29418, USA

ISBN: 978-3-639-00881-4

ACKNOWLEDGMENTS

I am very grateful to Rodney Tiffen, Rodney Smith, John Henningham and Fran Humphryis for their generous and creative contributions to this project. I am also very grateful to those people who made themselves available for interviews.

My wife Sarah deserves very special thank you for her love, patience and support.

TABLE OF CONTENTS

Appendix 2: Coding for Television Content Analysis June-July 2004.

TABLES

Chapter 4

(nil)

Chapter 5

(nil)

Chapter 6

Conclusion

(nil)

INTRODUCTION

This research arises from a central conundrum: television news and current affairs is the most used and most credible source of information for people in western societies, such as Australia,[1] and the nature of business and economic practices, policies, institutions and controls are central to the well-being of those people and societies. The quality and nature of information provided by journalists is an important part of decision-making and the exercise of power in those societies. Yet it has been argued that television journalism has great, perhaps insuperable, obstacles in covering business and economic developments. These obstacles include television's need for visual material and appetite for dramatic events, the complexity of some business and economic issues, the impressionistic nature of television, and the personalisation of issues. A major question is how these considerations have influenced economic and business debate.

News and Current Affairs Television in Australia

Television in Australia marked its first half-century in 2006. Sydney's TCN 9 commenced broadcasting on 16 September 1956. The first news program went to air the following evening. Current affairs programming started in 1961 with the ABC's *Four Corners* program. Australians looked to the United States and Britain for news and current affairs models and echoed what was being done in those countries. The resources committed to news and current affairs television in Australia, however, were relatively limited. Commercial and government interests imposed further constraints on content on the commercial stations and public station respectively.

This book will explore why news and current affairs on Australian free-to-air television developed as they did. It will consider some related issues in economic and business reporting in print and developments in pay television and the internet and identify some

---

[1] Pearson, Mark, and Brand, Jeffrey (2001). *Sources of news and current affairs*, Sydney, Australian Broadcasting Authority. p. 236.

issues that are media specific or media common. It will look at how technology shaped news and current affairs coverage and how political elites turned technological developments to their advantage. Who benefits from the access politicians have to television? How does this access differ from that of business elites? The oil shocks of the 1970s, globalisation and economic reforms of the 1980s and 1990s - such as the float of the Australian dollar, banking deregulation and changes to superannuation - altered the economic environment of Australians with economic coverage becoming an important part of political coverage. How are these different developments related?

The direct ownership of shares by Australians has soared over the past two decades from 9% in 1986 to 20% in 1997 to 44% in 2004. Total direct and indirect ownership has risen from 16% in 1991 to 55% in 2004.[2] Australia has one of the world's highest levels of private share ownership.[3] As this growth accelerated in the 1980s Australians needed financial and economic information. The business community needed ways of reaching the public to market their products and for the support of their activities. Television was by then already regarded as presenting the fairest and most unbiased news[4] but what are the news values television brings to economic and business news and information?

Propositions

The research and analysis for this project was informed by a number of propositions. First among them is that television is driven by technology. It cannot exist without the means to allow vision and sound to be captured, stored, manipulated and transmitted. Television is the result of newsworkers endeavouring to use this technology to organise the limited images of all that is happening in the world and to present those images in a brief and coherent manner. Those images are therefore framed in two ways; in the narrow sense of what is actually in the viewfinder of the television camera and in the broader sense of where the camera is pointed. Television can also carry several levels of meaning. Some are intended and consciously

---

[2] Australian Stock Exchange. Shareownership in Australia. 2004 Study (for 2004 figures). Downloaded 15 March 2006. http://www.ask.com.au/research/market_info/history/share_ownership.htm
[3] Australian Stock Exchange (2005). International Share ownership 2005. Downloaded 7 Sept. 2006. http://www.asx.com.au/resources/pdf/international_share_ownership_summary_05.pdf
[4] Western J.S. and Hughes, Colin A. (1971). *The mass media in Australia – use and evaluation*. St Lucia, University of Queensland Press. p. 119.

recognised and others might be unintended and sub-consciously recognised. This book will explore those meanings.

These limits of television run the risk that the remote, the unexpected, the un-recognised, the non-visual and the not-looked-for go unreported. News values are biased toward the exceptional and the visual demands of television magnify this. Television newsworkers operate with limited resources in terms of technology (the utilization of scarce camera crews), time (for research, to travel to locations and to edit material), and the limited on-air time that is available to them (that requires brevity in reporting). Newswork on daily programs is process-driven and repetitive in terms of broadly following the same steps: identifying (discovering or being assigned) a report topic, researching the developments, finding interviewees and locations, shooting footage and finding vision, preparing the script and editing the report.

A second proposition is about the nature of the television industry. The Australian television model is of mixed commercial and public broadcasting. The argument that the media *is not* 'just another business' has resonance for those who are concerned about the impact of the media on, for example, national debate and attitudes.[5] However for others the media *is* 'just another business' and subject to similar cost and profit equations, consumer demands and shareholder judgements as any other business. Commercial considerations help shape what is presented in television news and current affairs just as they do in other media forms and other commercial activities. The Australian Broadcasting Corporation (ABC) does not have to attract advertising support but the ratings for the ABC are scrutinised and are largely used to measure the success of programs. The ABC is funded by government and is subject to political influence through the government's selection of board members and political pressures such as comment by politicians and interests groups and parliamentary activity. The commercial and public broadcasters alike therefore see their interests best served by broadly supporting political, social, cultural and economic orthodoxy.

A third proposition is about the nature of interviewees who appear on television. Politicians value the exposure that television gives them and the public has come to expect politicians as

---

[5] For further consideration of this see Schultz, Julianne (ed.) (1994). *Not just another business: journalists, citizens and the media*. Sydney, Pluto Press.

generally having to submit themselves to media scrutiny. How politicians manage this - by restricting their appearances to brief occasions such as doorstop interviews, by restricting their appearance to one medium or one program, by appearing and attempting to avoid particular topics and to shape the nature of interviews or reports - is part of political management and influences what audiences receive. Business leaders are less accountable and might seek to appear only when coverage is positive but the importance of their media performance has been growing.

A final proposition is that television news and current affairs (and television overall) is capable of making major contributions to ideational change. The combination of a strongly crafted message and powerful visual material can have enormous impact despite the relative brevity of news and current affairs reports. Ideas do not always require lengthy explanation or detailed analysis. As television news reports and the narratives presented by interviewees or newsworkers however, are not of uniform quality, well presented material will have a strong impact but badly presented material will have little or negative impact.

Research Design

This book results from three major research strategies. The first examines the history and continuing development of television and its relationship with other mediums such as print and the internet. This research draws on the major histories of broadcast and print media and journalism, as well as biographies and other memoirs and newspaper articles. This material reveals general and specific issues surrounding political and economic and business journalism at particular junctures in Australian history. This literature also identifies perspectives - for example the emphasis on conflict and consensus or the primacy of celebrity - for the examination of Australian television.

The content analysis of economic and business reports in five generalist and specialist programs that went to air in Sydney from 1 June to 4 July 2004 is the second research strategy. The generalist programs are the weeknight 6.00pm *Channel 9 News*, the top-rating commercial news, the weeknight 7.00pm *ABC News*, the main news program on the major public broadcaster, and *The 7.30 Report* on the ABC because of its reputation as Australia's leading serious weeknight current affairs program. The specialist business programs are

Business Sunday, at 8.00am on TCN 9, the longest-running business program on Australian television, and *Inside Business*, at 9.45am Sundays on the ABC as the national broadcaster's major business program.

The economic and business reports in these programs are examined by quantitative categories such as the topic of the report, the number and role of interviewees, the nature of the institutions represented, the nature of interview events, the origin of vision, graphics and durations. The reports are also examined for qualitative characteristics such as how the elements in specific reports come together, the nature of the vision (for example the relationship of the visual material to what is being reported or how Prime Minister John Howard uses the Australian flag as a backdrop) and specific terms (for example loaded language) used by interviewees and newsworkers. This combination of objective and subjective analysis is necessary because the visual and aural nature of television means communication takes place in a number of different ways.

The third strategy of this research is 15 elite interviews conducted by the author. The interviewees have experience in economics, politics, business or the media. Their perspectives are presented on political, economic and business events they have participated in or observed or television programs they have been involved with. The interviewees' more general impressions about the nature of television's coverage of economic and business affairs are also considered.

Organisation of Book

Television is both criticised and praised but few commentators doubt its influence. For example Postman[6] asserts that television turns discourse into entertainment and makes serious debate a nonsense. Norris, however, disputes the claim that television causes civic disengagement and writes: "... the direct effects of watching television news are either neutral or else serve to encourage political interest, efficacy and knowledge."[7] Of television's influence Iyengar and Kinder comment: "... television news obviously possesses the

---

[6] Postman, Neil (1985). *Amusing ourselves to death: public discourse in the age of show business*. New York, Viking.
[7] Norris, Pippa (1998). *Blaming the messenger: television and civic malaise.* Paper for the Public Trust and Democratic Governance in the Trilateral Democracies. Bellagio, Italy, 29 June - 3 July. p.1.

potential to shape ... public opinion profoundly ..."[8] and McClure and Patterson state: "...TV can dramatically increase salience of some issues ...".[9]

In examining and reflecting this debate in terms of economic and business news on Australian television this book is organised into six chapters. These examine the overall development of news and current affairs on Australian television and the emergence of economic and business coverage in particular. The influences that shape economic and business coverage are considered, as is the contribution of television news and current affairs programs to economic and business debate.

Chapter 1 considers the history of news and current affairs programs on Australian television and the influence of developments in the US and Britain. The supply of programs is shaped by factors such as management decisions, budgets, television schedules, technology, sources of news material, newsworkers and production processes. Shifting, and sometimes conflicting, demand from different groups such as audiences, advertisers and sources, such as politicians, also shapes programs. These supply and demand forces always influence television but in particular fuelled a boom in economic and business coverage on Australian television during the 1980s.

What is currently presented in economic and business coverage in generalist and specialists programs on Australian television is analysed in Chapters 2 and 3. The news values that newsworkers apply, consciously or otherwise, influence which issues or events are covered and how they are presented to audiences. Visual material is crucial to television yet newsworkers are constrained by costs and logistics and the visual images audiences see are influenced by handout and file footage and the convenience of events and pseudo-events. News sources - individuals and institutions - compete for air time and impact and individual reports and programs contain varying numbers of points of view. Overall politicians are the dominant voice.

Television viewers are presented with carefully orchestrated visions of the political processes

---

[8] Iyengar, Shanto and Kinder, Donald R. (1987). *News that matters - television and American opinion.* Chicago, The University of Chicago Press. p.1.
[9] McClure, Robert D. and Patterson, Thomas E. (1976). Print vs. network news. *Journal of Communication.* April 1976, 26.2. p. 23.

and economic decision-making and capitalism. But who does the orchestrating? Chapters 4 and 5 discuss the contribution news and current affairs on television makes to the debate on economics, politics and business. Politicians and business leaders alike are accorded celebrity status by television. Members of both groups employ techniques such as controls on access by newsworkers and manipulation of issues by media advisors to obtain beneficial coverage or to slant the debate to their point-of-view and present contrasting casual narratives to promote perspectives on history or to support policy options. Television takes full advantage of the information subsidy offered by both these groups and there is evidence that television newsworkers are willing to limit the scope of their questions in order to obtain access to newsmakers.

Recent developments in broadcasting and the internet are examined in Chapter 6 for an indication of the nature of economic and business news in the future. Specialist business channels such as CNBC and Bloomberg have been developed for pay television and are delivered via satellite and cable. Channels such as these are available in most parts of the world and their audiences are growing, particularly in developing nations. Pay television and the internet are making economic and business news, information and comment available to audiences that would not have been exposed to this material in the past. Critics of these outlets say they are exporting US-style capitalism and threaten existing values and communities. At the same time these developments are blurring the distinction between news and information, altering and challenging the role of newsworkers and forcing change on media organisations.

CHAPTER 1

THE DEVELOPMENT OF TELEVISION NEWS IN AUSTRALIA

No journalistic age was ever given a weapon for truth with quite the scope of this
fledgling television.

Edward R. Murrow[10]

BACKGROUND

The first decade, from the mid-1950s to the mid-1960s, of television in Australia laid the
foundations for what Australians see on television today. At the end of that period news
programs featured an authoritative presenter behind a desk introducing reporter-packaged
items; a format that remains the standard today. Current affairs programs such as *Telescope*,
Four Corners and *This Day Tonight* introduced longer-form reports and interviews on topics
that ranged through political, economic, social and cultural material and laid the basis for this
constantly shifting genre. The technology developed by the end of this period - videotape for
storage and coaxial cables and satellites to transfer material - made immediate national and
global television available.

The 1980s brought a boom in the coverage of economics and business on television. The
factors behind this growth included greater public participation in investment, greater
awareness of economic issues, the ambition of television stations to widen their appeal and
maximise revenue and, in Australia as in Britain and the United States, as Parsons and Hird
comment " … significant cultural change in attitudes toward money and profits, as well as

---

[10] Bernhard, Nancy E. (1999). *U.S. television news and cold war propaganda*. Cambridge, Cambridge
University Press. p. 51.

reflecting the perceived 'usefulness' of economics."[11] These economic and business programs drew on the established news and current affairs genres to create a general look and approach that is still used. The 1980s also highlighted the challenges of reporting economics and business. These challenges remain and provide a framework for examining current programs and journalism throughout this research.

Different aspects of television in Australia are documented in a range of material. The reports of the Australian Broadcasting Control Board (ABCB)[12] and its successors offer a year-by-year perspective on the development of television. Inglis,[13] on ABC television, and Souter,[14] on the television activities of John Fairfax and Sons, offer broad institutional histories. The relationship between television and politics is explored by Curthoys,[15] Grattan,[16] Tiffen[17] and Western and Hughes.[18] The nature of television in Australia and its social impact is examined in a variety of works by Cunningham and Turner,[19] Hall,[20] and Windschuttle.[21] News process and newsworkers are examined by Henningham[22] and Schultz.[23] Television ratings are examined by Gerdes and Charlier.[24] Popular histories included Beilby[25] and Davies.[26] Some of these are straight-forward historical accounts of television, for example Inglis, while others

[11] Hird, Christopher (1989) referred to by Parsons, Wayne. *The power of the financial press: journalism and economic opinion in Britain and America.* Aldershot, Edward Elgar Publishing Limited. p. 209.
[12] For example: Australian Broadcasting Control Board (1957). *Ninth Annual Report.* Canberra. Commonwealth Government Printer.
[13] Inglis, K.S. (1983). *This is the ABC.* Melbourne. Melbourne University Press.
[14] Souter, Gavin (1981). Company of heralds – a century and a half of publishing by John Fairfax Limited and its predecessors 1831-1981. Melbourne, Melbourne University Press.
[15] Curthoys, Ann (1991). Television before television. *Continuum: the Australian Journal of Media and Culture.* Vol. 4 No. 2.
[16] Grattan, Michelle (1996). Sharing the same kennel; the press in Parliament House. in (eds.) Disney, Julian and Nethercote, J.R. *The house on Capital Hill - Parliament, politics and power in the national capital.* Leichhardt, The Federation Press.
[17] Tiffen, Rodney (1989). *News & power.* North Sydney, Allen & Unwin.
[18] Western J.S. and Hughes C.A. (1971). *The mass media in Australia - use and evaluation.* St Lucia, University of Queensland Press.
[19] Cunningham, Stuart and Turner, Graeme (eds.) (1993). *The media in Australia – industries, texts, audiences.* St Leonards, Allen & Unwin.
[20] Hall, Sandra (1976). *Supertoy: twenty years of television.* South Melbourne. Sun Books.
[21] Windschuttle, Keith (1984). *The media – a new analysis of the press, television, radio and advertising in Australia.* Ringwood, Penguin Books Australia Ltd.
[22] Henningham, John (1988). *Looking at television news.* Melbourne, Longman Cheshire.
[23] Schultz, Julianne (1993). *Reporting business – a report into the attitudes, values and practice of business, finance and economics journalism in Australia.* Sydney, Australian Centre for Independent Journalism.
[24] Gerdes, Peter and Charlier, Paul (1985). *TV news – that's the way it was.* North Ryde. Australian Film and Television School.
[25]Beilby, Peter (1981). *Australian TV – the first 25 years.* Melbourne. Thomas Nelson Australia.
[26] Davies, Brian (1981). *Those fabulous TV years.* North Ryde, Cassell Australia.

offer more ideological assessments, such as Windschuttle's perspective that the media should be seen "… as arenas of conflict between the social classes …"[27],. These works, along with international material, also inform the examination of the current practices of television journalism today.

There are both practical and theoretical challenges in examining the history of television and of a particular program area, such as news and current affairs. The practical problems of the preservation of television material are highlighted by Alysen who writes, for example, that the Australian government ScreenSound Australia archive holds only one news item from 1956, two from each of 1957 and 1958 and six from 1959.[28] This writer also has first hand experience of the difficulties in finding television news archive material. These difficulties come from technical difficulties in recording the news reader links and the insert items of news bulletins until the advent of videotape, the decay of archive formats, material not being returned after being accessed for a later report, changes in shooting format from film to tape in the 1980s, changes in tape formats since then, practical difficulties in storing large amounts of archive news material and archive news material being lost, destroyed or discarded when television stations move locations as many have in recent years. The use of print archives to study television poses questions as to how affiliations and rivalries between print and television organisations may have influenced coverage and the attitudes of newsworkers in one medium to a rival medium.

Jacka considers challenges such as the kind of history being undertaken, the standpoint and stakes of the examination and the 'common sense' ways television offers itself for historical study, such as by chronology, and how the theorisation of television history is limited.[29] This chapter looks at news and current affairs on television from a demand and supply perspective. The key players are media owners, media institutions, the electronics industries, newsworkers, unions, politicians, political institutions, interest groups and audiences. The factors driving greater coverage of economic and business issues are also explored.

---

[27] Windschuttle. op cit. p. x.
[28] Alysen, Barbara (2001). Today's news tomorrow: researching archival television. *Media International Australia incorporating Culture and policy*. No. 99 – May 2001. p. 17.
[29] Jacka, Liz (2004). Doing the history of television in Australia: problems and challenges. *Continuum: Journal of Media & Cultural Studies*. Vol. 18, No. 1, March.

SUPPLY OF NEWS

News on TV

There is no requirement under legislation for commercial television stations to supply news programs.[30] Program standards for news however were set out ahead of the introduction of television by the Australian Broadcasting Control Board. The voluntary nature of news programming is emphasised in Section 22 of the standard that states " ... a station which undertakes to provide a news or newsreel service ..." then adds news should be presented accurately and impartially, that each news session should be well-balanced and comprehensive, that commentary and analysis should be clearly distinguished from news, that news should be in good taste, that pictorial representation should not be misleading or sensational and carefully selected to ensure fairness, that no advertising matter should be offered as news or included in the contents of a news bulletin or newsreel although advertisements during 'natural breaks' are accepted.[31]

Richard Boyer, the ABC chairman, and Frank Packer, the proprietor of TCN 9, illustrate some of the attitudes toward news around the time of the introduction of television. Boyer believed the news could not be televised and that radio news - without visual material - should be read on television. Petersen summarises Boyer's concern as:

> The "visual showmanship" of the "production boys in the TV studios" would undermine the proven principles of news. Radio news could be tightly edited and controlled. TV news, in his view, could not because many of those involved, editors, cameramen, graphic artists, were not journalists.[32]

Boyer's concerns over televising the news may have been right, but for the wrong reasons.

---

[30] For example see Australian Broadcasting Control Board (1973). *Twenty-fifth annual report*. Commonwealth Government Printer. Canberra. p. 116. This is supported by the paragraph no. 451 "Although there is no formal obligation on stations to provide news programmes, all but one metropolitan station (TVQ Brisbane) televised a service of this type during the year."

[31] Australian Broadcasting Control Board (1956). *Television program standards. Determined by the board in pursuance of the Broadcasting and Television Act 1942-1956*. Canberra, Commonwealth Government Printer. p. 12.

[32] Petersen, Neville (1999). *Whose news? organisational conflict in the ABC, 1947-1999*. Australian Journalism Monographs, numbers 3&4, May-November 1999. Brisbane, Department of Journalism, University of Queensland. p. 9

Journalists, as well as editors, cameramen and graphic artists, are all subject to television's demand for visual material and the appetite that creates for staged events or handout footage as well as news values oriented to the visual. Boyer relented somewhat in 1956 when the ABC commenced television broadcasting and for the next three years two minutes of film could be used in the 15 minute bulletin.[33] Petersen examines how ABC television news values were dictated by radio news values developed by W.S. Hamilton, editor-in-chief of news, who " ... reinforced the role of ABC news in legitimating authority and supporting established values and sanctions of society."[34]

Packer was committed to news on television and saw television as an "extension of journalism". Packer thought the guiding principles for a controller of a television station were:

> ... to give the public what they want by way of entertainment, provided it is not obscene and does not transcend the bounds of decency, and to see that you provide news up to the moment as quickly as it can be obtained and, generally, to keep people informed by visual media in addition to the printed word in the Press.[35]

Learning from the United States and Britain

Australian television figures such as Boyer and Packer could look to the US and Britain where, during the 1950s, television news was being developed and television journalism was finding its voice and look. A review of what was happening in those countries illustrates the influences Australians were exposed to. Television news in the US commenced in 1946 with the three-nights a week, fifteen-minute program *The Esso Newsreel* on NBC. Newscasts of the era were, according to Barkin, " ...a pastiche of some information, some advertising, and

---

[33] ibid.
[34] ibid p. 7.
[35] Whitington, R.S. (1971). *Sir Frank – the Frank Packer story*. North Melbourne, Cassell Australia Ltd. p. 217. Note: Whitington thanks Frank Packer for his co-operation in preparing this book however it is not made clear if this quote is from an interview with Packer or from another source. It is also difficult to know if this was Packer's attitude from the first days of television although the emphasis on news in the 1956 reporting in *The Daily Telegraph* might indicate this was the case.

some comment that today is virtually inexplicable."[36] A detailed examination of *The CBS-TV News* on 7 April 1949 reveals the reports covered: price supports for wheat, the United Nations, guerrilla fighters in Greece, an FBI investigation of bond market fraud, Army Day in Washington, a visit by the Brazilian minister for war to the US military academy at West Point, protests in Reykjavik, Iceland, photographs of the nineteen-week-old Charles, the Prince of Wales, and a report on the United Mine Workers Union. Some characteristics of television news discussed elsewhere in this book are already apparent; for example the wheat report uses generic footage of farming, Army Day and the visit by the Brazilian minister are scheduled events that make it easy for cameras to be in place, the Greek guerrillas and the Reykjavik protests display an emphasis on conflict, and the photographs of Prince Charles display a focus on celebrity. Barkin writes " ... there is clearly an emphasis on film for its own sake ... the application of news judgement is not really in evidence, either in the order of stories presented or in the time allotted to each story."[37]

How US television news evolved further is considered by Cox, who was to become the editor of Britain's Independent Television News from 1956 to 1968. Several years after those programs reviewed by Barkin, Cox writes of being in the CBS studio to watch the coverage of the 1953 coronation of Queen Elizabeth II on the cigarette company-sponsored CBS *Camel News Caravan*, presented by Douglas Edwards. Edwards' reading of a commercial for cigarettes, with a picture of a pack on the screen, immediately after the headlines, is first criticised by Cox. Cox however then adds news presentation has become more coherent:

> ... the bulletin which followed had pace and vividness and indeed authority ...
> filmed news reports and interviews were interspersed with the spoken material to
> illustrate and emphasise the news, with visual material presented because it was
> news rather than because it was visual ... stills and diagrams helped out the
> spoken word where no film was available.[38]

Other material in the bulletin included footage of French Foreign Legionnaires in Vietnam, a baseball preview, street interviews about a new roadway in Brooklyn and tornado damage in

[36] Barkin, Steve M. (2003). *American television news – the media market place and the public interest*. Armonk, M. E. Sharpe Inc. p. 28.
[37] ibid.
[38] Cox, Geoffrey (1995). *Pioneering television news*. London, John Libbey & Company Ltd. p. 33.

the Midwest.

The role, impact and nature of news on television was debated in those early days, as it continues to be today. Bernhard writes:

> In its earliest years, denigrated by print and radio journalists, television struggled to establish itself as a legitimate news medium. On the one hand, the technology promised to enhance democracy. It offered unprecedented access for citizens to see government officials at work, to observe their faces, and to evaluate their character. On the other hand, television threatened democracy because it concentrated so much power to shape public opinion into such few hands.[39]

Differing views of television news in the United States during this period are contrasted by Bernhard. For example, A.M. Rosenthal, then the *New York Times* United Nations correspondent, said "Television is not interested in news but in entertainment." On the other hand CBS broadcaster Edward R. Murrow, remembered today for his *See it Now* series and his challenge to anti-communist campaigner Senator Joseph McCarthy, said "No journalistic age was ever given a weapon for truth with quite the scope of this fledgling television." Bernhard concludes:

> The service television offered to high-ranking officials by granting them immediate access to large audiences soon made earlier predictions of the failure of television news sound like sour grapes. Broadcasters earned acceptance as news gatherers, if not credibility as journalists, partly by making themselves indispensable to prominent public figures.[40]

In Britain during the early 1950s the BBC television news was a summary of events prepared by the radio news room and read by an unseen announcer with the only images a clock or a static graphics card. Visual material was left to separate newsreel programs that were judged by BBC management as being more entertainment than news. In 1954, ahead of competition from the newly-created Independent Television, the newsreels were moved to follow the

---

[39] Bernhard, Nancy E. (1999). *U.S. television news and cold war propaganda*. Cambridge, Cambridge University Press. p. 49.
[40] ibid. pp. 50-51.

news and in June 1955 the newsreaders were seen for the first time but remained anonymous - to avoid personalising the news - until they were identified by name 15 months later.[41]

Independent Television started in Britain on 22 September 1955,[42] almost a year before TCN 9 was to go to air in Australia. The news division, Independent Television News (ITN), presented three news programs on weekdays; bulletins of eight-and-and-half minutes at noon and 7.05pm and the main thirteen-and-a-half minute bulletin at 10.00pm with the final five minutes a newsreel. Cox writes that ITN's policy - unlike the BBC but similar to the CBS approach - was to have the news presented by 'newscasters'. These newscasters were people with a distinct personality who would not only present the news but also help decide what would be covered and who would also go out and prepare reports. Cox adds of the bulletins themselves:

> The components of those early television news programmes still reflected their different origins, with radio techniques dominating the spoken word, with film being seen not only, or even primarily, as a visual expression of the news of the day, but having an added pictorial element in its own right, an element which reflected not only the techniques but the news values of the cinema newsreels.[43]

The news values of the newsreels saw events such as flower carnivals or the Shrove Tuesday pancake races included not only because of their visual nature but also because "… they were predictable, and therefore could be sure of providing a story on a thin news week."[44] Predictability of events remains a key element in news coverage today.

Content and Nature of News

Australian media proprietors, program makers and newsworkers looked overseas - via travel or training by visiting experts - to develop their Australian news programs. The programs they developed included the authoritative news reader behind a desk, the use of footage over the news reader and still pictures and graphics and models.

---

[41] Cox. op. cit. p. 45.
[42] ibid. p. 43.
[43] ibid. p. 44.
[44] ibid.

The first television news program went to air on TCN 9 on 17 September 1956 at 7.00pm to 7.15pm.[45] This was just one day after TCN 9 became the first station to go to air with regular programs in what is generally accepted to be the start of television in Australia. *The Daily Telegraph* reported:

> Michael Ramsden, TCN Channel 9 news director, introduced the session. He said dramatic pictures of a bombing and of street-fighting in Cyprus - air-mailed to TCN Channel 9 yesterday - were typical of overseas film material arriving for television. Ramsden introduced Charles Faulkner, news reporter, who told of the end of the [Sydney] postal strike. Other highlights of the news session were films of the Air Force Week display at Richmond, including a fly-past by the Vulcan jet bomber, last Saturday's Rugby Union final, and the Olympic swimming trials. In the last three minutes of the news session Faulkner reported the weather. On a big map of Australia he pointed out the two main weather "highs" and a cold front.[46]

Another item in the bulletin was an interview with former film star Grace Kelly and Monaco's Prince Rainier in New York.[47]

The second bulletin on TCN 9, on 18 September, was also covered in *The Daily Telegraph* and carried reports on then Prime Minister Robert Menzies' return to Australia, an item from the Suez Canal (nationalised by Egyptian President Nasser), footage of Rosewall and Hoad in the US Open tennis singles and footage of the Royal Australian Navy's new Daring Class warship. Of most interest here is Menzies' return and the paragraph: "The telecast showed Mr Menzies' arrival by Super Constellation, police clearing the demonstrators from the airport, and Mr Menzies talking about his mission to Egypt."[48] This paragraph is of interest because of the relative emphasis, as reported by the newspaper, of the television report on the demonstrators. The coverage of Menzies' arrival in the evening news bulletin ahead of the print media reporting the same event the following morning is an early illustration of the same pattern that is repeated today. This is an example of television boosting the salience of newspaper reports that is discussed later.

---

[45] Religious talk and news on TCN Channel 9. *The Daily Telegraph*, 18 Aug. 1956. p. 1.
[46] ibid.
[47] TViewers (sic) hail news telecasts, *The Daily Telegraph*. 18 Sept. 1956. p. 9.
[48] P.M. on Channel 9. *The Daily Telegraph*. 19 Sept. 1956. p. 1.

The report in *The Daily Telegraph* indicates that "police clearing the demonstrators from the airport" was one of the three prominent points in TCN 9's coverage of Menzies' return, or at least one of the three prominent points in the eye of the *Telegraph* reporter. These same demonstrators received no coverage at all in the *Telegraph's* own front page report on Menzies' return. Coverage by *The Sydney Morning Herald* of the same event carried the headline "Not contemplating force – Menzies on Suez Canal"[49] with the demonstrators receiving only seven paragraphs at the end of the 43 paragraph *Herald* report. The emphasis on the demonstrators in TCN 9's report compared to either zero or slight coverage in the print reports illustrates television's appetite for conflict. The *Herald* report continued:

> About 50 university students dressed as Arabs staged a minor demonstration in the public enclosures. They carried banners with the slogans "Take Suez to the U.N.O.", "Our children not for war" and "Ming for King". One of the students said later: "This is nothing political. We just thought we'd come along for a lark."[50]

Almost 50 years after the event it is possible to surmise that the students may have watched the introduction of television and predicted, correctly, that a television crew would be at the airport to record Menzies' arrival. Whatever their motivations, within two days of the introduction of television news it was already recording staged protest events and reporting them in a political context.

The main values that influence newsmakers are consequence, proximity, conflict, human interest, novelty and prominence.[51] Those first two television bulletins display conflict (Cyprus fighting, the postal strike, Menzies' return and the Suez Canal) as the most frequent value, followed by novelty (Air Force Week and the Australian Navy's new ship), then prominence (Grace Kelly). Sport features strongly in the two bulletins with three reports. Event-driven journalism - attractive to television with its limited resources because it is scheduled, predictable and often pictorial - is noticeable in reports such as the postal strike, Menzies' return, the Air Force and Navy reports and the sporting events.

---

[49] Not contemplating force – Menzies on Suez Canal. *The Sydney Morning Herald*. 19 Sept. 1956. p. 1.
[50] ibid.
[51] Masterton, Murray and Patching, Roger (1997). *Now the news in detail. A guide to broadcast journalism in Australia*. 3rd edition. Geelong, Deakin University Press. pp. 15-18.

Just as Cox had found at the start of ITN a year earlier, those first Australian bulletins displayed a taste for the predictable and the pictorial although this was limited as a comment from the 1957 Australian Broadcasting Control Board (ABCB) report reveals: "At times the availability of pictures seems to have influenced the news content, but this has not been so dominant a factor as was expected."[52] News judgement was clearly influenced by visuals and footage although the ABCB report continued that the TV stations had no objection to showing the news presenter when no visual material was available. The report added that the stations were running their news programs at different times to give viewers a choice.

By 3 December 1956 both planned commercial stations, TCN 9 and ATN 7, and the ABC, ABN 2, were on air in Sydney. The television program schedule - a brief three paragraphs in a single column compared to the multi-column guides of today - from *The Sydney Morning Herald* on that day illustrates the prominence of news in the station line-ups. ABN 2 featured 15 minutes of news, newsreel and weather between 7.00pm and 7.15pm. ATN 7 featured 15 minutes of news between 8.00pm and 8.15pm. TCN 9 featured 15 minutes of news and weather between 7.00pm and 7.15pm.[53]

The new stations devoted considerable efforts to their news programs in that first year with the Australian Broadcasting Control Board (ABCB) commenting in the 1957 annual report:

> One of the special features of television is its presentation of news and weather information. It was thought likely that, at least in the early stages, news would be limited to periodical newsreel programmes and a brief summary of the headlines, but all four commercial television stations [note: two each in Sydney and Melbourne] have organised quite extensive news coverage which is supplemented by pictures from local and world sources.[54]

The new licence holders offered news programs to attract viewers and stressed the speed and breadth of television news. The news on ATN is going to be "efficient" with "alert and expert

---

[52] Australian Broadcasting Control Board (1957). *Ninth Annual Report*. Canberra, Commonwealth Government Printer. p. 45.
[53] Today's TV. *The Sydney Morning Herald*. 3 Dec. 1956. p. 8.
[54] Australian Broadcasting Control Board (1957). *Ninth Annual Report*. Canberra. Commonwealth Government Printer. p. 45.

coverage". Fox-Movietone is the "foremost supplier" of newsreels and United Press "has built up a newsreel organisation designed to cover news specially for television". The newspapers have large staffs and correspondents around the world that will be drawn on. Speed and comprehensiveness is of the essence; the cameramen are "a flying squad", the film can get to air in under an hour, Fox-Movietone footage will be "rushed" to Sydney and the news copy will be "flashed" to ATN by teleprinter.[55]

The ABCB made no comment on news programs in the annual reports from 1959 through to 1962. In 1963 the Board reported:

> Coverage of news and current events has been competently undertaken by most stations, which have realised the attraction for viewers of news illustrated with pictorial matter. This type of news programme is in marked contrast to those in which news items are read by an announcer on camera, with no other form of illustration. Most stations operate small film units which, in addition to their news gathering activities, have produced some informative documentary programmes on matters of current interest in Australia and abroad.[56]

The report continued that some stations added depth to news programs with commentary and " ... these statements of editorial policy indicate an awareness by stations of the responsible position they share with the other mass media."[57] Some of the visual images going to air came under scrutiny with the Board commenting it had found it necessary to question the suitability of material such as close-ups of accidents.

By 1966, a decade after television was introduced to Australia, the main evening news programs had much the same style, content and program slot that they do today. ABN 2 had a half hour of news, sport and weather at 7.00pm. TCN 9 and ATN 7 were competing in the same slot at 6.30pm - only half an hour later than today - each with a half hour of news sport and weather. Channel 10 had a five-minute news program at 6.25pm; taking a different approach as it does today with its 5.00pm hour-long news. In moving to a half hour bulletin

---

[55] Fully equipped Services For News. *The Sydney Morning Herald ATN Supplement*. 3 Dec. 1956. p. 5.
[56] Australian Broadcasting Control Board (1963). *Fifteenth Annual Report*. p. 63.
[57] ibid. p. 64.

Channel 9 and 7 were behind the United States where a half hour was introduced in 1963 but ahead of the UK where ITN introduced the half hour bulletin in 1967.

Even as Australian television news developed it was slow to recognise economics and business. Schultz writes "In the 1970s it was rare for the nightly television news bulletins to include information on the day's trading on the stock exchange, or the relative value of the Australian dollar and international currency."[58] Gerdes and Charlier indicate that television did not devote much time to economics and business. Their survey of television in 1978 and 1983 considers business affairs as including primary and secondary industry, takeovers and mergers, economic statistics and reports, trade, money markets, tourism, finance reports and discoveries and new products.[59]

Table 1.1
Business affairs in Australian television news 1978 and 1983
(% of time)

Year	Region	ABC	ATN	TCN	TEN	SBS
1978	Aust.	4.5	1.0	0.9	0.9	-
	Foreign	0.2	0	0	0	-
1983	Aust.	3.9	2.1	2.9	2.1	1.3
	Foreign.	0.4	0.1	0.6	0	0.4

(source Gerdes and Charlier)

The survey indicates that in 1978 the ABC devoted less than 5% of news programming to business affairs yet this is still more than four times as much coverage as the commercial channels. The amount of ABC coverage fell slightly in 1983 while the commercial channels more than doubled their coverage. This expansion of business coverage, although still slight, is due to the interest generated by the entrepreneurs and the business boom of the 1980s. (The categories of the Gerdes and Charlier survey, that excludes government actions such as tax and spending, make comparisons between 1978 and 1983 and the survey categories for this research in 2004, which takes economics and business together, difficult. However, as discussed in Chapter 2, economic and business reports in news programs [excluding sport and

---

[58] Schultz, Julianne and Matolcsy, Zoltan (1993). Business boosters or impartial critics. in Schultz (ed.) *Reporting business – a report into the attitudes, values and practice of business, finance and economics journalism in Australia.* Sydney, Australian Centre for Independent Journalism. p. 9.
[59] Gerdes, Peter and Charlier, Paul (1985). *TV news – that's the way it was.* North Ryde, Australian Film and Television School. pp. 11, 32, 55.

weather] during the June 2004 survey make up 13.7% of news on the ABC and 7.4% on Channel 9.)

News Programming

The quality of the news programs surprised the ABCB, as reflected in the 1957 annual report quoted earlier, but the amount of news programming declined in the following year as the stations established themselves and came to grips with the economics of television. In 1958 the Australian Broadcasting Control Board commented:

> The Board had originally expected that owing to the high cost of collection and presentation of pictures, news programmes would be limited. The surprisingly elaborate news services which were presented in the early stages of programme development have mostly disappeared and the presentation of news services is now much more restrained.[60]

The amount of news and current affairs programming on Australian television is not fixed and varies with the station's programming priorities, sources, news values and budgets. In 1957 news content on all the Sydney stations was 6%, falling to 2.8% in 1959 and climbing again to 3.7% in 1960.[61] The four commercial television stations made losses in the first two years of operation and first turned a profit in 1958-59. It is likely, but not stated in the report, that the funding available for news and current affairs is a function of a station's profitability.

The competition for funding between news and current affairs and other programming strands is illustrated by Peach and his experiences with the current affairs program *Telescope* on Network 10. Peach writes that within the first year of the network going to air:

> ...Ten had underestimated its costs and overestimated its likely revenue, and by the end of 1965 the station was running out of money. It tried to cut costs by cutting local production and went into a tailspin ... The news would disappear in 1966 to be replaced by spot bulletins, and *Telescope* would have to survive with

---

[60] Australian Broadcasting Control Board (1958). *Tenth Annual Report.* p. n/a.
[61] Australian Broadcasting Control Board (1957, 1959, 1960). *Ninth, Eleventh, Twelfth Annual Report (s).*

its existing resources by moving to a later night spot twice a week.[62]

News reports were not restricted by program schedules and big news stories were able to interrupt programming from the earliest days of television. An example of this was ATN 7's coverage of the recapture of jail escapee Kevin John Simmonds on 15 November, 1959, after 37 days on the run. *RTN: Radio Television News* reported on 20 November:

> Simmonds' 37 days of freedom had aroused excited interest everywhere and radio and television stations had provided some graphic broadcasts during the intense police search. TV viewers were well served by films which arrived form the scene of the recapture and dramatic shots of Simmonds and his captors during afternoon and evening programmes.[63]

The ability to supplement the fixed evening bulletins with shorter scheduled headline services and news flashes when needed became a feature of television news in the mid-1960s.[64]

The shifting time slots of the early news programs on the first commercial stations and the ABC was considered previously. Some of the factors that influence the placement of news programs are illustrated by the third commercial station, Channel TEN 10. Channel 10 commenced broadcasting in 1965 and opted for a mid-evening news bulletin that followed the evening feature film. The films however varied in length by up to half an hour so viewers never knew exactly what time the news would start. Peach writes "This is the first law of television ....attracting the evening audiences to your news bulletin and holding them with the programs that followed ... we [also] broke the second law of television, which is that audiences want regularity in their television schedules."[65]

Twenty years later the ABC flouted another law of television, running a news program over the 7.00pm divide, when it tried a major experiment - and failed - in news programming. In March 1985 the ABC dropped the 7.00pm news - the ratings of which had declined from

---

[62] Peach, Bill (1992). *This Day Tonight: how Australian current affairs TV came of age.* Sydney. Australian Broadcasting Corporation. p. 21.
[63] Wide cover of manhunt. *RTN: Radio Television News.* 20 Nov.1959. p. 3.
[64] Australian Broadcasting Control Board (1965). *Seventeenth Annual Report.* Canberra, Commonwealth Government Printing Office. p. 72.
[65] Peach. op. cit. p 20-21.

thirteens in 1978 to 9s in 1984 - and *Nationwide,* the current affairs program that followed the news, to launch a new hour-long program from 6.30pm to 7.30pm called *The National.* The program's key segments were two national news segments and one current affairs segment separated by promotions for upcoming stories. Economics was an important part of the mix with Max Walsh moving from Channel 9 to present comment pieces on political/economic issues. Walsh was joined by ABC political commentator Richard Carleton.

The Australian Financial Review reported:

> *The National* is certainly a great deal better - technically, as well as being more
> attractive and informative - than the old ABC television news and it does show
> promise. But what it will never be is the "equivalent of a high-quality newspaper",
> as its executive producer was reported by *The Australian* as claiming for it. The
> program will apparently be trying to background and analyse events - a function
> which is clearly going to fall largely on Walsh and Carleton. But television is not
> a very suitable medium for doing that job during a news program.[66]

The National was criticised within a week of going to air by veteran ABC newsreader James Dibble[67] and attracted comments such as going "... from disaster to disaster ..."[68] and was taken off air later the same year.[69]

Television scheduling is a black art. The final word on news programming, and why many Australian television news programs hover around the 6.00pm to 7.00pm slot, should go perhaps to Senator James McClelland who, in an aside to Myles Wright, ABCB chairman, reflected on one aspect of Australian culture. McClelland said "The 7.00 o'clock news

---

[66] Solomon, David (1985). Aunty's new show is promising but it must keep the faithful. *The Australian Financial Review.* 12 March. p. 4.

[67] Dibble, James (1985). ABC news is dead, *The Australian Financial Review.* 15 March. p. 41.

[68] Williams, Graham (1986). The fiscal grind goes on ... the ABC will bleed yet again. *The Australian Financial Review.* 17 June. p. 8.

[69] The author was working in commercial television at the time and recalls that several reasons put forward for the failure of *The National* were the difficulty in ordering reports by prominence across the hour, the difficulty in presenting local, national and international news to a national audience and the problem of retaining viewers - who were used to selecting news and current affairs in half hour slots - for a full hour and against competing programs that started at 7.00pm.

probably owes its origin to the fact that hotels used to close at 6.00pm."[70]

Pressures on News: Advertisers, Management and Politicians

The difficulty of distinguishing between news and promotional material, staged events or spin and competing national interests was only partially recognised in the early days of television. For example the one paragraph that deals with news in the 1954 *Report of the Royal Commission on Television* states:

> The Australian Broadcasting Commission informed us that a large pool of documentaries and films produced by large commercial undertakings for public relations purposes, many of which are suitable for television, would be available for national television programs. [71]

The apparent acceptance of " … documentaries and films produced by large commercial undertakings for public relations purposes … " suggests little regulatory concern over the promotional aspects of this type of material.

By 1956 however, the Television Program Standards stated:

> No advertising matter should be offered as news or included in the contents of a news bulletin or newsreel. This does not prevent the televising of short advertisements during natural breaks between recognised sections of a news programme: but no advertisement in the form of a "story", or which could be mistaken by viewers for a news item, should be accepted.[72]

At the ABC it was not advertising but management that restricted television news. Inglis describes ABC managers as "the men in suits"[73] who sought to control the journalism in ABC news. Television news, like radio news, was under the control of the ABC Editor-in-

---

[70] *Senate Standing Committee on Education, Science and the Arts.* Canberra, Commonwealth Government Printing Office. 4 June 1972. p. 89.

[71] *Report of the Royal Commission on television* (1954). Paragraph #296 (of 499) Newsreels and Documentary Films. Canberra, Commonwealth Government Printer. p. 108.

[72] Australian Broadcasting Control Board (1956). *Television program standards.* Section 22f. Melbourne, Commonwealth Government Printer. p. 12.

[73] Inglis, Ken (1992). in Peach, Bill (1992). *This day tonight – how Australian current affairs TV came of age.* Sydney, ABC Enterprises. Foreword. p. 3.

Chief Wally Hamilton, a former chief sub-editor of the *Sun* newspaper. Petersen writes that while Hamilton supported the use of visuals in television news " ... news criteria and reporting were firmly left in the hands of radio."[74] Television had to follow radio's selection of the five or six major stories of the day, radio managers decided what stories were to be covered and how reporters were assigned; there were no reporters assigned full-time to television. Petersen adds that Hamilton:

> ... reinforced the role of ABC news in legitimating authority and supporting established values and sanctions of society. News of good deeds, or "progressive news" had priority. Crime was downplayed, divorce and rape was ignored. There was to be no concentration on "anti-social aspects" of community life. There was to be no criticism of the police ... News of strikes was deliberately limited to state news for fear they might spread.[75]

The editorial failings of ABC television news and related coverage in the early years are also recalled by Raymond:

> There was straight news - read with BBC-like solemnity by former radio announcers in dinner jackets - plenty of sport, a weekly 'news magazine' of non-topical items, and an occasional, brief, illustrated lecture by a university political scientist on 'some faraway place of which we know little' ... Topical background, contemporaneous comment, helpful interpretation was not just in short supply; there simply wasn't any.[76]

The two Sydney commercial stations, TCN 9 and ATN 7, are also criticised by Raymond for failing to do the " ... powerful television journalism that Ed Murrow was doing for the top-rating US commercial network, CBS."[77]

Interference in news and current affairs started at TEN 10 on its opening night, April 5 1965.

---

[74] Petersen, Neville (1999). *Whose news? organisational conflict in the ABC, 1947-1999.* Australian Journalism Monographs, Numbers 3&4, May-November 1999, Department of Journalism, University of Queensland. p.9.
[75] ibid. p. 7.
[76] Raymond, Robert (1999). *Out of the box. An inside view of the coming of current affairs and documentaries to Australian television.* Henley Beach, Seaview Press, p. xiii.
[77] ibid p. 4.

Peach recalls that Reg Fox, then general manager of 10, instructed him that Sir Robert Menzies, the prime minister, was to be at TEN for the opening and that "Sir Robert Menzies was not to be annoyed." Peach, the presenter of a current affairs program called *Telescope,* writes: "To my discredit, I reconstructed the program ... I told [author and interviewee] Donald Horne that the management were anxious that he should not criticise Menzies personally ..."[78]

Management interference at the commercial channels was still in place in 1974 with Stone commenting:

> ... commercial managements too often seemed to regard their news departments as little more than publicity machines to churn out free plugs for other programs or to lend a favour here or there for an important advertiser or business contact. Sir Frank Packer certainly wasn't alone among proprietors in making sure newsroom staff knew which stories were 'safe' and which were too hot to handle.[79]

The willingness of management to interfere with the news was highlighted on 16 August 1974 when TCN 9 and ATN 7 decided not to run a report from the Joint Parliamentary Committee on Prices because they did not want to alienate their advertisers. The report said that Colgate-Palmolive and Unilever were making excessive profits in an industry that lacked price competition and relied on excessive advertising. Stone adds that Sam Chisholm, then TCV 9's sales director, criticised John Foell, then TCN 9's news director, for assigning the story and that:

> Foell was a victim of his era, when a phone call from Sir Frank or one of his senior executives could halt coverage in its tracks or spin a story against the rotation of the facts. He allowed himself to give way to Chisholm's wrath and kill the story.[80]

---

[78] Peach. op. cit. p. 19.
[79] Stone, Gerald (2000). *Compulsive viewing - the inside story of Packer's Nine Network.* Ringwood, Viking. p. 274.
[80] ibid. p. 279.

The ABCB held a public inquiry into the failure of the stations to report on the findings and ruled that " … decisions regarding the news are entirely the responsibility of the news editor, subject only to managerial direction in matters involving questions of taste or legal requirements."[81] Stone hails this as a "journalistic magna carta".[82] That view however ignores the possibility of proprietors and managements hiring news editors who understand the attitudes of proprietors and are willing to follow these without specific direction.

Technology

In the first news program on TCN 9 viewers saw footage of a bombing and street fighting in Cyprus; material that was specifically introduced as having arrived in Sydney by airmail.[83] Two months later, on 6 November, the inclusion of footage of the 1956 Hungarian revolution in the bulletin was noteworthy enough to warrant a report in *The Daily Telegraph* with the headline "Hungary revolt on TCN". The report read:

> The first newsreel of the Hungarian revolt to reach Australia was shown over Channel 9, TCN last night. The newsreel arrived in Sydney late yesterday afternoon. The film was taken late last week in a lull in the Budapest fighting. The cameraman risked his life to secure close-up shots of the devastated city.[84]

The details of how the news footage came to Australia illustrates not only the novelty of the overseas film but also one of the technological limitations of television in the 1950s; the need to physically transport footage meant the Budapest footage arrived at least three or four days after it was filmed. The emphasis on the first footage of an event, even though it has been reported in print and radio previously, is still a feature of television today and another is the emphasis on conflict such as the Budapest fighting.

The technology behind ATN 7's local coverage was the subject of a report in *The Sydney Morning Herald* ATN supplement on 3 December 1956. Headlined 'Fully Equipped Service

---

[81] ibid. p. 281.
[82] ibid.
[83] Religious talk and news on TCN Channel 9. *The Daily Telegraph*. 18 Sept.1956, p 1.
[84] Hungary revolt on TCN. *The Daily Telegraph*. 6 Nov. 1956. p 5.

For News'[85] the report details that newsreels would come from ATN's own cameramen " …
a flying squad of newsreel cameramen equipped with the latest movie and sound and film
cameras. They will rove throughout Sydney continuously shooting vision of outstanding
events."[86] The newspaper report indicates that ATN had the ability to process, edit and air
film in under one hour. As well footage from Australia and New Zealand would be provided
by the Fox-Movietone organisation which was a supplier of newsreels to theatres. Overseas
footage would come from a number of sources including the world-wide United Press.

Another report in the same year illustrates the technology available for news gathering.
Melbourne's GTV Channel 9 inaugurated a 'Nightwatch' van. *RTN: Radio Television News*
reported:

> A special van has been provided with a sound camera, a cluster of adjustable
> spotlights and a two-way radio link with the GTV studios at Richmond. It is this
> unit which is being used in GTV's new Sunday night feature, "*Nightwatch*", an
> on-the-spot round-up of dramatic news occurring in the metropolis on Saturday
> nights.[87]

Developments in camera technology assisted news production. Newsreels relied on 35mm
sound cameras that required the cameraman and the soundman to be linked by a cable and
this restricted movement. The cameras were also heavy and this further reduced the
cameraman's flexibility.[88] This type of arrangement is best suited for covering set pieces
where coverage can be planned ahead of time. The style of filming was often slow and
considered. Cameramen however experimented with smaller, lighter cameras, among them
the clockwork Bell and Howell, but as these did not record audio some of the impact of
events was lost.[89] Film has to be returned from the field and developed – a process that
requires 30 to 60 minutes for the average news report – before it can be put to air. Film

---

[85] Fully equipped Services For News. *The Sydney Morning Herald ATN Supplement*. 3 Dec.1956, p. 5.
[86] ibid.
[87] "Nightwatch" van chases the news. *RTN: Radio Television news*. 4 Dec. 1959. p. 10.
[88] MacGregor, Brent (1999). Making television news in the satellite age. In MacKay, Hugh, and O'Sullivan,
Tim (eds.) *The media reader: continuity and transformation*. London, Sage. p. 251.
[89] 16mm cameras that recorded audio without the need for the cameramen and the soundman to be linked by a
cable, such as the Cinema-Products CP-16, were developed in the early 1970s and gave cameramen greater
freedom and allowed more spontaneous footage.

cameras are restricted from covering events live and are limited by the expense of film and processing.

Despite the promotional claims of the television stations the technology of news gathering was limited; the inaugural producer of the 1963 ATN 7 current affairs program *Seven Days*, John Pringle, writes:

> Our technical equipment was hopelessly inadequate. Only too often the sound failed altogether or was so bad that nothing could be heard except the sound of the wind or the roar of the traffic. Hours of work could be wasted in this way.[90]

The invention of videotape in the US in 1956 overcame one of television's big technical problems - how to record and transfer material. Prior to videotape, events such as studio interviews and performances, sporting matches, political gatherings and the like were transmitted live or recorded by film cameras capturing the images off a television screen, a process known as kinescope or telerecording. This was limiting as film, as discussed above, was expensive and required processing. Videotape allowed events to be recorded and played back at will, for example in the news program that evening.

Videotape was vital for playback and recording when coaxial cable and then satellites were introduced. Sydney and Melbourne were linked by coaxial cable in 1962 with the ABCB commenting:

> Regular use is made of the Sydney-Canberra-Melbourne coaxial cable by stations TCN Sydney and GTV Melbourne to provide an interchange of topical items and news commentaries originating in the three cities.[91]

Satellites were first used to bring foreign material to Australia in 1967 via a transportable earth station operated by the Department of Supply for NASA outside Toowoomba in Queensland. Free from the restrictions of film transported by aircraft Australian television audiences saw special programs such as *Expo 67* on 7 June 1967 and a BBC program called

---

[90] Pringle, John Douglas (1973). *Have pen: will travel*. London, Chatto & Windus. p. 159.
[91] Australian Broadcasting Control Board (1964). *Sixteenth Annual Report*. Canberra, Commonwealth Government Printing Office. p. 70.

Our World on 26 June. Programs such as these encouraged Australians (and audiences in other countries) to think of themselves as global citizens. The opening of a permanent earth station by the Overseas Telecommunications Commission (OTC) at Moree, New South Wales, allowed full-time commercial satellite access.

The first commercial use of the Moree earth station saw Australian television stations take relays of US President Lyndon Johnson's speech on 31 March 1968 announcing the reduction of bombing in Vietnam and the end of his campaign for re-election. Australians also got direct coverage of events following the assassinations of Dr Martin Luther King Jr and Senator Robert Kennedy. There was also direct coverage of sporting events such as the America's Cup yachting, the World Heavyweight Boxing Championship and the Indianapolis 500 motor race. Foreign sporting events such as these also add to the supply of material for news programs.[92] In 1969-70 satellite relays allowed Australians to see immediate reports of the investiture of the Prince of Wales, the space exploration of Apollo 11, 12 and 13, the principal statements made by US President Richard Nixon on policy on the war in Vietnam and Cambodia and the official opening of the Australian pavilion at Expo 70 in Japan.[93] A ten-minute daily feed of footage from Visnews - that grew out of the Commonwealth International Newsfilm Agency formed in 1957 by the ABC and other broadcasters - was also delivered via satellite from 1975 for a joint cost of about $500,000 (about $4.4 million in 2004) that was shared between the ABC and the commercial broadcasters.

Inglis writes:

> This arrangement reduced the difference between the ABC's news bulletins and those of its rivals, all of whom took the same pictures and the same commentary (principally from the BBC and the American NBC network). The ABC used more of the Visnews material, however, the commercials had no equivalent to the

---

[92] Australian Broadcasting Control Board (1968). *Twentieth Annual Report*. Canberra, Commonwealth Government Printing Office. p. 21-23.
[93] Australian Broadcasting Control Board (1970). *Twenty Second Annual Report*. Canberra, Commonwealth Government Printing Office. p. 107.

filmed stories from the ABC's own correspondents, who now reported for News
and Public Affairs from twelve centres ...[94]

In summary, a little more than a decade after Australian television commenced broadcasting
the key elements were in place to allow the further development of television and television
news. Australia's dual-structure of commercial and public stations was established.
Advertising was sustainable and profitable for the commercial stations. News bulletins were
an established and popular strand of programming. Portable and (relatively) light-weight
cameras made news gathering feasible. News footage could be sent over long distances: via
co-axial cable within Australia and via satellites from the rest of the world. Politicians made
regular appearances and filmed press conferences and election broadcasts foreshadowed the
increasing influence television would have on politics.

Ongoing technical developments in television include the introduction of colour in March
1975, the introduction of electronic news gathering (ENG) in the early 1980s, and Channel 9
building its own earth station with the US material it received contributing to 25 hours a week
of news and current affairs programming by 1985.[95] The introduction of ENG at the ABC
became a significant industrial issue. The ABC had the first full-time ENG crew in Australia
in 1977.[96] Staff bans and demarcation disputes however stopped its use until mid-1984 when
it was used to a significant extent for the news program *The National*. The union action cost
the ABC any first mover advantages - such as the ability to put late-breaking footage to air or
to cross live into the news - over the commercial stations. Those stations obtained the new
technology after the ABC but were able to make use of it immediately with TEN 10 obtaining
an added advantage by avoiding the first generation three-quarter inch tape and instead opting
for the later and better Betacam.[97] This period was also a financially buoyant one for the
commercial networks with Tiffen commenting " ... advertisers [were] seemingly willing to
sustain any rises in the rates they were charged ... "[98] that assisted in the acquisition of new
technology.

[94] Inglis. op. cit. p. 352.
[95] Fell, Liz (1985). Impacts of AUSSAT. *Media Information Australia*. No. 38. p. 108.
[96] McElvogue, Louise (1985). Making immediacy the measure. *New Journalist*. December. No. 46. p. 22.
[97] ibid.
[98] Tiffen (1989). *News & power*. North Sydney, Allen & Unwin. p. 26.

The launch of the first Aussat satellite in 1985 allowed satellite delivery of television services. The ABC first used the satellite to broadcast to remote areas through its Homestead and Community Broadcasting Services (HACBSS) scheme[99] and there was an expectation the satellites would be used for pay television.[100] In 1993 however, after several changes in thinking - on issues such as the preferred delivery method, the number of services, the roles of the ABC and the commercial networks, foreign ownership, advertising and program content - the Labor government awarded the new satellite television licences to the highest bidders.[101]

Newsworkers and News Production

Television stations need staff to work on the news and other programs but in a country with no history in the medium the supply of experienced people was limited. Frank Packer commented about staff inexperience on the eve of TCN 9 going to air "Our staff has a newspaper background, and knows more about producing newspapers than television."[102] The new licence holders looked to people with a broadcasting background in radio, newspaper workers who were willing to be trained in television techniques[103] and workers with overseas television experience.

A group from TCN 9, including Bruce Gyngell, who would become the first face on Australian television and later program manager, Alec Baz, who became station manager, and Mike Ramsden, who became news director, went to the United States to study television. Gyngell, a former ABC radio announcer who worked with the advertising department of Australian Consolidated Press, did a television course with New York's Columbia University before studying with TV networks in the US.[104] Ramsden was a former *Daily Telegraph* journalist, a Korean War correspondent and worked in Washington D.C. for AAP-Reuters.[105]

---

[99] Jacka, Elizabeth and Johnson, Lesley (1998). Australia. in Smith, Anthony and Paterson, Richard (eds.) *Television - an international history*. Oxford, Oxford University Press. p. 217.
[100] Tiffen, Rodney (1994). in Brett, Judith et al (eds.) *Developments in Australian politics*. Melbourne, Macmillan Education Australia. p. 345.
[101] ibid.
[102] Packer, Frank (1956). We are proud pioneers in Australian TV. *The Sunday Telegraph*, 16 Sept. 1956. p. 7.
[103] Lloyd, Clem (1985). *Profession - journalist; a history of the Australian Journalists' Association*. Marrickville, Hale & Iremonger. p. 283.
[104] Behind the TV screen. *The Daily Telegraph* 18 Sept. 1956. p. 9.
[105] ibid.

Chuck (Charles) Faulkner, TCN's first newsreader and 'personality' was a veteran of US radio.[106] At ATN 7 C.G. Alexander, a former NBC station manger from the United States, was appointed general manager.[107] At the ABC staff such as Clement Semmler, the Assistant Controller of Programs, travelled to England between 1954 and 1956 to study television at the BBC and trainers from the UK, the US and Canada came to Australia to teach the techniques of television to about 120 ABC staff.[108]

The Australian observers could adopt from the techniques pioneered overseas; the use of stills and graphics and of filmed reports interspersed with spoken material to create bulletins with coherence. They could avoid both advertising that was indistinguishable from news material and the early BBC model of ignoring visuals entirely. The Australians faced the same restrictions as the Americans and British: the need for events and celebrity, the use of generic footage because new footage was difficult to obtain and news values dictated by visuals. Australians faced another restriction; because they relied on overseas sources for foreign coverage the emphasis and angle was American or British. In Australia television journalism would also be seen as a poor cousin of print journalism. It is likely however that criticism of television in mainstream print was muted by the cross-ownership of print and television interests with individual print owners promoting their television interests.

At TCN 9, and the pattern followed by other stations in Australia, Chuck Faulkner represented the personality side of the newscaster model. Stone however comments that Frank Packer resisted promoting TCN 9's other news personalities and did not allow them to identify themselves on air because this could lead to their asking for higher wages.[109] However the Australian adoption of the newscaster model largely stops with the personality. Few Australian news presenters have a real role in shaping the news bulletins or going out to do reports.[110]

[106] Hall, Sandra (1976). *Supertoy – 20 years of Australian television*. South Melbourne, Sun Books. p. 29.
[107] Gavin, Souter (1981). *Company of heralds – a century and a half of Australian publishing by John Fairfax Limited and its predecessors 1831-1981*. Melbourne, Melbourne University Press. p. 315.
[108] Inglis. op. cit. p. 197.
[109] Stone. op cit. pp. 283-284.
[110] Stepping outside that first decade of Australian television there are some exceptions to this such as the news specials prepared by TEN 10's Katrina Lee during the 1980s, some news presenters such as Mary Kostakidis at

Journalists with newspaper backgrounds were also on air in programs other than news. For example journalist and commentator Eric Baume presented a commentary program " ... a racy roundup of the passing scene, based on personal impressions ..." in a nightly program on ATN 7 at 8.15pm.[111] On TCN 9 the program *Meet the Press*, on air on Sunday at 7.00pm for 30 minutes, was hosted by David McNicoll, editor-in-chief of Australian Consolidated Press. The program was described as " ... a press conference of the air where a panel of journalists quiz a personality who plays a vital role in Australian and international affairs." [112] McNicoll recalls that in the early years of the program he was not paid and writes "For us it was an ego trip."[113] *Meet the Press* is an early example of television offering prominent politicians and business leaders direct access to a wide audience and letting them avoid critical examination by the print media that commentators such as Michelle Grattan would draw attention to four decades later.[114]

The television newsrooms turned to the newspapers for news copy. ATN 7 material came from the Fairfax newspapers *The Sydney Morning Herald*, The *Sun* and The *Sun-Herald* with " ... large staffs in New York and London and correspondents in every part of the world."[115] The news material would first go to the newspaper offices in Sydney then via teleprinter to the ATN newsroom at Epping:

> "The television news staff [at Epping] will specially edit the news to conform with television practices. A typical newscast will include newsreel, still photographs, and other illustrative material. Graphs, diagrams and even models will be used where they would give the viewer a better appreciation of the news. ATN is anxious to develop television news techniques specially suited to Australian conditions."[116]

SBS conducting short interviews within the news and, as illustrated during the survey period, TCN 9's Jim Waley presenting the news from Iraq in June 2004, but these are not the norm.
[111] Views on the news. *Sun-Herald television supplement*. 2 Dec. 1956. p. 41.
[112] Meet the Press sponsored by electrical co. *RTN: Radio Television News*. 31 May 1957. p.4.
[113] McNicoll, David (1979). *Luck's a fortune*. Sydney, Wildcat Press. p. 137.
[114] For example see Grattan, Michelle (1996). Sharing the same kennel; the press in Parliament House. In (eds.) Disney, Julian and Nethercote, J.R. (1996). *The house on Capital Hill - Parliament, politics and power in the national capital*. Leichhardt, The Federation Press.
[115] Fully equipped Services For News. *The Sydney Morning Herald ATN Supplement*, 3 Dec. 1956. p. 5.
[116] ibid.

DEMAND FOR NEWS

The development of news on television was driven by the recognition by a variety of different groups that news was something they could benefit from. The uses and gratifications approach asks: "Why do people use media and what do they use it for?" McQuail's four leading gratifications for audiences are: information and education, guidance and advice, diversion and relaxation and social contact.[117] News meets audience demands for information which has developed from societal pressures to stay up to date with events and the need to differentiate between a range of rivals for their political support, expenditure or investment. News also lets individuals compare their circumstances with those of others. The photograph on the front page of *The Daily Telegraph* at the launch of Channel 9 on 16 September 1956 "… Mr. Russ Wild is with Mr. and Mrs. Ian Mitchell, guests at a party in his Kogarah home."[118] displays another aspect to television - the social side; television viewing was something people did together, at least in the early years of the medium.

Politicians, interest groups, manufacturers of consumer goods, providers of financial services and others recognise the importance of both the news itself as promotion for their interests through editorial content and as an attractive programming strand for commercial spots. As television news developed these groups added to the demand for news and other air time. Politicians (despite an apparent and complex initial reluctance by then Prime Minister Robert Menzies to embrace television[119]) realised the potential of television in general and news in particular and came to both appreciate and attempt to manipulate television as a vehicle to put their messages directly to the public. Interest groups have increasingly turned to news to promote their interests and attempt to influence not only what is in the news but also the standards that are applied to news. As the demand for news has increased, news programs have grown to accommodate it, expanding from just a few minutes a day when television started in 1956 to morning, evening and late evening bulletins on free-to-air television and round-the-clock news on pay television.

---

[117] McQuail, Denis (2005). *McQuail's mass communication theory. 5th edition.* London, Sage. p. 428.
[118] It's here, at last! (1956). *The Daily Telegraph.* 17 Sept. p. 1.
[119] Gorman, Lyn (1998). Menzies and television: a medium he 'endured'. *Media International Australia incorporating Culture and Policy.* No. 87 – May 1998. p. 49.

Television news bulletins satisfied several demands of the television stations. Because much of their non-news product was imported the competing commercial stations had a similar look. Hall writes:

> The process of station identification began to devolve on the news service and a small number of showcase productions by which house personalities could be promoted. TCN did no drama because it was too expensive and too much of a gamble, so it built what distinctions it had on the style of its news bulletin and a series of variety shows resulting from [TCN Chief Executive Ken G.] Hall's show business contacts.[120]

Audiences

Australians knew of television in the United States and the United Kingdom and its introduction to Australia was considered by a wartime committee in 1941. In early 1953 a Gallop poll indicated that 80% of those polled wanted television to be introduced, 51% of these after a "careful enquiry".[121] About 3,000 Sydney homes had television sets when TCN started broadcasting in 1956.[122] Nationally about 1% of homes had a television. The strong demand for television is demonstrated by 55% of homes possessing television in 1961, rising to 87% in 1966, 91% in 1971 and 99% in 1993.[123]

The early demand for news is displayed by viewer reaction to the first news program on TCN 9 reported in *The Daily Telegraph*, owned by Channel 9 co-owner Frank Packer. The headline read "TViewers (sic) hail news telecasts" and the report began:

> Viewers who saw their first television news programme last night described it as "something we can't afford to miss each night." Typical comments were: ... Mr J. Wayne, of Killara: "The whole family enjoyed the news tonight, especially the

---

[120] Hall, Sandra (1976). *Supertoy: twenty years of television*. South Melbourne. Sun Books. p. 31.
[121] Curthoys, Ann (1986). The getting of television, dilemmas in ownership, control and culture, 1941-56. in Curthoys, Ann and Merritt, John (eds.). *Better dead than red – Australia's first cold war 1945-1959*. p. 141.
[122] 100,000 crowd sets for Aust. television debut. *The Daily Telegraph*. 17 Sept. 1956. p. 1.
[123] Australian Bureau of Statistics (1995). *Australian social trends 1995. Culture and leisure – special feature leisure at home*. Downloaded 6 Mar. 2006.
http://www.abs.gov.au/websitedbs/D3310114.nsf/home/home?opendocument.

shots of the air show at Richmond. My wife liked the interview with Grace Kelly and the Prince in New York, and I enjoyed the sporting shots.[124]

Television news, according to *The Daily Telegraph*, was a hit with viewers. The following day the *Telegraph* reported "Viewers want more TV news". The report continued:

Many television viewers would like TCN Channel 9 to run a longer news programme each night. After seeing their first two news programmes - last night and Monday night - they said they have found them possibly the most interesting. One set-owner, Mrs Z. Vincent, of 23 Grand Parade, Brighton-le-Sands, said last night: "I thought tonight's shots of the interview with Mr Menzies and the demonstration when he landed at Mascot were excellent ... Mrs. A. Nassar, 103 Dowling Street, West Kensington, said: "All the programmes from TCN are good, but the news is wonderful." Mrs. T. Kramer, 18 Walker Avenue, Mascot said she had found the news programmes "absorbing."[125]

The demand for news continued as a survey taken in 1966 by Western and Hughes reveals:

... news was the most popular category, news programmes being watched regularly by 33% of the sample. Drama was also popular: crime and suspense programmes were watched regularly by 24% of the sample, and "other drama" by 21%. Serious drama, adventure programmes, westerns, and domestic and comedy programmes were named relatively infrequently. Current affairs programmes were named by 16% of the sample and information programmes by 9%; no one admitted to watching political programmes regularly - perhaps a function of programming rather than taste.[126]

By 1961 the news on the ABC was attracting twice the number of viewers watching other ABC programs.[127] In 1968 the combined audiences of Sydney's TCN 9 and Melbourne's

[124] TViewers (sic) hail news telecasts. *The Daily Telegraph*, 18 Sept. 1956. p. 9.
[125] Viewers want more TV news. *The Daily Telegraph*, 19 Sept. 1956. p.5.
[126] Western J.S. and Hughes, Colin A. (1971). *The mass media in Australia – use and evaluation*. St Lucia, University of Queensland Press. p. 52.
[127] Inglis, K.S. (1983). *This is the ABC*. Melbourne. Melbourne University Press. p.212.

GTV 9 took the news program into the national top ten of programs for the first time.[128]

Print and Television

The benefits of cross-promotion - including topics for newspaper reports and advertising opportunities - are made clear by examining the Australian Consolidated Press and the Fairfax newspapers ahead of the launch of TCN Channel 9 on 16 September 1956 and of ATN Channel 7 on 2 December 1956. This examination makes it clear that commercial considerations - the promotion of the newspaper owners' associated television interests - take precedence over the news values of newsworkers.

The Daily Telegraph, owned by TCN 9 co-owner Frank Packer[129], started to promote Channel 9's 'test' broadcast ahead of the 16 September broadcast date. For example on 15 September one story was headlined "Opening of TCN, Channel 9 - thousands plan to attend TV parties". [130] A second story, headlined: "Where you can see TV", listed about 60 locations, including electronic retailers, restaurants, RSL clubs and town halls, where the public could go to see the broadcast. [131] On Sunday 16 September itself, a page one story told readers 'TV "takes to the air" tonight' while there were other reports on pages two, seven, eight and 18.[132]

The Daily Telegraph promoted ideological views and self-interest as well as the launch of TCN 9. The editorial on page two commented: "Today the people of Sydney, Wollongong and Newcastle add something new to their way of life. And free enterprise brings it to them first under a Federal policy which makes for healthy competition and the public benefit."[133] In a major story on page seven, Frank Packer used his paper to buy into the debate over Australian versus foreign talent on television writing "… it would be unfair and, in fact impossible, to expect TV, which is after all a movie theatre in your own home, to be

---

[128] Beilby, Peter (ed.) (1981). *Australian TV – the first 25 years*. Melbourne, Thomas Nelson Australia. p. 33.
[129] Note: The Theodore family was an early but brief shareholder in TCN 9 with N.B. Theodore the managing director of Television Corporation when TCN commenced broadcasting.
[130] Thousands plan to attend TV parties. *The Daily Telegraph*, 15 Sept. 1956. p. 4.
[131] Where you can see TV. *The Daily Telegraph*, 15 Sept. 1956. p. 4.
[132] TV "takes to the air" tonight and other reports, *The Sunday Telegraph*, 16 Sept.1956. p 1.
[133] TV Day, *The Daily Telegraph*, 16 Sept. 1956. p. 2.

restricted by impossible demands for the use of local talent."[134]

The reports covering the lead-up to the introduction of television also display how television was used to promote the print interests of the proprietors. At the time rival newspapers ran highly competitive cash giveaways to lure readers. On the eve of the launch of TCN 9 the Packer-owned *Sunday Telegraph* had just completed a 'Goldwords' competition and the £10,000 prize ($231,394 in 2004 terms) was won by Bondi housewife Mrs J.E. Starr. The *Sunday Telegraph* of 16 September 1956 featured Mrs Starr on the front page and promised readers that she would appear and be interviewed on television that evening.[135]

The night of the launch itself was covered extensively in *The Daily Telegraph* on Monday 17 September. Much of the front page was devoted to a photograph of Kogarah locals toasting the first broadcast with drinks in hand and the caption "It's here, at last!". [136] The headline for the story itself was "100,000 crowd sets for Aust. television debut," with a first paragraph that read "More than 100,000 people last night saw Australia's first regular television programme - from Station TCN Channel 9." The launch of the station was also covered in an editorial on page two, all of page three with photographs and reports, and all of the non-advertising space on pages four and five.

The first news broadcast on TCN 9 - and Australian television - was broadcast the following night from 7.00pm to 7.15pm. Again *The Daily Telegraph* reported this on the front page with the headline 'Religious talk and news on TCN Channel 9', and a first paragraph that read "Television station TCN Channel 9 last night scored two more firsts - the first Australian religious programme and the first news session."[137]

For its part, Fairfax, that controlled 37.7% of Channel 7 owner ATS,[138] promoted Channel 7 when it began broadcasting. On Sunday 2 December 1956 *The Sun-Herald* ran a page two news report[139] and a six page supplement promoting ATN 7's launch that evening. Half of the supplement was advertising material from companies such as television manufacturers

[134] Packer, Frank. We are proud pioneers in Australian TV. *The Daily Telegraph*. 16 Sept. 1956. p. 7.
[135] Goldwords £10,000 goes off and TV "takes to the air" tonight. *The Sunday Telegraph*. 16 Sept. 1956. p 1.
[136] 100,000 crowd sets for Aust. television debut. *The Daily Telegraph*, 17 Sept. 1956, p. 1.
[137] TViewers (sic) hail news telecasts. *The Daily Telegraph*, 18 Sept. 1956. p. 9.
[138] Souter. op. cit. p. 315.
[139] Opening of ATN tonight *The Sun-Herald*. 2 Dec. 1956. p. 2.

including Astor, Kriesler and STC Television and retailers including David Jones and H.G. Palmer. The promotional nature of the copy is displayed by articles quoting Mr Justice Maxwell, chairman of the board of Amalgamated Television Services (ATN's parent company), praising the social benefits of television, and C.W. Davidson, postmaster-general, praising ATN 7's policies.

On Monday 3 December, the day after the launch, *The Sydney Morning Herald* ran a front page report headlined 'Television Station ATN Channel 7 Opened by PMG', with a photograph of W.C. Davidson and Mr Justice Maxwell cutting the ribbon to open the station. The report noted that ATN's news service was the final part of the opening night's programming: "The highlight of the news service was a film of the station's opening ceremony which had been processed at the studio and presented within two hours of the opening."[140]

Inside *The Sydney Morning Herald* two more photographs of the launch and a report headlined 'Street Crowds For Opening Of ATN: Live Show Praised' demonstrated Fairfax's determination to promote ATN and the public response to television. The report began: "Thousand of people stood outside city and suburban shops last night to watch the first programmes of television station ATN, Channel 7. Many set-owners held parties in their homes for the occasion.".[141] As in *The Sun-Herald*, the commencement of ATN 7 broadcasts were marked by a special supplement in *The Sydney Morning Herald*. This supplement ran for ten pages and again advertising accounted for well over 50% of the space.

The Daily Telegraph also reported the start of broadcasts by rivals the ABC and ATN 7, but much more briefly, and in the case of ATN 7 more negatively, than the coverage the paper gave to TCN 9. The debut of ABN 2, on 5 November, was reported on page five with the headline: "A.B.C. television station opens". The report began "The Australian Broadcasting Commission's Sydney television station, ABN, made its first telecast last night. Station ABN was the third Australian television station to begin transmission."[142] ATN 7's commencement, on the evening of 2 December, was reported on page four with the headline:

---

[140] Television Station ATN Channel 7 opened by PMG. *The Sydney Morning Herald*, 3 Dec. 1956. p. 1.
[141] Street Crowds For Opening Of ATN: Live Show Praised,. *The Sydney Morning Herald*, 3 Dec. 1956. p. 5.
[142] A.B.C. television station opens. *The Daily Telegraph*, 6 Nov. 1956. p. 5.

"Storm hits new TV" and the opening paragraph: "An electrical power failure last night hindered the opening of Sydney's third television station, ATN."[143]

That restricted coverage, however, was more than Packer's Consolidated Press rival John Fairfax gave to the first broadcast of TCN 9. The unofficial 16 September start of television broadcasting in Australia - a major news event by most standards - received no coverage on the day of the event by *The Sun-Herald* or the day after by *The Sydney Morning Herald*. The official opening of TCN 9 on Saturday 27 October was recorded by a brief three paragraph report on page five with the headline 'Opening of TV station'. The report read:

> Television station TCN (Channel 9) opened officially last night. TCN, operated by Television Corporation Ltd, has been transmitting experimental programmes since September 16. In a brief ceremony last night, messages of goodwill were telecast by national and state leaders, including the Prime Minister, Mr R.G. Menzies.[144]

Advertisers

There was a demand for television as a platform for advertising. N.V. Nixon, president of the Australian Association of Advertising Agencies, told the 1953 Royal Commission on Television that advertisers would support television once an adequate number of television receivers had been sold because "the existing advertising media to-day are overburdened with advertising". Nixon added that while existing media would probably lose revenue to television, new advertising spending would also come from economic growth. Clive Ogilvy, of the Macquarie Broadcasting Service, indicated that his organisation: "had already been approached by a number of national advertisers who require time and programmes on television", and that these advertisers were willing to spend money even though the initial audience would not justify the expenditure.[145] The advertisers did support the new medium and television station earnings from advertising grew rapidly. The Australian Broadcasting Control Board (1963) states that "gross earnings from televising of advertisements" grew

---

[143] Storm hits new TV. *The Daily Telegraph*, 3 Dec. 1956. p. 4.
[144] Opening of TV station. *The Sun-Herald*, 28 Oct.1956. p. 5. Note: *The Sydney Morning Herald* did devote a report (TV era has started to change Australian's way of life) to the introduction of television some days later on 22 September. However while the report was an overview of television and considered ATN 7's rivals almost 40 percent of the report was devoted to ATN 7.
[145] *Report of the Royal Commission on television* (1954). Canberra, Commonwealth Government Printer. p. 90.

from £692,744 in 1956-57 to £9,058,405 in 1961-62, a 13-fold increase.[146] Television's share of the advertising dollar grew from 6.5% of total metropolitan advertising in 1956-57 to 75% in 2004.[147]

News is a major attraction for advertisers because of its key place in the prime time slot that starts at 6:00pm when the number of adult male and female viewers increases dramatically. But in the formative years of Australian television the programming and advertising model was still being developed. Programmers were experimenting with the best place for the news. When all three networks were on air in December 1956, the ATN 7 news program was at 8.00pm and the TCN 9 news program at 7.00pm. In 1959 the ATN 7 news was at 6.56pm for four minutes with a 15-minute bulletin at 11.00pm and the TCN 9 news was at 6.45 for 15 minutes. ABN 2 was at 7.00pm in both years.

Advertisers were so impressed by television that the Australian Association of National Advertisers later argued for advertising on the ABC with the rationale that ABC audiences " … are in the upper socio-economic group which are themselves significant consumers of goods and services and ideas but more importantly take decisions on behalf of major companies, organisations, associations and governments." This was not accepted.[148]

Politicians

Prime Minister Robert Menzies, as reported in *The Daily Telegraph*, was the first Australian politician to receive television coverage. On 18 September, three days after TCN 9 commenced broadcasts, and on the second day of TCN 9's news program, Menzies was filmed on his return to Australia. The *Telegraph* carried a page one photograph of viewers

---

[146] Australian Broadcasting Control Board. *Fifteenth Annual report 1962-63*. Canberra. Commonwealth Government Printer. p. 32.

[147] The industry group FreeTV Australia states that total expenditure on advertising on metropolitan television was $2.46 billion in 2004. Downloaded 10 Jan. 2006. http://freetvaust.com.au/Content_Common/pg-TV-Advertising-Expenditure.seo. The inflation calculator at http://www.rba.gov.au/calculator/calc.go was used to obtain adjusted dollar figures. The author accepts that gross earnings from televising of advertisements used by the ABCB and television advertising expenditure used by FreeTV are slightly different but believe they provide a fair illustration of the trend.

[148] Committee of Review of the Australian Broadcasting Commission, The ABC in Review: National Broadcasting in the 1980s, Volume 2, Report (Dix Report), AGPS, Canberra, 1981. p.494. in Windschuttle, Keith (1984). *The media – a new analysis of the press, television, radio and advertising in Australia*. Ringwood, Penguin Books Australia Ltd. p. 62.

watching Mr Menzies on screen during the TCN news. The headline read "P.M. on TV Channel 9" and the first paragraph reported "This is one of the thousands of homes into which television took the Prime Minister (Mr Menzies) last night." Further down the report said: "The telecast showed Mr Menzies' arrival by Super Constellation, police clearing the demonstrators from the airport, and Mr Menzies talking about his mission to Egypt. He became the first Australian politician to go on television in Australia."[149]

Menzies was known to dislike journalists, and in the airport press conference that was part of his television appearance he demonstrated this dislike by making a statement then declining to answer questions from journalists.[150] Inglis illustrates Menzies' view of television with an account from the early 1950s - when Menzies told a visitor from the BBC: "I hope this thing will not come to Australia in my term of office." - and comments that Menzies delayed television's arrival " ... as long as he could easily manage."[151] This delay, Curthoys comments, was due to economic problems in 1950-53 and because of opposition to television from church, rural, academic and artistic interests. She adds: " ... the Menzies government chose to step slowly and warily while such groups were placated with a system of regulation."[152]

On the other hand, Gorman argues that Menzies had previously demonstrated his understanding of the political opportunities of broadcasting and the possibilities it offered for circumventing journalists and newspapers. He presented weekly broadcasts on radio during 1942 and 1943 when he was in opposition and from 1949 he used radio as "a public communications model without peer", including broadcasts seeking public support against communism during the 1951 referendum campaign.[153] Menzies's television appearances started on the BBC Press Conference program in 1955 and continued in the UK the following year during the Suez crisis.

---

[149] P.M. on Channel 9. *The Daily Telegraph*. 19 Sept. 1956. p. 1.
[150] Not contemplating force – Menzies on Suez Canal. *The Sydney Morning Herald*. 19 Sept.1956. p. 1.
[151] Inglis. op. cit. p. 193.
[152] Curthoys, Ann (1986). The getting of television: dilemmas in ownership, control and culture 1941-56. in Curthoys, Ann and Merritt, John(eds.). *Better dead than red – Australia's first cold war: 1945-1959*. Vol 2. Sydney, Allen & Unwin. p. 153.
[153] Martin, A.W. (1993). *Robert Menzies: a life Vol. 1, 1894-1943*. Carlton. Melbourne University Press. p 399. in Gorman, Lyn (1998). Menzies and television: a medium he 'endured'. *Media International Australia incorporating Culture and Policy*. No. 87 – May 1998. p. 50.

Menzies then made regular appearances in the new medium. He appeared, along with other dignitaries, on the first television program transmitted by the ABC on 5 November 1956.[154] Also during the first decade of television Menzies took part in four telecasts during the 1958 election campaign with more broadcasts during the 1961 election. Menzies chose a television (and radio) broadcast over a conventional public meeting for his policy speech for the 1963 federal election campaign. Hughes and Western comment: "It seemed certain that the Prime Minister's speech would be a venture in a political technique new to Australia …".[155] And: "Generally politicians and the interested public were convinced that there was a magic about television which made it a particularly effective means of political communication. In fact there was little in the literature of mass communication to support such an expectation."[156] We can conclude that Menzies valued the political impact of appearing on television yet was wary of the political and structural issues surrounding its introduction.

Other politicians of the era also acknowledged the impact of television and displayed a readiness to accommodate its requirements. There was a five-minute program *The Premier Speaks* on television in South Australia during the early 1960s in which " … the premier of South Australia deals with matters of public interest" (and by doing so presented his case to the public).[157] Robert Askin (NSW premier 1965-1975) revealed his view of the first decade of television with this comment:

> In nine years television has radically changed politicians' approach to political life
> … we may still have our hall and street corner meetings, but they now play a very
> small part in a political campaign. The politician now appeals to the family group.
> What he has to say is discussed by parents and children.[158]

CURRENT AFFAIRS

A distinction has to be made between newsreel-type programs and current affairs television.

---

[154] Inglis. op. cit. p. 193.
[155] Hughes, Colin A. and Western, John S. (1966). *The prime minister's policy speech – a case study in televised politics*. Canberra. Australian National University Press. p. 1.
[156] ibid p. 132.
[157] The Australian Broadcasting Control Board (1963). *Fifteenth Annual report*. p. 60.
[158] Federation of Australian Commercial Television Stations submission to the Senate Standing Committee on Education, Science and the Arts, 18 July1972. p. 346.

Newsreel-type programs might be best defined as containing reports on events and issues that are timeless and often driven by visual values such as the flower carnivals and pancake races as identified by Cox.[159] Australian television, like British television, has a history of newsreel programs whose origins lay with cinema newsreels, such as the long-running ABC *Weekend Magazine*, but those are not covered here. The term current affairs ideally interprets and comments on the news and explores important political, economic or social issues but the nature of current affairs programs has become confused with tabloid, lifestyle programs such as Channel 9's *A Current Affair* or Channel 7's *Today Tonight*.[160]

In August 1961 the ABC's *Four Corners* first went to air. Inglis describes *Four Corners* as the ABC version of the BBC's *Panorama* program that was "... a nimble weekly investigation of current affairs ... ".[161] The presenter was Michael Charlton, a former ABC radio reporter and announcer and the first presenter on ABC television who had watched as much BBC material as possible.[162] The producer was Robert Raymond, an Australian who had worked in journalism in Britain and film-making in Africa and done a 'crash course in television production at CBS'[163] in New York. Both admired the *See It Now* program with Ed Murrow on CBS and *Panorama* with Richard Dimbleby on BBC and Raymond adds "There was nothing remotely like that on the ABC (never mind the two commercial channels)."[164]

The first 45 minute *Four Corners* had a mix of eight national and international reports. The program evolved into " ... an odyssey, having fewer items and taking viewers with Charlton as he pursued current issues in corners few [viewers] had visited - places such as Marble Bar, Moonie and Queenstown - and corners of the world never before explored through Australian eyes."[165] At a site called Moonie, near Tara in southern Queensland " ... Charlton stood in a drab grey plastic mac in pouring rain in front of a pounding oil rig and told the story of

[159] Cox, Geoffrey (1995). *Pioneering television news – a first hand report on a revolution in journalism.* London. John Libbey & Company Ltd. p. 44.
[160] See Turner, Graeme (2005). *Ending the affair - the decline of television current affairs in Australia.* Sydney, University of New South Wales Press Ltd. and Pearson, Mark and Brand, Jeffrey (2001). *Sources of news and current affairs,* Sydney, Australian Broadcasting Authority. p. 68.
[161] Inglis (1983). op. cit. p. 215.
[162] Raymond, Robert (1999). *Out of the box - an inside view of the coming of current affairs and documentaries to Australian television.* Henley Beach, Seaview Press. p. xiii
[163] ibid. p. 4.
[164] ibid p. 23.
[165] Inglis. op. cit. p. 217.

Australia's first commercial oil strike."[166] In that first year Raymond and Charlton worked with a cameraman and assistant, an editor and a researcher/secretary. They were also able to draw material from overseas programs. The early *Four Corners* programs had to be physically transported around Australia because of the lack of videotape and microwave or coaxial links with the result that viewers in Hobart saw the program 11 days after viewers in Sydney.

The program introduced comments from ordinary citizens on the street in 'the voice of the people' or vox populi (abbreviated today to 'vox-pop') segment[167] and the use of a 'piece to camera' that shows the reporter addressing the camera on location[168] both of which have become standard techniques in Australian television news and current affairs. As well the ABC management directed that political balance had to be maintained and the test of this was that interviews with opposition spokesman could only be used if there was an interview with the relevant government minister; if the minister declined, then the opposition interview could not go to air. Raymond and Charlton disregarded this rule in a campaign to free up political debate on television. On one occasion, in May 1963, following a report on public housing, ABC management instructed Raymond to give William Spooner, minister for Public Housing, a right of reply even though Spooner had refused an opportunity to be interviewed previously. Raymond writes "Political pressure had been applied, and the ABC had buckled."[169]

These restrictions meant the early *Four Corners,* like the ABC news discussed previously, presented an incomplete view of the world. ABC management refused to let Charlton go to go to Indonesia or China and he was prevented from going to West New Guinea in 1963 when Australia was agreeing to the Indonesian take-over. Inglis writes:

> Charlton was not surprised by interventions ... it was second nature for him to accept the constraints imposed on everybody who worked for [the ABC]; he knew

---

[166] Raymond. op. cit. p. 38.
[167] ibid. p. 29
[168] ibid. p. 37
[169] ibid. p. 61.

that *Four Corners* was eroding old inhibitions, and he was having too many good innings week by week to fret much over the odd duck.[170]

Charlton and Raymond left *Four Corners* after two years and the program became more "troublesome" for management with a report on the Returned Services League (RSL) and another on capital punishment ahead of the execution of murderer Eric Edgar Cooke in Western Australia.[171] A *Four Corners* report on the right of journalists not to disclose sources of information resulted in an uproar over political interference and questions in parliament. Alan Ashbolt, manager of the program, John Power, producer, and John Penlington, reporter, were transferred. Despite, or because of, these controversies, *Four Corners,* which remains on air today, helped inspire other current affairs programs on both commercial television and the ABC.

The first current affairs program on commercial television was a weekly program called *Seven Days* launched on ATN 7 in 1963. Again illustrating television's habit of drawing on print journalists the producer of that program was John Pringle, an Anglo-Scot who had been editor of *The Sydney Morning Herald* from 1952-57. Pringle had gone back to Britain and been deputy editor of *The Observer* for five years - where he was presumably exposed to television and the debates about its nature - before he returned to Australia. In 1963 Pringle was in charge of starting a weekly current affairs program along the lines of *Four Corners*. The resources, however, were limited:

> The truth was that the commercial stations did not have the resources to do the job. One cannot run a public affairs program effectively without at least three teams, each consisting (as a minimum) of a reporter, a film cameraman and a sound-technician, British programmes like '*Panorama*' may have as many as ten. We had one.[172]

Pringle did not stay with the program for long and was ultimately succeeded by academic Peter Westerway. Davies, a reporter on the program, recalls:

---

[170] Inglis. op. cit. p. 218.
[171] ibid, p. 219.
[172] Pringle. op. cit. pp. 158-9.

Westerway's 'White Paper' programmes on *Seven Days*, examining government policies, were particularly successful. Otherwise, like *Four Corners*, *Seven Days* ranged over Australia geographically and across the canvas of the nation's social issues ... the two programs portrayed Australia and the issues with a frankness that sometimes offended audiences and special interest groups, not least politicians.[173]

At TCN 9 Robert Raymond, and others who had worked with him on *Four Corners*, produced *Project 64* in 1964 and its derivatives for the next five years. The *Project* programs covered a different single-topic documentary each week and were not a multi-report current affairs program. Despite this, *Project* did take an in-depth look at Australian and world issues. Inglis comments "For once the dual system of broadcasting was working benignly: a serious initiative from the national system had proved so successful that the commercials judged it good business to follow."[174]

Channel TEN 10 commenced broadcasting on 5 April 1965 and the schedule included the current affairs program *Telescope*. Bill Peach - with experience in ABC radio and BBC radio - was the producer and presenter and there was a secretary, a cameraman, an assistant and a film editor. Peach writes that *Telescope* covered parochial issues such as a scandal with a beach at Dee Why or a drain at Denistone, and more controversial issues that made TEN 10's "... conservative management pop the buttons off their suits. Homosexuality, child abuse, prostitution, mental illness and the menopause were not the staple diet of Australian television in the 1960s."[175] Peach and Douglas Fleming, Channel 10's then program manager, drew the inspiration for *Telescope*, and also access to reports, from the BBC program *Tonight*, started in 1957. Peach left *Telescope* in 1966 and recalls " ... whether the management realised it or not, the station had actually begun a revolution. It had pioneered the first nightly current affairs program on Australian television."[176]

In 1966 the ABC had several weekly current affairs programs. There was *Watch This Space* in Melbourne, *Week* in Hobart, *S.A. Magazine* in Adelaide and *West Coast* in Perth. In Hobart

[173] Davies, Brian (1981). *Those fabulous TV years*. North Ryde, Cassell Australia. pp. 153-4.
[174] Inglis. op. cit. p. 222.
[175] Peach. op. cit. p. 21.
[176] ibid. p. 23.

there was also *Line-Up*, a program with " ... pace, variety, controversy and teamwork ..." according to its originator David Wilson, the Supervisor of Talks in Hobart.[177] Peach writes that "*Line-up* had been promoted as a topical program, ranging as widely as imagination and the camera lens would allow, and including a dash of bite and a pinch of wit."[178]

Line-up, was a Tasmanian pilot for a national program. The ABC had overseas models, including the BBC's *Panorama* and *Tonight*, and their local derivatives, ATN 7's *Seven Days*, Channel 10's *Telescope* and the variety of ABC state-based weekly programs including *Line-up* - to draw on in creating a new, national, nightly program. That new program was *This Day Tonight (TDT)*. (*TDT* is one year outside the first decade of television in Australia because it went to air in 1967. *TDT's* inclusion here is warranted because of the impact the program displays on current affairs television.)

TDT was the brainchild of Ken Watts, the ABC's federal director of television programs. Like other Australian news and current affairs programs *TDT* owed a lot to foreign influence. Peach comments:

> Like every other high ABC executive who had spent time on secondment to the BBC in the previous ten years (and that must have been practically all of them) Watts had seen the *Tonight* program with Cliff Michelmore. Like them all, he had thought, "We could do that." Unlike them all, he had done something about it.[179]

TDT started with relatively large resources; a team of nearly 50 people; including producers, reporters, studio directors, research assistants, cameramen, technical producers, designers, film editors, floor managers and typists.[180] The journalists had differing backgrounds; Frank Bennett came from one of the ABC television weekly programs, Sam Lipski from commercial television and *The Bulletin*, Ken Chown from ABC news, and Peter Luck and Gerald Stone from newspapers.[181] Bill Peach was the presenter.

---

[177] Inglis. op. cit. p. 266.
[178] Peach. op. cit. p. 27.
[179] ibid. p. 25.
[180] Inglis. op. cit. p. 267.
[181] ibid. p. 267.

The first program of *This Day Tonight* went to air on 10 April 1967. Peach writes " ... *(TDT)* grew into a program of breaking news, hard-hitting interviews and comment, and daring satire which was forthrightly and uniquely Australian."[182] The program caused controversy from the first day. A spoof telegram said to have come from Dr James Darling, the chairman of the ABC, caused Dr Darling to " ... go rigid with rage ...". [183] On the third day Harold Holt, the then prime minister, was critical of the program for using comment from Allan Fraser, a former ALP MP, and employing Mike Willesee because his father was a Labor senator.[184] Those first days shaped the pattern of *TDT's* editorial values clashing with those of politicians and ABC management. Turner writes "Dogged by management's fear of the political consequences of its work, *TDT* was subject to a high degree of central control and interference."[185]

Peach believes *TDT* - that was to last for 12 years - changed censorship law, shamed Australians into voting 'yes' in the Aboriginal referendum of 1967 and made politicians feel " ... obliged to explain and defend their policies in the public forum of television."[186] He also believes the program opened up areas of debate, particularly relating to sex, politics and religion. And he adds that *TDT* " ... advanced the idea of multiple points of view in a society which was used to accepting single points of view."[187] Other commentators share Peach's view of the impact of the program, an impact that displays the power of television. Turner writes that *TDT* played an important role in institutional change:

> *TDT* provides us with a window on to a national community that was politically conservative; at the same time the public structures available for the prosecution of political change were extremely primitive. TDT became an important part of renovating and modernising those structures.[188]

TDT helped bring about a:

---

[182] Peach. op. cit. p. 242.
[183] ibid. p. 2.
[184] Inglis. op. cit. 268.
[185] Turner, Graeme (2005). *Ending the affair - the decline of television current affairs in Australia.* Sydney, University of New South Wales Press Ltd. p. 40.
[186] Peach. op. cit. p 242.
[187] ibid.
[188] Turner. op. cit. p. 46.

... new regime of public accountability for public officials ... this regime is so well established now that it has spawned a whole new sphere of professional activity to counter its effects - the spin doctors and PR flacks who surround the public officials of today.[189]

TDT also helped the development of a number of journalists – such as Michael Willesee, Gerald Stone, Kerry O'Brien and others – who would have major roles in Australian current affairs television. And Inglis adds that the genes of *TDT* can be found in later current affairs programs.[190]

ECONOMIC AND BUSINESS NEWSWORKERS AND PROGRAMS

Australian life generally has revolved around sport, politics and business. But business has never been fully covered by television. What is happening now is that people are taking more direct control of their financial affairs and not just leaving it to a bank or an insurance company to invest their money for them. As a result, they are hungry for information.

Max Walsh[191]

Economic and Business Newsworkers

Economic and business coverage in print or within television news, current affairs or dedicated economics and business programs requires journalists with specialised knowledge yet these have not always been available. Schultz considers the Australian media overall in her review of business, finance and economic journalists[192] and illustrates the changing nature of this type of journalism with the report of Don Henderson, a former finance editor of *The Daily Telegraph*, who gave evidence to a Senate Committee in 1970. Henderson drew on

---

[189] ibid.

[190] Inglis foreword p. 3. in Peach. op. cit.

[191] Verrender, Ian (1995). Business returns with a better deal. *The Guide. The Sydney Morning Herald.* 20 Feb. p 3.

[192] Schultz, Julianne (ed.) (1993). *Reporting business – a report into the attitudes, values and practice of business, finance and economics journalism in Australia.* Sydney, Australian Centre for Independent Journalism. pp. 5 - 12.

coverage of the financial results of Australian Consolidated Industries (ACI) for 1952 and 1970. The 1952 report on ACI contained:

> ... a brief one column report noting net profit, tax, provision for depreciation and dividends. Don Henderson noted, "It did not elaborate beyond the directors' report. It was common practice 'not to go into' financial reports in the publication of financial news.

By contrast 18 years later:

> The 1970 news report described ACI's operations, discussed its expansion and international operation and reported the profit, tax and depreciation. This report was more story-like, and the significance of particular details was emphasised with the liberal use of adjectives.[193]

Finance journalists are an elite among journalists. Schultz found that finance journalists are more highly educated than their non-finance colleagues (although fewer television finance journalists had a degree than their print colleagues).[194] Henningham found that finance journalists are better paid, better educated and more likely to be from middle class socio-economic backgrounds.[195]

As business and economic coverage in Australia in print and on television expanded during the heady times of the 1980s some weakness in this sector of journalism were displayed. The concentration of ownership of the Australian media is identified by Kitchener as discouraging " ... a diversity of viewpoints or insightful reporting."[196] Marshall and Kingsbury comment that a combination of newsworkers being too accepting of orthodoxy, inexperience and conflict of interests made dispassionate reporting and analysis increasingly difficult.[197] Journalists are criticised by Nagy for failure " ... to exercise critical thinking, accepting too

---

[193] ibid. p. 5.
[194] ibid. p. 12
[195] Henningham, John (1997). Characteristics and attitudes of Australia's finance journalists. *Economic Analysis & Policy*. Vol. 27 No. 1 March 1997. p. 45.
[196] Kitchener, Jennifer (1999). in Curthoys, A. and Schultz, J. (eds.), *Journalism: print, politics and popular culture*. St Lucia, University of Queensland Press. pp. 240-241.
[197] Marshall, Ian, and Kingsbury, Damien (1996). *Media realities: the news media and power in Australian society*. South Melbourne, Addison Wesley Longman Australia Pty Limited. pp. 157-166.

readily that what they were being told was correct."[198] Schultz and Matolcsy survey finance journalists to find almost half felt there was a bias in favour of business in business reporting and that they were "... a voluntary mouthpiece for Treasury ..."[199] One third of finance journalists said they would " ... not pursue a story that was potentially damaging to my employer's commercial interests as actively as a story about an unrelated company."[200] Tiffen comments that " ... advocacy for their sources would seem most a danger in business and economic reporting."[201] Advocacy and a celebratory reporting style is highlighted by Toohey who blames many journalists of the era for creating " ... heroes of some of the most recklessly incompetent executives ever to control a public company."[202]

The particular orthodoxy of the 1980s that is criticised by, in particular, Nagy, Schultz and Toohey, is what Schultz summarises as " ... the trinity of privatisation, deregulation and economic rationalism ...".[203] Schultz adds "'The economic' was elevated above the social, and became the bedrock of politics."[204] Further, Schultz writes that Paul Kelly, then editor-in-chief of The Australian, believes that journalists of the era had a zeal for economic rationalism that was shared by the government and opposition and other members of the national and international elite. Nagy, Schultz, Toohey and others are critical of economic rationalism for the social, business and economic disruption they believe it caused.

The supporters of economic rationalism however believe it transformed and updated the Australian economy. Kelly, for example, cites average economic growth of 3.8% during the 1990s, seven years of sustained recovery, low inflation and interest rates and a more reliable banking system than Japan and the US and concludes "All these are genuine achievements, and they did not occur by accident. They result from the lessons learnt and the reforms made in economic policy over the past 15 years under the governments of Hawke, Keating and

---

[198] Nagy, Joe (1997). In over our heads. Pymble, HarperBusiness. p.262.
[199] Schultz, Julianne and Matolcsy, Zoltan (1993). Business boosters or impartial critics. in Schultz, Julianne (ed.) (1993). Reporting business – a report into the attitudes, values and practice of business, finance and economics journalism in Australia. Sydney, Australian Centre for Independent Journalism. op .cit. p. 27.
[200] op. cit. p. 25.
[201] Tiffen (1989). op. cit. p. 45.
[202] Toohey, Brian (1994). Tumbling Dice, Port Melbourne, William Heinemann Australia. p. 232.
[203] Schultz, Julianne (1992). in (eds.) Horne, Donald. The trouble with economic rationalism. Newham, Scribe publications Pty Ltd. p. 84.
[204] ibid. p. 88.

Howard."[205]

The debate over economic rationalism during the 1980s came at a time when television coverage of economics and business was increasing. Economic rationalism and more economic and business coverage were both influenced by those features considered previously: better communications through technology, the growing realisation of the importance of economic issues, and the growth of global markets. Each influenced the other; the debate over economic rationalism supplied material for television reports and key players used television to present their arguments for economic change.

In support of this it seems fair to include television under the umbrella term of the press when Parsons writes:

> The development of the press and price system are ... inextricably linked both with one another and with the political system since economic and financial commentaries and news events impact upon and communicate themselves to the business community. The press serves as a crucial mediator between the business men and men of ideas to set the parameters of ruling opinion.[206]

The role of television is reinforced by Walsh who believes:

> Television has played an absolutely pivotal role. Not so much the role played by the journalists in television, but particularly during the 80's when you had a Labor government, with two particularly articulate political performers like Hawke and Keating. They really put economics out there into the market place. They got constantly pushed because they were arguing for a cause ... they had the platform and they had the ability.
>
> Max Walsh[207]

---

[205] Kelly, Paul (1999). The paradox of pessimism, in Waldren, Murray (ed.). *Future tense – Australia beyond election 1998*. St Leonards, Allen & Unwin, p. 4.
[206] Parsons, Wayne (1989). *The power of the financial press: journalism and economic opinion in Britain and America*. Aldershot, Edward Elgar Publishing Limited. p. 3.
[207] Walsh, Max (2000). Editor-in-Chief, *The Bulletin*. Personal interview 18 July.

The coming together of economic and political coverage in the 1980s accelerated a trend started several decades before. For example, Maxwell Newton, a political correspondent in Canberra for *The Sydney Morning Herald* and *The Australian Financial Review* in the late 1950s and editor of *The Australian Financial Review* and *The Australian* and proprietor of his own newsletters in the 1960s, pursued this connection in his campaign against tariffs.[208] Walsh recalls that defence and foreign affairs were important during the Cold War era, that social issues then became important but that economic issues attracted limited attention:

> In the years of the Cold War a great deal of [political debate] was about defence and foreign affairs but that is long forgotten that's really passed into history. Then it became social issues and is still largely social issues, but more and more business is penetrating into the day-to-day business of politics and the day-to-day business of news ... in '66 inflation wasn't even a problem. We had a Liberal government still, we had one since 1949 and economics was not regarded as of any significance what so ever. The budgets were not covered the way they are now.

> Max Walsh[209]

Walsh's own career - he started commentating on politics and economics from *The Australian Financial Review* Canberra bureau in 1966 for Channel 7 and has appeared on the ABC, Channel 9 and Channel 10 - illustrates the growing contribution to television by senior journalists dealing in politics and economics. Hywood adds:

> A new political elite has evolved in Australia - its members not politicians, but living off politics and living well. They are the new breed of television's political analysts who earn prime ministerial salaries in the vicinity of $100,000 and beyond to explain the latest machinations in Canberra to an increasingly politicised Australia. Laurie Oakes, Max Walsh, Robert Haupt and, most recently,

---

[208] For more on this see McCarthy, Nigel (2000). Alf Rattigan and the journalists: advocacy journalism and agenda setting in the Australian tariff debate 1963-1971. *Australian Journalism Review*, v.22, no.2, Dec 2000, pp. 88-102 and Newton, Sarah (1993). *Maxwell Newton; a biography*. South Fremantle, Fremantle Arts Centre Press.
[209] Walsh. op. cit.

Paul Kelly are a product of the 1980s, having moved from long and influential careers in newspaper to television: to some degree exchanging power for money and public recognition.[210]

Economic and Business Programs

The opening of the coaxial cable that linked Sydney and Melbourne via Canberra in the early 1960s allowed the television stations to take a more national view of news. Channel 7 did this in 1966 with a morning program (name unknown) hosted by Bruce Webster and featuring a regular spot with Max Walsh and Fred Brenchley, both journalists in the Canberra Bureau of *The Australian Financial Review*. Walsh recalls "I don't know if anyone watched ... it was essentially about politics and economics".[211]

Three years later, in February 1969, Channel 9 trialled a morning program called *Today* that included some business content. Robert Raymond, the executive producer, wanted the program to be "Like a television newspaper - something along the lines of *The Australian* ... [we felt] that at that time of day we had a better chance of getting hold of the decision makers - politicians, businessmen, scientists, academics ... viewers liked the news bulletins and weather reports every half hour, topical political interviews, the short snappy contributions by well-known journalists, overnight stock market news, arts reviews, live musical interludes ....".[212]

Today was also an early bid by a commercial channel to use business content to attract advertisers. Raymond recalls that Bruce Gyngell, head of Channel 9, used "His connections at the Bank of New South Wales - a heavyweight in the corporate market we were aiming for - to talk them into becoming our first advertiser." [213] *Today* however was short-lived in the face of Channel 10 launching a cartoon program that saw children challenge, and beat, their parents for control of the television set.

---

[210] Hywood. Greg (1985). Taking the money and the box. *The Australian Financial Review*. 27 Feb. p. 15.
[211] Walsh, Max (2000) Personal interview. 18 July.
[212] Raymond. op. cit. p. 119 p.121.
[213] Raymond. op. cit. p. 121.

Commercial media organisations seek to attract an audience which they then sell to advertisers. As Seaton puts it: "Commercial television produces audiences not programmes. Advertisers in purchasing a few seconds of television time, are actually buying the viewer."[214] Business and economic programs contribute to this by turning around low revenues in time slots such as weekday or Sunday mornings, which previously carried low rating or children's television, and replacing them with audiences in the highly sought-after high-income AB demographic that attract higher advertising rates. Newsworkers try to shape their programs to fit the perceived needs of audiences and to make their information appealing.

As illustrated by the comment from Max Walsh at the start of this section, business and economic programs are a response to audience demand for financial, business and economic information resulting from changes to the Australian economy such as compulsory superannuation and increased investment by Australians. At the same time economic and business programs are meeting television network demands for greater revenue. This presents a risk of newsworkers ignoring news values for revenue. Parsons warns:

> Ever in pursuit of the affluent reader to boost advertising income, newspapers geared to high income groups have eagerly given over features to pull in the appropriate sponsors. Such developments have proved a subtle form of distorting economic news values and the economic agenda itself.[215]

Parsons draws on Curran's 1978 research of advertising in newspapers that shows this results in "economic comment is overwhelmingly given to tipping, investment advice, company news and gossip, rather than to critical analysis. The actual national economy comes a poor third."[216] There is no reason why advertising on television should be any different.

The first oil shock of 1973 - when the members of the Organisation of Petroleum Exporting Countries (OPEC) cut supplies to those nations that supported Israel in the Yom Kippur War

---

[214] Seaton, Jean (2003). How the audience is made. in Curran, James and Seaton, Jean. *Power without responsibility: the press, broadcasting and new media in Britain*. London, Routledge. p. 179.
[215] Parsons. op. cit. p. 209.
[216] ibid.

and raised prices - made the world and Australians realise that economics and economic news was important. Walsh comments:

> ... of course the world changed with the first oil shock ... [that] created global inflation and a commodities boom ... and that coincided to a large extent with the deregulation of the banking system and financial systems which enabled that recycling of petro-dollars to occur ... very soon afterwards came the globalisation enhancement of technology and then the personal computer, which democratised financial transactions ... there was a total revolution in the way in which we thought about business and thought about economics and the way it impinged on our lives.

Max Walsh[217]

The growing interest in economics and business during the 1980s was illustrated in November 1981 when Channel 9 launched the *Sunday* program. *The Bulletin,* also owned by Packer, reported the program was:

> The first attempt by television in this country to produce an electronic equivalent of a quality Sunday newspaper for a national audience. For two hours, from 9 am to 11 am, a team of leading journalists and commentators will combine to give news, views, reviews, comment and opinion on national and international events.

Economics and finance were among the target topics of *Sunday* with Allan Hogan, the producer, saying: "We'll be covering everything ... such as an examination of the gap between rich and poor countries ... [and] topics such as the arts, science, film and business." Max Walsh was a compere, heading a panel " ... interviewing whoever the person in the news may be - politician, businessman, sportsman ...". Political journalist Alan Reid was a commentator and Jim Waley the presenter.[218]

Max Walsh left the program and went to the ABC and *The National* when that program commenced in 1985. Walsh and Richard Carleton survived the demise of *The National* to

---

[217] Walsh. op. cit.
[218] Bell, Glennys. (1981). Quality for the Sunday morning slot. *The Bulletin.* 17 Nov. p. 56.

present *The Carleton-Walsh Report* on ABC television three nights a week at 9.30pm. In 1987 *The Carlton-Walsh Report* was pushed back to 10:00pm. Later that year Carleton left to join Channel 9 and Max Walsh moved to Channel 10.

Channel 9 boosted its business coverage in November, 1985, with the launch of the 20-minute *Business Today* segment at 6.40am within the *Today Show*. The host was Michael Pascoe who, *Australian Business* magazine reported:

> ".. will inform sleepy-eyed business people across the nation of the latest stock and currency moves overnight; present a story on a local event or trend; interview someone who has made headlines that morning and give a preview to the business day ahead.[219]

Business Sunday, launched in 1986, was a further bid by Channel 9 to attract the business audience. The launch of *Business Sunday* caused Freeman reflect on the appeal of Sunday morning television to advertisers. She observed that just 6% of households tuned into Sunday morning current affairs programs and added "Most of them are soundly thrashed in the ratings by the ABC's *Couch Potato*."[220] The reasons the Sunday morning current affairs programs survived:

> Is that this heavy-duty early morning programming is a Sabbath cash cow. Shows such as *Sunday* and *Meet the Press* may not have mass appeal but they do attract the viewers advertisers love - people with high disposable incomes who can be targeted while frowning attentively (if sleepily) at their television screens.[221]

Australian Business magazine asked "So is there a TV business boom on the horizon?" The response of Steve Cosser, *Business Sunday's* producer, was "Most other networks follow the Nine approach to news, current affairs and sport and I can only see that happening in the business area." Max Walsh added "… it is not that business has discovered television, it is

[219] Johnstone, Roger (1986). TV gets taste for business. *Australian Business*. 9 April pp. 23-24.
[220] Freeman, Jane. (1987). The battle for the big spenders. *The Sydney Morning Herald The Guide*. 11 Aug. pp. 4-5.
[221] ibid.

that television has discovered business."[222] Channel 10 introduced a similar weekly business program called *Business Week* in 1986 hosted by John Barton.

Channel 7 launched its contribution to business programs in May 1988 with the morning business program *TVAM*, which John Barton joined as presenter. Christopher Skase, chairman of the Australian Television Network, owners of Channel 7, and a former finance journalist, commented "*TVAM* - at last the business community in Australia has on television what it expects and receives from the print media. *TVAM* is the first daily television program to comprehensively cover the business, finance and political scene in Australia and overseas."[223]

Television business and economic programs fare better in boom economic times than they do in the busts. In 1987 world share prices, including the Australian market, collapsed. This caused a big reduction in Australian television business programs. *The Sydney Morning Herald* television guide reported in January 1990 "It's a bleak bear market for business television. Network Ten's, *Business Week*, hosted by finance journalist Max Walsh, is the latest of the 80s rush of business programs to kiss the dust of the cutting room floor." Toward the end of 1989, Channel 9 had dropped the morning weekday segment *Business Today*. Channel 7 cancelled *TVAM*. The *Herald* explained it this way "The problem, it seems, is that Australians love their heroes - sporting, business or both - but reports of receivers and liquidators carving up once-great corporate empires is a turn-off for viewers."[224] In 1990 *Business Week* on Channel 10 finished and Max Walsh moved slots to *The Walsh Report*, airing at 8:00am on Sundays. The new program was a combination of *Business Week* and the politics program *Face to Face*. Walsh commented:

> We've all suffered, there is no doubt, from the collapse of the entrepreneurial bubble which is working its way through the system now ... [Business failures are] cheerless news. Increasingly one looks at the prospect of running programs

---

[222] ibid.

[223] TVAM Seven means business. *The Bulletin*. 4 June 1988. Advertising supplement.

[224] Wright, Lea (1990). Back in business. *The Sydney Morning Herald The Guide*. 22 Jan. p. 7.

on liquidators. So I think that's been one of the problems for business programs - they have been caught up in the very cycle they reported.[225]

With the gloss off the big players, Channel 9 decided to go after mum and dad investors with the *Money* program that started in 1993 and would run for almost a decade, ending in September 2001. *Money*, presented by Paul Clitheroe, a non-journalist and partner in the investment firm ipac, was unlike most of the other programs considered here in that it was an infotainment program rather than a serious economic or business program.[226] *Money* was a rating success with a national viewing audience of 3 million people and became the most popular program on Australian television.[227]

Presenter Clitheroe believes the appeal of the program came from the need for Australians to finance their own retirement. He says "What I think has happened is that nearly all Australians have become aware of the fact that, like every other western society, we're an aging society; basically we're living longer and we're tending to retire earlier."[228] Clitheroe adds that Australians retiring at the age of 55 were likely to be retired longer than they had worked and needed to be financially independent to have a reasonably comfortable lifestyle. A decade previously, the view was "You work, you pay off the house, you educate the kids and when you retire you go on the pension.". This had generated new public interest in money with Clitheroe commenting "If I'd mentioned the budget deficit 10 years ago, 90% of the people wouldn't have known what I was talking about, whereas now I think 90% of the people do know."[229]

The success of *Money* allowed Channel 9 to charge $9,500 for a 30-second advertisement in Sydney or $29,000 for five capital cities during 1994 and Miller writes "With seven minutes of advertising during the show, companies are queueing (sic) for a spot." [230] Channel 10 did

---

[225] ibid.

[226] *Money* prompted a successful magazine of the same name. Clitheroe also presented money segments on Nine's *A Current Affair*, became a regular on radio, wrote a weekly column that appeared in 60 newspapers around Australia and wrote several books with sales would of more than 500,000 copies.

[227] Miller, Gretchen (1994). Shooting from the hip pocket. *The Sydney Morning Herald The Guide* 11 July. p. 2.

[228] Lawrence, Mark (1993). Money – a winner boom or bust. *Green Guide. The Age.*. 26 Aug. p. 1.

[229] ibid.

[230] Miller. op. cit. Note if all seven minutes of available advertising were sold at the five-city price the total revenue would be $406,000 or $552,734 in 2005 using the Reserve Bank of Australia inflation calculator at http://www.rba.gov.au/calculator/calc.go

less well with a look-alike program *Your Money and Your Life*, presented by David Koch, that was discontinued after a short run in 1995.

The Small Business Show on Channel 9, 7.30am on Sundays, set out to capture a different audience by targeting the 95% of businesses in Australia that, in the early 1990s, were small businesses employing 2.8 million people. The problems of small business, problems the program aimed to address, included getting a loan or government grant or incentive to start up, taxes and levies. Presenter Janine Perrett said:

> ... we see ourselves as crusaders for small business, the voice of small business ...we'll be going to the right people and trying to get answers out of them, push them, cut through all that red tape and try to do something for them.[231]

The Small Business Show was cancelled in August 2002 as Channel 9 sought to reduce costs.[232]

Business Success, was launched by Channel 9 two years later. On air at 7.30am on Sundays *Business Success* was first presented by Jason Cameron and later by Charles Slade. The program echoes the trend of recent years to reality programs by sending " ... consultants into small firms to help them overcome problems or just find ways to become more successful."[233]

The ABC decided to launch a business program in 1994 and again it was in an unlikely time slot. *The Bottom Line* first went to air at the end of February at 8:00am on Saturdays. Again Max Walsh was a presenter and Maxine McKew a co-host. The ABC was, and is not, dependent on ratings to attract advertisers but uses ratings as an indication of how successful it is in identifying an audience. The ABC was therefore seeking to attract the same audiences as the commercial channels and was unlikely to present a different perspective. McKew said the program wanted to attract:

---

[231] Hooks, Barbara (1994). Crusading for better odds in small business. *The Age. Green guide.* 22 Sept. p. 9. Downloaded 11 Dec. 2005. http://global.factiva.com.ezproxy.library.usyd.edu.au/ha/default.aspx
[232] ibid.
[233] Jackson, Sally (2004). Business steals the show. *The Australian.* 29 April. p. 20.

... the economic decision makers, the corporate heavies and, if you like, the informed amateurs. There is an increasing army of people who have taken a reasonable redundancy package and decided to retire early, or people who want to manage their own super payout. [They] are quite hungry for a lot of information about the movements of things.[234]

The *Bottom Line* finished at the end of 1995 with "budget cuts" given as the explanation.[235]

There was a gap of seven years before the ABC again attempted a specialised business program with the launch of *Business Breakfast* in June, 2002 on air between 6:30 and 7:00 each weekday morning. Presenter Emma Alberici, who worked with Channel 9 before the ABC, said she thought the program would have "broad appeal" because a "huge proportion of Australians own shares". Alberici added: "On top of that you have people who have indirect investments through managed funds, and then more again through superannuation. That means virtually everybody has some kind of shareholding."[236] In mid-2003 *Business Breakfast* moved from its early morning slot to replace the *World at Noon* at mid-day.

Also in 2002, in August, the ABC started another program, *Inside Business*, hosted by Alan Kohler, a veteran finance journalist and former editor of *The Australian Financial Review*. Running for half an hour at 9:45am on Sundays, the program features "analysis and comment".[237] Max Uechtritz, head of ABC news and current affairs told *The Sydney Morning Herald* the ABC is keen to challenge the long-running Channel 9 programs. "They've had it easy for a long time now, haven't they?" Uechtritz adds "We're the national broadcaster ... why wouldn't we want to continue to showcase the outstanding journos and the repository of knowledge we have in business ...?".[238]

SBS started *The Business Show* in August 2001. The presenters of the program were Richard Ackland and Emiliya Mychasuk and the program went to air on Sunday evenings. In 2003 *The Business Show* moved to 7:30pm on Friday nights before it was cancelled mid-2003.

---

[234]Martin, Louise (1994). ABC does business on Saturday. *The Age. Green Guide*. 9 June. p. 8.

[235] Jackson, Sally (2004). Business steals the show. *The Australian*. 29 April. p. 20

[236] Tabakoff, Jenny. 2002. 'Testing the market'. *The Sydney Morning Herald The Guide*. 27 May. p. 2.

[237] Torpy, Kathryn (2002). ABC gets up to business. *The Courier-Mail*. 10 July. p. 28.

[238] Buchanan, Matt (2002). It's the politics, stupid. *The Sydney Morning Herald The Guide*. 20 July. p. 2. Downloaded 19 Jan. 2006. http://global.factiva.com.ezproxy.library.usyd.edu.au/ha/default.aspx

Channel 10 started *Bread*, about small business, in August 2004 and then, from February 2006, followed it in the 8.00am Sunday slot with *Inside Franchising*. The promotion on the Network Ten website reads "Don't work hard to make them rich. Make yourself rich. What's it really like to buy a franchise? We take a look at the pros and cons and what makes them successful." *Bread* is listed on the Network Ten website as a light entertainment program.[239]

At the time of writing (September 2006) *Business Sunday* had recently merged with *Sunday*. Former *Business Sunday* presenter Ali Moore moved to the ABC to present *Lateline Business*, a half-hour program running Monday through Thursday nights after the *Lateline* program. Moore's transitions between commercial television and the ABC, like Max Walsh and others before her, illustrates that the same newsworkers are acceptable to both commercial and public television. Channel 9's *Business Success* and the ABC's *Inside Business* remain on air on Sunday mornings. Channel 10's *Inside Franchising* is not on air although a second series is planned.

Most of the twenty or so programs that have been or are devoted to business and economics have been scheduled outside prime time - for example early in the morning, late in the evening or on Sunday - displaying the perception of programmers that these programs are of limited general appeal yet able to attract a good demographic. The programs seem to proliferate during boom economic times - for example during the 1980s and early 2000s. This is not always the case as Channel 7 made a substantial commitment to the five-days a week *TVAM* in 1988, one year after the 1987 crash.

Programs such as *Money, The Small Business Show* and *Inside Franchising* emphasise the finance and business activities of individuals; people who are actively involved in managing their money or running a business. This is in contrast to more traditional programs such as *Business Sunday* that are about the 'big end of town.'

Television's own program cycle - the time it takes to develop a new program and the difficulty in filling the slot if the program is cancelled - operates somewhat independently of the business cycle. First-mover advantage and brand strength is displayed by the longevity of

---

[239] Bread. Downloaded 24 Jan. 2006. http://.ten.com.au

Channel 9's *Business Sunday* which was one of the first dedicated business programs and lasted for twenty years.

The content of the programs has varied from the emphasis on national economic and business and political issues of *The Carleton-Walsh Report* to the personal investment and finance style of *Money* to the small business approach of the *Small Business Show* or *Inside Franchising*. The style of the programs follows broader television trends; for example the programs of the 1980s and 1990s and most today echo news and current affairs style while recently launched programs such as *Business Success* echo the current popularity of reality programs.

The reality approach is taken further in *The Apprentice*, an NBC America program aired in Australia by Channel 9 from 2004. This is a reality program based loosely on business. Contestants are divided into two teams and asked to perform a business-related task such as selling, negotiating prices or managing a business with the ultimate winner being offered a job with Donald Trump's company. Other reality programs with a money and business theme include home make-over shows such as Channel 9's *The Block* in 2003 and Channel 7's *Hot Property* in 2005 and the restaurant management program *My Restaurant Rules* on Channel 7 in 2004.

Businessmen Donald Trump in the United States and Sir Alan Sugar in the UK are the key figures in *The Apprentice*. The reasons why corporate leaders accept, and even court, the attention of the media are varied. Business leaders may seek public support to preserve or promote their company share price. They may also need shareholder support in corporate challenges, such as takeovers, restructuring, or internal struggles.

Alternatively business leaders may be driven by more than commercial goals and are seeking to project their activities and personalities and win recognition. This might help explain the flamboyant, media-attracting behaviour of Australia's most notorious entrepreneurs of the 1980s who provided much of the material for newspaper reports, magazine articles and television reports. Sykes recalls this flamboyance; Alan Bond's big toys such as a corporate jet, an airship and a four-masted schooner, George Herscu's Toorak home modelled on Tara from *Gone With the Wind* and boasting double jacuzzis, Christopher Skase's headquarters painted in ice-blue and with antiquities such as a Egyptian cartonage mask (circa 1300 BC) and a Greek vase (circa 300 BC).[240] This behaviour might also explain why these business leaders made themselves available to the media. David McNicoll, editor-in-chief of Australian Consolidated Press, is quoted previously in this chapter as saying the reward for hosting the television program *Meet the Press* was ego. Lionel Tiger, an anthropologist with an interest in business studies, told the *Harvard Business Review* " ... the attention structure of a primate group, not the distribution of resources, will tell you who is the leader. It's not who gets the most bananas - it's who gets looked at." [241] (Business leaders and television are discussed in Chapter 4, including the greater willingness of business leaders to deal with the media when the news is positive and reduced willingness when the news is negative.)

As business coverage on television started to expand from the mid 1980s business leaders accepted television's growing interest in their activities. Johnstone comments that "Most chief executives are comfortable with the medium (many have done media training courses) and it offers them a fairly accommodating vehicle to get their point across to a large audience without the hard analysis of the financial press."[242] This view of television's non-critical approach to business is backed up by Michael Pascoe, presenter of *Business Today* on Channel 9, who said many business leaders appear on the program "Because they know the show understands business. For years there was a line of journalistic questioning based on the proposition that you (the company) made too much profit."[243]

CONCLUSION

By the mid-to-late 1960s the practices of news and current affairs television were in place and they remain largely the same today. There has been little change to the studio presenter, interviewee and reporter model of programs or the voice-over, interview grab and sound effects manner of packaging reports. The early Australian newsworkers imported the techniques of television from the US and the UK and there is little that is unique to the

---

[240] Sykes, Trevor (1996). *The bold riders*. St Leonards, Allen & Unwin. pp. 201, 267 and 305.
[241] Tiger, Lionel (2001). in Collingwood, Harris and Kirby, Julia (eds.) All in a day's work. *Harvard Business Review*. December 2001. p. 64.
[242] Johnstone, Roger (1986). TV gets taste for business. *Australian Business*. 9 April. pp. 23-24
[243] ibid.

Australian method of presentation. Improvements in technology since that period have made it simpler and cheaper to shoot material and to move it around the nation and the world.

Television has had a dramatic impact. For example, in the US television highlighted coverage of the civil rights movement, the 1963 assassination of President John F. Kennedy and opposition to the Vietnam War.[244] In the UK television helped erode class barriers by finding fascination with ordinary everyday life.[245] *Four Corners* showed viewers parts of remote Australia and let them look at and listen to themselves with the voice of the people segment. ATN 7's *Seven Days* scrutinised government policies with the 'White Paper' segment. TCN 9's *Project* programs helped Australians " … overcome our cultural cringe and take enormous pride in the uniqueness of our native flora … to recognise the eco-systems …".[246] *TDT* challenged Australian institutions and perceptions and *TDT's* first presenter Bill Peach signalled the start of the end of BBC voices dominating the ABC. [247] In short television helped Australians to look at themselves for what Tom Fitzgerald called "the shock of self-recognition".[248]

The reporting of economic and business news has shifted from debate over the national economy to wealth creation. Television has helped bring about an acceptance of wealth and legitimised the ambition to be wealthy, as illustrated by the top ratings achieved by Channel 9's *Money* program. This probably goes hand-in-hand however in creating discontent. Some of the features of television news and current affairs, in particular its appetite for visuals and celebrity, can emphasise the material and this is particularly so in the coverage of economics and business. As Frey finds "Long hours spent in front of a TV are linked to higher material aspirations and anxiety and therewith lower life satisfaction."[249]

---

[244] Barkin, Steve M. (2003). American television news: the media marketplace and the public interest. Armonk, M.E. Sharpe, Inc. p. 28.
[245] Cox. op. cit. p. 57.
[246] Gyngell, Bruce (1999). in Raymond op. cit. p. ix.
[247] Peach. op. cit. p. 11.
[248] Appleton, Gil (1988). How Australia sees itself: the role of commercial television. in Australian Broadcasting Tribunal. *The price of being Australian*. North Sydney, Australian Broadcasting Tribunal. p. 202.
[249] Frey, Bruno, Benesch, Christine and Stutzer (2005). *Does watching TV make us happy? Working Paper No. 2005-15*. Centre for Research in Economics, Management and the Arts. Downloaded 20 Feb 2006. http://www.crema-research.ch/papers/2005-15.pdf

Television broadcast Prime Minister Robert Menzies' comments on the evening news just hours after his press conference and put politicians into Australian living rooms. Since then politicians have attempted to present their messages directly to voters. The benefits of politicians speaking without journalistic mediation is offset by their speaking without challenge. Menzies's Suez press conference was an early display of several effects of television: emphasis on the political leader, issues examined in the glare of publicity, pressure for speed in the decision making process and focus on one issue.[250]

---

[250] Donovan, Robert J. and Scherer (1992). *Unsilent revolution: television news and American public life.* Cambridge, Cambridge University Press. pp. 163-164.

CHAPTER 2

ECONOMIC AND BUSINESS NEWS ON AUSTRALIAN TELEVISION

The news media are naturally attracted to the financial markets because, at the very least, the markets provide constant news in the form of daily price changes. Nothing beats the stock market for sheer frequency of potentially interesting news items.

Robert Shiller[251]

NEWS CONTENT

The irony of television news is that moving pictures are both its strength and weakness. Television, as the literature examined in this chapter will reveal, revolves around good visual material.[252] This and newsroom structures in turn create a predisposition among television newsworkers to cover pseudo-events.[253] Economic and business coverage on television in particular is criticised for having difficulty in dealing with the complexities of economics and business.[254]

This chapter will examine the economic and business reports on the *Channel 9 News*, the *ABC News* and *The 7.30 Report* that went to air in Sydney from 1 June to 30 June 2004. *Channel 9 News* was selected as the top rating commercial network news, the *ABC News* because it is the flagship television news program on the major national broadcaster and *The 7.30 Report* because of its reputation as Australia's leading nightly serious current affairs

---

[251] Shiller, Robert (2000). *Irrational exuberance*. Princeton, Princeton University Press. p. 86.
[252] Schlesinger, Philip (1978). Putting reality together - BBC news. London, Constable. p. 128-129.
[253] Boorstin, Daniel (1962). *The image*. Harmondsworth, Penguin. pp. 22-23
[254] Goddard, Peter, Corner, John, Gavin, Neil T. Richardson, Kay (1998). Economic news and the dynamics of understanding: the Liverpool project. in Gavin, Neil T. (ed.) *The economy, media and public knowledge*. London, Leicester University Press. p. 11.

program. Weekday programs only are included and are examined to the first sport report in the rundown so sport and weather are excluded from the item count. The three programs are compared and contrasted to explore what issues and events are covered, the sources that are used and the role and techniques of the journalists.

This chapter will consider issues such as the reliance by television news on events and pseudo-events and diary items, news values, the use of file material, the combination of script and vision, economic terms, sources, institutions and newsworkers.

The processes of newswork and the values of newsworkers will be examined to see how they influence the criticisms above. Television news content displays a consistent set of news values that are applied to broadcast journalism.[255] But do these values contribute to or overcome the criticisms? And do news processes and techniques - such as graphics, economic terms and jargon and reporters' pieces-to-camera - also contribute to or overcome the criticisms?

> I suppose the bread and butter of television news coverage of business and economic affairs is the movement up and down of interest rates because that has direct relevance to their viewers. And it's become a cliché now the way they film [interest rate related issues], film houses being newly built and people accessing their money through the ATM. Those are the pictures that inevitably crop up when they are running stories about the rise and fall of interest rates.

> Elliot Taylor[256]

> ... I think actually television has a comparative advantage over print in equities and in foreign exchange and interest rates. There is a combination of fast moving stories and short comments from talking heads and a bit of visuals and direct immediate impact on people's fortunes.

> John Edwards[257]

---

[255] Masterton, Murray and Patching, Roger (1997). *Now the news in detail. A guide to broadcast journalism in Australia.* 3rd edition. Geelong, Deakin University Press. pp. 15-18.
[256] Taylor, Elliott. Editor, *Media, The Australian.* Personal interview 3 Aug. 2000.

Content and Regular Finance Segments

There are many different ways for television news producers to package material in news bulletins. The stand-alone report or package (prepared by a journalist and generally containing a voice-over and interview grabs) is the main building block for news bulletins and the main element in the following content analysis. The other presentation options that producers can employ include presenter read-only items (where the presenter remains on screen), live voice-overs (where footage or graphics are played over the presenter's voice), sound-on-tape items (where an interview grab is butted up to a presenter's read), and different combinations of these. How newsworkers use those building blocks and other techniques of television reporting, such as graphics and reporter pieces-to-camera, are vital in overcoming those problems identified by Goddard et al above.

Economic and business reports on *Channel 9 News* accounted for 7% of items during the survey period with viewers seeing a report of this nature on six of the 22 days (27%). *ABC News* viewers saw more with reports of this nature accounting for 14% of all items during the period for an economic or business report on 15 out of the 22 days (68%). On two different days there were three economic or business reports in the ABC bulletin and on one of those days (22 June) economic and business reports made up 42.9% of the packaged items before the sport break.

Table 2.1
Economic and business reports 1 - 30 June 2004

Channel 9 News %	ABC News %	The 7.30 Report %
7.4	13.7	21.1
n = 135	n = 176	n = 71

(Economic and business reports defined: Reports that deal predominately with monetary policy, fiscal policy, trade, business, commodities and related topics.)

The much greater amount, in both relative and absolute terms, of economic and business

---

[257] Edwards, John (2000). Chief Economist, HSBC. Senior Advisor (Economics) to Prime Minister Paul Keating, 1991-94. Personal interview 21 July.

material on the *ABC News* compared to *Channel 9 News* is the first of a number of differences the content analysis reveals and reflects the different nature of the two networks.

> I think the Board believes there should be more business and finance on the ABC. I don't know why that is necessarily, I can only guess. It could be because they see it as a growing area on rival networks ... It could be because there may be more influence on the Board from the right in politics, the right side of the political spectrum, I don't know. There is that stereotyped image, more Liberal Party appointees may be more interested in business. After all, the Liberal government has been doing, has done, a lot or privatisation has taken place, although that happened under the Labor governments as well. So there is interest on both sides of politics.

Philip Lasker[258]

The 7.30 Report shows a much higher percentage than either of the two news programs with 21% of items substantially about economic and business issues. Like the news programs *The 7.30 Report* is aimed at a general audience without a specific interest in, or knowledge of, economic and business issues. Viewers saw at least one economic or business report on eight of the 18 days, 44%, of the survey period.

The 7.30 Report sets out economic coverage as one of its goals:

> The program's imperative is to provide up-to-the minute, balanced coverage of the most important issues of the day whether they be political, economic, medical, environmental, social, sporting or cultural.[259]

The two news programs have a regular finance segment each week night. On the *Channel 9 News* the segment is presented by the news reader and has a duration of about 20 seconds. Channel 9 uses two sets of full-frame graphics to describe share market moves (with brief comments about individual companies) and currency moves; in both sets of graphics green arrows represent a gain and red arrows a loss. This brief, market highlights approach is

[258] Lasker, Philip (2000). Finance Reporter, News, ABC Television, Sydney. Personal interview 28 July 2.
[259] http://www.abc.net.au/7.30/aboutus.htm

similar to that used by television stations around the world for a number of years. On four evenings brief economic or business items, several with graphics or overlay, were presented as live items ahead of the finance segment.

ABC News by comparison has a regular finance slot, presented by finance commentator Alan Kohler, that runs approximately 1:30 minutes. Standing in a studio in front of a chroma key screen Kohler details movements in key indices such as the Australian ASX 200, US S&P 500, the exchange rates for the Australian dollar and other data that is making news such as commodity prices, housing and employment statistics and so on.

Kohler also focuses on particular issues or events with explanations of what they mean and why they are important. Kohler's style is conversational and inquiring. For example he looks at topics such as the historical price of oil to tell viewers the current price is not as high as it appears. House prices are examined with Kohler explaining the differences between Reserve Bank and Australian Bureau of Statistics (ABS) figures, then presenting a graphic of capital city price movements with the comment "And I'll just give you a chance to check out yours ... " ahead of a slight pause to allow viewers to absorb the data relevant to their city (2 June).

The 7.30 Report does not include a regular finance segment.

Topics

Not only is there a difference in the amount of economic and business news *Channel 9 News* and the *ABC News* present, there is also a difference in the focus of the reports. The table below displays the dominance of fiscal topics, with the number of reports on government spending, by Channel 9 (50%) and *The 7.30 Report* (44%). The *ABC News* emphasises business, covering the activities of a variety of companies, (25%) as the dominant category.

Table 2.2
Topics - economic and business reports 1 - 30 June 2004

	Channel 9 News %		ABC News %		The 7.30 Report %	
Fiscal	**1**	**50.0**	2	20.8	**1**	**43.8**
Business	2	20.0	**1**	**25.0**	2	18.8
Resources	2	20.0	3	16.7	3	12.5
Other	4	10.0	5	12.5	3	12.5
Trade	-	-	3	16.7	5	6.7
Monetary	-	-	6	8.3	5	6.7
	n = 10		n = 24		n = 15	

(Topic categories defined: Fiscal - decisions and actions taken by the federal or state governments on fiscal policy or other issues relating to fiscal policy. Business - issues relating to large and small business. Resources - issues relating to Australia's management of natural resources but excluding trade issues. Other - economic and business issues outside the defined categories. Trade - issues relating to Australian trade with the rest of the world. Monetary - decisions and actions taken by the federal government on monetary policy or the release of data and other issues relating to monetary policy.)

The emphasis on fiscal topics by Channel 9 and *The 7.30 Report* include the NSW state property tax, the NSW budget, the cost of medicines through changes to the Pharmaceutical Benefits Scheme (PBS), changes to superannuation, federal government advertising spending and the baby bonus. These topics have the potential to impact on many viewers' incomes and spending and so touch the hip pocket nerve although *The 7.30 Report* also focused on the national policy perspective of these issues. The program also considers the unintended consequences of the energy plan on the niche sector of bio-diesel production (24 June).

The *ABC News* has reports on topics such as the James Hardie asbestos inquiry, the inquiry into the Panthers football club, the Telstra share price rise, plans by QANTAS to base staff in London, the reorganisation of Westfield and staff cuts at winemaker Southcorp. The ABC news also shows a greater distribution of material across topics than Channel 9 with at least one item in each of the six categories compared to Channel 9's topics confined to four of the six categories. The *ABC News's* top two topics make up 46% of the total compared to Channel 9's top two topics making up 70% of the total items.

Many of the ABC news reports touch on secondary topics. For example the James Hardie and Panthers reports raise questions of corporate governance and the Telstra and QANTAS reports explore the progress of now-privatised or partly-privatised former state-owned enterprises that carry a legacy; the expectation that Telstra provides equal service, at equal prices, to all Australians and that QANTAS remains a national flag carrier that, in the words of ACTU President Sharan Burrow (22 June), enjoys a 'loyalty' from Australians.

Economic Terms

A rule of journalism is to avoid specialist terms, technical language and jargon. George Orwell wrote: "Never use a foreign phrase, a scientific word, or a jargon word if you can think of an everyday English equivalent."[260] The three programs under consideration in this chapter are all aimed at a general audience yet all contain economic, business or management terms and jargon.

The economic literacy, or illiteracy, of Australians is examined by Schultz with a qualitative survey that asked one white collar and one blue collar group to describe the following terms: macroeconomic policy, microeconomic policy, fiscal vs. monetary policy, gross national product/gross domestic product, balance of trade, balance of payments, current account deficit, economic growth, all-ordinaries index, CPI, corporatisation and privatisation. While all the terms were familiar to both the groups, they were not necessarily understood. Schultz writes:

> Respondents admitted that whilst they heard many of these descriptions frequently, they had little or no understanding of their true meaning ... In addition, respondents actually cared little about this lack of understanding and showed little inclination to become more informed.[261]

In another survey, 29% of *The Sydney Morning* readers said they knew little, or had only limited knowledge, of finance matters, 27% had some knowledge and wanted more, 35% had

---

[260] Orwell, George. 1945. *Politics and the English language.* http://www.k-1.com/Orwell/pol.htm
[261] Schultz, Julianne (1992). in (eds.) Horne, Donald. *The trouble with economic rationalism.* Newham, Scribe publications Pty Ltd. p.4.

a reasonable amount of knowledge while 9% said they knew a lot about finance matters.[262] So economic and business reports are unlikely to make sense to audiences if they contain terms that viewers - only 44% of whom have a reasonable or good knowledge of finance matters – do not understand.

Table 2.3
Reports with economic/business terms 1 - 30 June 2004

	Channel 9 News %	ABC News %	The 7.30 Report %
Reports with eco/bus. terms	50.0	29.2	30.0
Explained	20.0	28.6	25.0
Not explained	80.0	71.4	75.0
	n = 10	n = 24	n = 15

(Economic/business terms defined: The terms identified are those likely to be outside the daily use of average Australians as informed by the 1991 Quadrant Research Services qualitative survey of economic terms[263] that included macroeconomic policy, microeconomic policy, fiscal vs. monetary policy, gross national product/gross domestic product, balance of trade, balance of payments, current account deficit, economic growth, all-ordinaries index, CPI, corporatisation and privatisation.)

The economic and business terms in the *Channel 9 News* reports include deficit, capital gains tax, negative gearing, (superannuation) co-contribution and (company) listing. Only deficit is explained as meaning 'in the red'.

Almost 30% of the reports on the *ABC News* contain one or more economic, business or management terms. Only two of the reports contain an explanation of one or more terms. Among the terms used are GDP growth, retail sales figures, contracting business investment, growth rate, unregulated lending, building approvals, a hard or soft landing, consumer sentiment survey (explained), dividends, capital management framework, after tax profits, share buy-back, special dividends, (budget) deficit (explained as in the red), free trade, (stock market) list.

There are no economic terms in 70% of the items on *The 7:30 Report* which may indicate a

---

[262] *Money* (1997). Sectional survey, August 1997, Detailed Findings, Taverner Research.
[263] Schultz op. cit.

conscious awareness by journalists and producers of the general nature of their audience. Of *The 7.30 Report* items that do contain economic terms - household debt to income ratio, consumption, soft landing, OPEC, roll-out lags, excise, leverage, impediments to commercial development, profit margin - only one item, household debt to income ratio, is explained.

Other terms such as 'MRET' (Kemp interview *The 7.30 Report* 15 June) do not fall into the category of economic and business terms but are more 'jargon'. The term 'MRET' was used by Environment Minister David Kemp during a studio interview with presenter Kerry O'Brien. Neither Kemp nor O'Brien explained the term, nor did O'Brien ask Kemp for an explanation.[264]

SOURCES

As news reporters depend on government sources to "break" or fill out stories, these sources play a fundamental role in shaping the media agenda and in slanting their stories.

Douglas Kellner.[265]

Interviewees, Interview occasions, Different Voices and Gender

Newsworkers and the production process of television shape what issues and events will be covered and who will be interviewed. The gatekeeper model of news selection by individual journalists was first put forward in 1950.[266] Newsworthiness - consequence, proximity, conflict, human interest, novelty and prominence[267] - is considered elsewhere. More recently the ABA/Bond University *Sources of news and current affairs* adds:

---

[264] Research into the term discovered an interview with the newly-appointed Environment Minister Ian Campbell on the ABC television program *Insiders* (25 July) . Campbell said "… the establishment of what the boffins called MRET, which is mandatory renewable energy targets …" suggests that many people - other than the boffins - might not be familiar with the term.

[265] Kellner, Douglas (1990). *Television and the crisis of democracy.* Boulder, Westview Press. pp. 105-106.

[266] White, D.M. (1950). The gatekeeper: a case study in the selection of news. *Journalism Quarterly,* 27(4). pp. 383-390.

[267] Masterton, Murray and Patching, Roger (1997). *Now the news in detail. A guide to broadcast journalism in Australia.* 3rd edition. Geelong, Deakin University Press. pp. 15-18.

Several factors influence news producers in their work beyond the basic 'newsworthiness' of an item. They include their own views, pressure of audiences, ratings and circulation; commercial interests such as advertising; ownership; public relations operatives; politicians and government; and other journalists and media.[268]

Politicians are by far the largest group appearing in economic and business reports in all three programs under examination ranging from over 60% on the *Channel 9 News* to 44% on the *ABC News* and to over 30% in *The 7.30 Report*. This illustrates television journalists' perception of the leading role of politicians in economic and business issues and their role as idea promoters, policy makers and legislators. It also illustrates the preparedness of politicians to make themselves available to television and reflects news processes and logistics that make it easy for newsworkers to access politicians. The dominant presence of politicians highlights the potential for them to shape the media agenda and slant stories.

Table 2.4
Interviewees in economic and business reports 1 - 30 June 2004

	Channel 9 News %		ABC News %		The 7.30 Report %	
Politician	1	62.1	1	43.8	1	31.5
Spokesman	2	20.7	2	30.0	5	9.8
Worker/public	3	6.9	7	1.3	2	18.0
Analyst/comm.	4	3.4	3	7.5	6	6.5
CEO	4	3.4	4	6.3	6	6.5
Other	4	3.4	5	5.0	4	11.7
Business	-	-	5	5.0	3	14.9
Lawyer	-	-	7	1.3	8	1.1
	n = 10		n = 24		n = 15	

(Interviewee categories defined: Politician - representatives elected by voting at a state, territory or federal level. Spokesman - a catch-all category for representatives of non-business organisations such as interest groups or industry bodies. Worker/public - workers or members of the public presenting their personal point of view. Analyst/commentator - people employed by organisations, generally large financial organisations, to determine trends and/or to offer reflective comment (mostly economic and business but also social and political). Chief Executive Officers as identified by position. Other - interviewees outside the

[268]Pearson, Mark, and Brand, Jeffrey (2001). *Sources of news and current affairs.* Sydney, Australian Broadcasting Authority. p.7.

defined groups. Business - company employees identified by title other than CEOs for example chairman. Lawyers - legal practitioners.)

The central role of politicians in shaping the economic and business landscape is reinforced by comparing their presence with that of other groups. On the *Channel 9 News* politicians clearly exceed all other groups taken together (37.8%). On the *ABC News* the politicians' presence is only equalled by taking the next three categories - spokesman, analyst and CEO - together (43.8%). The combined business and CEO categories on *The 7.30 Report* (21.4%) make up the second largest group although still only two-thirds of the politician category. (Note: assessing the role of businessmen is made difficult by the practice of both Channel 9 and the ABC of often only identifying interviewees by their organisational affiliation and not by their title or job description.)

The prime minister, treasurer and other government ministers are interviewed during the survey period, as were the opposition leader and several opposition spokesmen. Premiers from all states have their say and the New South Wales treasurer made several appearances. Prime Minister John Howard accounts for 3.4% of the interviewee slots on *Channel 9 News*, 8.8% on the *ABC News* and 6.5% on *The 7.30 Report*. Howard is the politician most frequently interviewed on both news programs however his two appearances in reports on *The 7.30 Report* are exceeded by three appearances by Treasurer Peter Costello.

Politicians make their presence felt even when they do not appear in reports. For example although politicians are not interviewed in almost 40% of reports on *Channel 9 News* their influence is still apparent in three-quarters of those reports; Panthers CEO Roger Cowan (15 June) blames the state government for being behind the inquiry into the club. The rocket plane (22 June) is presented as "A first for private enterprise, the dawn of commercial space travel ..." in a sector that has previously been dominated - un-stated but implied - by government. The super debate (24 June) features industry and worker response to expected government changes to superannuation. Only one report on Channel 9, Undercoverwear (25 June), is free of the shadow of politicians.

The programs display varied results in giving ordinary people a voice. On the *ABC News* the lack of opportunity for individual workers or members of the public to have a say is displayed by their equalling the lowest representation (1%). Their appearance is greater on *Channel 9 News* (7%). On *The 7.30 Report* however the second largest category is worker/public and illustrates a good opportunity for the public to have a voice. Interviewing ordinary people is a feature of current affairs programs but as these are often vox-pops (interviews that run just a few seconds) the say of the ordinary person is limited.

How, where, and to whom interviewees make their comments reveals which politicians (and topics) are considered important by the media but also when politicians are prepared to make themselves available. A press conference attended by a large number of media illustrates the perceived importance of an individual or an issue. A one-on-one interview session could be indicative of only one media organisation having an interest in the interviewee. Alternatively the exclusive appearance could be caused by one of a number of other factors - for example a special relationship between the interviewee and the journalist or somebody else within the media organisation, payment, an attempt to manipulate the media by being accessible to one organisation but not others, or a specific reason such as the geographic, demographic or ideological reach of the selected media organisation - that influence the prominence of the politician. An elaborate stage-managed set-piece appearance may indicate promotion of an individual or an issue with a pseudo-event.

The interview occasions display a preference by Channel 9 for press conferences (45%) compared to the preferences of the two ABC programs for one-on-one interviews, *ABC News* (49%) and *The 7.30 Report* (73%).

Table 2.5
Interview occasions in economic and business reports 1 - 30 June 2004

	Channel 9 News %		ABC News %		The 7.30 Report %	
Press conf.	1	**44.8**	2	30.0	5	1.1
Interview	2	24.1	1	**48.8**	1	**73.4**
Set-piece	2	24.1	3	16.3	2	15.6
Vox-pop	4	6.9	5	1.3	3	6.4
Dramatic	-	-	4	2.5	-	-
Other	-	-	5	1.3	5	1.1
Studio	-	-	-	-	4	2.1
	n = 10		n = 24		n = 15	

(Interview occasions defined: Press conference - formal or semi-formal question-and-answer session between an interviewee and media representatives on a non-exclusive basis. Interview - one-on-one question and answer session between an interviewee and a media representative. Set-piece - interviewee making comment at a pre-planned and staged managed event that is not exclusively for the media. This includes events such as parliamentary sessions or annual general meetings. Vox-pop - vox populi or voice of the people interviews that are usually brief and informal with the interviewee not necessarily identified. Dramatic - a first-person account of an unexpected situation recorded in the heat of the moment. Other - interview occasion outside the defined categories. Studio - similar to interview above but conducted in a dedicated broadcast studio.)

'Hold it and they will come' could be a lesson from this category with a majority of the interviewees' comments in Channel 9 items originating from press conferences. A smaller but still significant number of the comments in the *ABC News* also originated in press conferences. The very small percentage of press conferences in *The 7.30 Report* and a large number of one-on-one interviews illustrates a major difference between news and current affairs programs. Rival news programs are often driven by the same daily news agenda with competitive pressures forcing them to cover the same events and attend the same press conferences. *The 7.30 Report*, a current affairs program, is better able to set its own agenda, pursue different or unique topics, and seek comment away from press conferences.

Press conferences generally indicate that the interviewee has made themselves available to all media. Press conferences range from formal, scheduled events organised by the interviewee and their supporters, to casual, impromptu events motivated by the media when and where they can gain access to the interviewee. A door stop is when the media approaches the interviewee - who may or may not be agreeable to answering questions - in a public place and asks for comment. It can be difficult for the viewer to judge if a press conference is scheduled, impromptu or a doorstop.

Press conferences are differentiated by factors such as their locations, backdrops, props, the interviewee's spatial control and the behaviour of the media. These factors can colour the message presented to audiences. For example, John Howard (water agreement 25 June), is seen within the restricted confines of Parliament House, with an Australian flag as a backdrop, behind a lectern with just two carefully placed microphones and with the media some distance away in what is clearly a scheduled press conference. By contrast Shadow Finance Minister Bob McMullan (drug backflip 22 June), appears to be doing a press conference on the run in a more public area outside Parliament house, with an array of microphones carrying large network logos and with reporters pressing close to him. The images support the thrust of the reports; Howard, presented visually as being in control, has successfully concluded an historic water agreement with the states, McMullan, interviewed on the run, is attempting to defend Labor's controversial abandonment of a long-held price-freeze of the Pharmaceutical Benefits Scheme.

Almost half of the comments in the *ABC News* are one-on-one interviews. These are also the largest category in *The 7.30 Report*. This is because current affairs reporters are usually chasing unique reports and are often seeking interviewees who are not available in press conferences and similar group events. Even if the interviewee has given a press conference, current affairs reporters often - and news reporters occasionally - want a separate interview to pursue unique topics or angles, to provide more explanation than is generally offered in news reports, or to distinguish their interview from other material. These one-on-one interviews are often conducted in a different location to press conferences to provide a different look to the report. As well, the in-depth nature of current affairs programs such as *The 7.30 Report* may mean it attempts to seek out - to a greater extent than news - the people who are feeling the impact of events, such as the eight mothers and mothers-to-be in the baby bonus report (30 June).

An informal pattern in television news and current affairs is that news interviews are often conducted standing up while current affairs interviews are conducted sitting down. Sit-down interviews can provide a more in-depth, reflective and analytical feel to the longer current affairs report.

The lack of studio interviews in both news programs illustrates a traditional feature of Australian television news; that the news studio is the domain of 'professionals' such as the news presenter and other presenters such as the finance, sport and weather presenters. Studio interviews however are a regular feature in current affairs and can provide an opportunity for extended discussion over a topic. *The 7.30 Report* carried two major studio interviews.

The number of voices (interviewees) in an item can be - but is not necessarily - a guide to the number of perspectives that are being presented.

Table 2.6
Distribution of voices in economic and business reports 1- 30 June 2004

Number of voices	Channel 9 News	ABC News	The 7.30 Report
1	2	1	-
2	1	7	-
3	3	4	-
4	**4**	**9**	1
5	-	2	2
6	-	-	**4**
7	-	1	1
8	-	-	1
9	-	-	2
10	-	-	1
11	-	-	1
Mean is:	2.9	3.3	7
	n = 10	n = 24	n = 13

Channel 9 News and *ABC News* both display four interviewees in the greatest number of reports (in bold) while *The 7.30 Report* with longer reports displays six interviewees in the greatest number of reports.

The greatest number of voices (interviewees) in the greatest number of items in the news programs is four people in both *Channel 9 News* and the *ABC News*. The average number of interviewees per item is 2.7 for Channel 9 and 3.3 for the *ABC News*. *The 7.30 Report* displays the greatest frequency of six people per item which should allow a topic to be explored at greater depth as would be expected in a current affairs program of this type. the average number of interviewees is in *The 7.30 Report* is 7.1.

In two reports on Channel 9, Panthers (15 June) and rocket plane (22 June) only one interviewee is presented. In the Panthers report, CEO Roger Cowan may have been the only person available to make a comment for legal reasons or conventions. In the rocket plane report, pilot Mike Melvill was the sole interviewee, possibly because as the man who flew into space, he was judged as the central and only necessary interviewee.

It is journalistic practice for reporters to sometimes ask the groups involved in an issue being reported to identify possible interviewees. For example in the industrial relations report (8

June) on *The 7.30 Report*, reporter Heather Ewart may well have asked the National Union of Workers to identify workers unsatisfied with workplace agreements and employer groups such as the Chamber of Commerce and Industry to identify workers satisfied with workplace agreements. Of the three workers who appeared in the report two are critical and one is satisfied with workplace agreements. This suggests that those groups who are best able to provide effective interviewees can build the strongest case for their position and causal narrative.

Some items on *The 7.30 Report* saw interviewees make comments without being identified by either a super or an introduction for example industrial relations report (8 June); a practice that makes it impossible for viewers to know the identity of the interviewee or their perspective unless their faces are very recognisable. One argument to support this technique is that television practice allows interviewees to initially appear without being identified as a tease to spark viewers' curiosity and keep them watching. Another argument is that when interview grabs are too short there is not enough time to identify the interviewees. Both arguments seem to come at some cost to comprehension. Alternatively this failure may rest with production difficulties; the sort of difficulties that see interviewees appear without being identified, identified as the wrong person or supers appearing at inappropriate times when no interviewee is speaking.

A heavy bias in favour of males is displayed on all three programs.

Table 2.7
Gender of interviewees in economic and business reports 1 - 30 June 2004

	Channel 9 News %		ABC News %		The 7.30 Report %	
Male	1	**86.2**	1	**91.3**	1	**73.4**
Female	2	13.8	2	8.8	2	26.0
	n = 10		n = 24		n = 15	

The representation of women among the interviewees reflects their limited public voice in economic and business affairs. By way of comparison females make-up 50.3% of the Australian population compared to 49.7% of males. Women number 25% of Members of

85

Parliament in the House of Representatives and 30% of Senators[269] while fewer than 8% of Australian company directors are women.[270]

Institutions

Exploration of the institutions represented in the television programs under examination offers an insight into the main institutions - as perceived by the media - in Australia in the debate over the economy and business. The media comments, including those made on television, by the spokespeople who represent these institutions are a public signal of their positions on issues. These signals are for both mass and elite consumption with the elites either consuming media directly or being advised of media content by their staff, or by media monitoring services, such as Rehame.[271] Government, combining state and federal, and opposition, combining state and federal, are the two most represented institutions on *Channel 9 News* (both 31%). Government, including state and federal, is the most represented institution in economic and business reports on both ABC programs; *ABC News* (33%) and *The 7.30 Report* (25%). Interest groups are the second most represented institution on *ABC News* and business is second on *The 7.30 Report*.

Table 2.8
Institutions in economic and business reports 1 - 30 June 2004

	Channel 9 News %		ABC News %		The 7.30 Report %	
Government	1	**31.0**	1	**32.5**	1	**24.5**
Opposition	1	**31.0**	4	11.3	6	9.6
Interest groups	3	13.8	2	18.8	5	13.0
Business	4	10.3	3	17.5	2	18.1
Other+non.inst.	4	10.3	6	5.0	3	14.1
Union	6	3.4	6	5.0	8	2.3
Finance	-	-	5	6.3	7	4.3
National	-	-	8	3.8	-	-
Academia	-	-	-	-	3	14.1
	n = 10		n = 24		n = 15	

---

[269] http://www.aph.gov.au/Library/parl/HIST/noswomen.htm
[270] http://www.womenonboards.org.au/news/media050406.pdf
[271] In 2001 Aged Care Minister Bronwyn Bishop made headlines when it was revealed her office had spent $350,000 on media monitoring in three months during the nursing home kerosene bath scandal. Gilchrist, Michelle (2001). Self-monitoring - Budget 2001 - The Aftermath, *The Australian* 26 May. p.6.

(Institution categories defined: Government - state and federal governments (note: no distinction is made on a party basis) and departments. Opposition - state and federal opposition politicians. Interest groups - organisations that represent specific interest groups and have the goal of bringing about particular policies or actions. Industry groups fall within this category although it is recognised they may play other roles. Business - large and small commercial enterprises operated with the aim of making a profit. Other - those institutions outside the defined categories. Union - trade unions, the ACTU and international labour movements. Finance - organisations such as banks, building societies, insurance companies, mortgage providers, and investment companies. National - non-government institutions with Australia-wide influence such as the Reserve Bank of Australia and the Australian Securities and Investments Commission. Academia - tertiary-level educators or researchers.)

Channel 9 News's equal ranking of government and opposition displays an apparent balance in reporting the perspective of these two groups. This balance however is not always achieved in individual reports, but instead fits the concept of balance over time. For example in some reports government interviewees are in the minority such as green power (15 June) where the government is represented by Prime Minister John Howard while opposition is represented by Labor's Shadow Family Minister Wayne Swan and the Green's Bob Brown. In the water agreement report (25 June) government is represented by state premiers Bob Carr and Peter Beattie and Prime Minister John Howard while no opposition figure is interviewed. However as this report looks at the nature of state-federal relations, the state governments and the federal government are presented as opponents.

The government white paper on energy (all programs 15 June) is a good example of the interplay between institutions. The plan, presented by the federal government, prompted responses from other political parties, the minerals sector, a conservation group, and the alternative energy industry. The report and the responses display some of the different groups - political, ideological and profit motivated - who have a voice on energy and environment issues.

The plan includes $1.5 billion in cuts to the diesel excise and $500 million for lower emission technologies. The *Channel 9 News* report has opposition MP Wayne Swan criticising the announcement as being political ahead of an election, Prime Minister John Howard describing the plan, Mitch Hooke, from the Minerals Council, praising the package and Greens MP Bob Brown criticising the package. *ABC News* carries John Howard describing the plan, criticism of the plan from Don Henry, the Australian Conservation Foundation, and

Susan Jeanes, from the manufacturers of alternative energy sources Renewable Energy Generators, and Opposition Leader Mark Latham. *The 7:30 Report* has John Howard describing the plan, Peter Cook, of the coal support group Greenhouse Gas Technologies, praising the plan, Don Henry, of the Australian Conservation Foundation, criticising the plan, Carl Mallon, from Wind Energy Australia, criticising the plan and Greens MP Bob Brown criticising the plan. Between them the three programs carry five interviewees supporting the plan and eight against. On an interviewee-by-interviewee basis - an uncertain method of judging balance - only Channel 9 has two for and two against the plan.

On the *ABC News* the second largest group is interest groups (19%). This illustrates the important dialogue between government and interest groups in economic and business debate. This also indicates that, on the *ABC News* at least, interest groups have a larger role in debating economic and business issues than the role of political opposition parties (11%).

Of the fifteen interest group appearances on the *ABC News*, five (33.3%) represent farmers' interests; the Fire Blight Task Force and the NSW Apple Growers Association (1 June) and the National Farmers Federation (8, 24 and 25 June). (Farmers actually receive greater representation than this with individual farmers appearing on three additional occasions but listed under the business category.) The Australian Conservation Foundation appears twice (15 and 24 June) and motoring interest groups - the NRMA and the Australian Automobile Association - also appear twice (both 7 June). Other groups are the Asbestos Diseases Foundation (4 June), the Property Council (18 June), the Shareholders Association (21 June), the Parents & Citizens Federation (22 June), the National Summit on Housing Affordability (28 June) and the Housing Industry Association (28 June).

The interest groups represented on *Channel 9 News* are the Minerals Council (15 June), the Property Council (18 June) whose constituency, policy and funding is not identified, and the Financial Services Association and the Superannuation Funds Association (both 24 June). At least three of these four groups represent industry rather than the public.

The national institution represented is the Reserve Bank with two appearances by Deputy Governor Glen Stevens (in two reports on 2 June) and one by Governor Ian MacFarlane (4 June). The two appearances by Glen Stevens on the same day illustrate another feature of television news; a single speech or press conference by a prominent person might range over a number of topics that are then included in several different news reports.

The representation of business as an institution is greater than indicated because it is also represented by groups appearing outside the category, for example by interest groups such as the Minerals Council and the National Farmers Federation. In its own right business ranks fourth on the *Channel 9 News* and third on the two ABC programs. This category includes reports such as QANTAS seeking to base staff in London to save costs (22 June). In speaking of the international cost pressures it is experiencing, QANTAS might also be seen to be reflecting the cost pressures of this nature on other Australian companies. It is uncertain, however, what message viewers might take away under the cultural theory model.[272] Viewers might receive the cost pressure argument, the management-labour conflict, how the issue might impact on their next overseas trip, or all three messages.

The management-labour issues in the QANTAS report introduces the representation of unions and television coverage. Unions ranked sixth on the *Channel 9 News* and the *ABC News* and ranked eighth on *The 7.30 Report*. The percentage of coverage given to unions, Channel 9 (3%), *ABC News* (5%) and *The 7.30 Report* (2%), falls well short of even the most pessimistic figures from the Australian Bureau of Statistics that show 17% of private sector workers belong to a trade union.[273] Workers' interests are also represented in several reports by the Asbestos Disease Foundation and the workplace reform item (28 June).

The 7:30 Report is a program seen in all states (unlike ABC news which generally has different versions for each state) and its goal is to make viewers in all states feel that their views are represented. In reports on national issues, such as water use (23 and 24 June), a number of states are represented with the NSW, WA and Victorian governments each represented twice.

---

[272] Hall, Stuart (ed.) (1980). *Culture, media, language: working papers in cultural studies. 1972-79.* London, Hutchinson. pp. 128-138. See discussion later in this chapter.

[273] This figure, and union claims that it is incorrect and does not represent a drop from 30% 12 months before, were reported on ABC Radio. Either figure shows a very limited representation compared to membership. http://www.abc.net.au/cgi-bin/common/printfriendly.pl?http://www.abc.net.au/worldtoday/content/2005/s1333496.htm

It is difficult to understand the nature or perspective of some of the institutions that are represented in some of the reports on *The 7.30 Report* because of a lack of information. In the energy policy report (15 June) for example, one interviewee is introduced by reporter Michael Brissenden with the line " … the fossil fuel industry thinks that's a pretty good approach." A super then identifies the interviewee as Dr Peter Cook, Greenhouse Gas Technologies. Viewers can identify Cook as speaking about the needs of the fossil fuel industry but it is unclear if Cook is a lobbyist, a corporate spokesman or an independent scientist. There is no explanation of what Greenhouse Gas Technologies is or its significance. The same report features another interviewee identified by a super as Dr Carl Mallon, Wind Energy Australia. Viewers are left with a similar lack of information as with Dr Cook. Television reporters struggle to fit a lot of material into a limited time and in that struggle context can be a victim.

The representation of different institutions on the different programs might have several explanations. It might indicate a editorial position taken by the journalists and news managers in terms of which institutions they judge as important. It might reflect an organisational structure and reach in which some networks are able to cover more institutions. For example does Channel 9 restrict its political coverage to those actors in Federal Parliament and is the ABC able to reach more institutions which may have to be interviewed away from Parliament House? The ABC's coverage of farm groups might illustrate a sensitivity to rural issues that has come from pressure from rural interest groups.

NEWSWORKERS AND PRODUCTION PROCESSES

… television journalists in Australia have firm professional attitudes. This is reassuring, given the capacity of television to distort reality …

John Henningham[274]

Their [television journalists'] grasp is not as good as say that of some of the print journalists but they are certainly more [than previously] au fait with who's who in business and some of the basic issues about business.

---

[274] Henningham, John (1988). *Looking at television news.* Melbourne, Longman Cheshire. p. 101.

Trevor Sykes[275]

I think [journalists' economic knowledge] is surprisingly good, considering that they have a mixed job if you like. They are both media people and they have to know a bit about their topic. But presumably they know, [that interviewees] know more than they do, but nevertheless they still have to ask you the right question. So the ones that interview you live, I think they do an amazingly good job. Occasionally, and again this is the nature of the business, because the economics reporter can't get out or whatever, they've sent the court reporter or whatever.

Chris Caton.[276]

Events and Pseudo-events, News Values and Report 'Triggers'

The three comments above display the need for newsworkers covering economics and business to combine professional attitudes with specialist knowledge and to work within news processes. In gathering news, attitudes and news values and processes attempt to make sense of the events and pseudo-events that are a major source for television news. The term 'pseudo-event' is used by Boorstin to explain the interviews, debates, press conferences, leaks and other manufactured events that are presented in the media. The four characteristics of a pseudo-event are 1. lack of spontaneity. 2. designed to be reported or reproduced. 3. having an ambiguous relation to reality. 4. devised with the intention of being a self-fulfilling prophecy. Boorstin suggests pseudo-events create a world where fantasy is more real than reality. [277]

That view is updated with an examination of postmodernism by Kellner. He writes:

The acceleration of media politics seems to support the postmodern media theory of Jean Baudrillard and others who claim that image has replaced reality in a contemporary media society and that the incessant proliferation of images

[275] Sykes, Trevor (2000). Senior writer and Pierpont columnist, *The Australian Financial Review*. Personal interview 17 July.
[276] Caton, Chris (2000). Chief Economist, BT Funds Management Australia. Former head of the Economic Division of the Department of Prime Minister and Cabinet. Personal interview 21 July.
[277] Boorstin, Daniel (1962). *The image*. Harmondsworth, Penguin. pp. 22-23

("radical semiurgy") has produced a state of affairs whereby individuals can no longer distinguish between the image and the real. In short, they contend, the image has come to constitute a new mass-mediated reality.[278]

Kellner, however, adds that "postmodern image fetishism" ignores institutional and commercial issues of network television.[279] Among these issues are some of the factors identified in the content analysis examined later in this chapter including the reliance of producers on diary events, television's need for visual material, production constraints such as limited camera crews and the logistics of travel and the convenience of file footage and handout footage. Statements by Baudrillard such as "... that TV is present precisely where it happens is not coincidental ..."[280] is illustrated in the day-to-day content of news based largely on non-coincidental events such as press conferences, meetings, demonstrations and the like. These events become news on television because television is there to cover them.

So, television is susceptible to pseudo-events because of its reliance on vision and this can be provided by events or pseudo-events. Because of their planned nature television can capture pseudo-events much more readily than many real events. Whale writes "Television is pictures. It feeds on them. It must always have them ... This is the first datum that all television journalists have to come to terms with."[281]

These two conditions - pseudo-events and television's need for pictures - come together in television news to create a preference for diary items. Diary items are those events known ahead of time such as press conferences, set pieces such as a political speech or an annual general meeting, inquiries, data releases,[282] anticipated announcements such as the Reserve Bank's announcements on interest rates and so on. Diary events do not always turn out as expected, some might provide stronger news stories than anticipated, while others might be judged as not warranting a report. Such items are generally carefully monitored by journalists

---

[278] Kellner, Douglas. 1990. *Television and the crisis of democracy*. Boulder. Westview Press. p. 159.
[279] ibid. p. 160.
[280] Baudrillard, Jean (translated by Shelia Faria Glaser) 1994, Simulacra and Simulation, Ann Arbor, University of Michigan Press. p. 53.
[281] Whale, John (1969). *The half-shut eye - television and politics in Britain and America*. London. Macmillan. p. 19.
[282] Quarterly earnings announcements and the expectations generated ahead of their release may be the ultimate pseudo-event in business according to Martin, Dick (2004). Corporate reputation: reputational mythraking, *The Journal of Business Strategy*, 2004, Vol. 25. Iss. 6. pp. 39-45.

but their inclusion in news bulletins depends on what is actually announced or takes place and what other newsworthy events are taking place on the day. An example from newsroom practice is how one news producer might ask another: 'What's in the diary for tomorrow?' As a survey category a diary event is known ahead of time; at least at the beginning of the day's work. Non-diary events are those events that are not expected and so cannot be planned for or anticipated.

Table 2.9
Diary/non-diary items in economic and business reports 1 - 30 June 2004

	Channel 9 News %		ABC News %		The 7.30 Report %	
Diary	1	60.0	1	70.8	2	26.7
Non-diary	2	40.0	2	29.2	1	73.3
		n = 10		n = 24		n = 15

(Diary/non diary categories defined: Diary reports - reports based on those events known ahead of time such as press conferences, set pieces, data releases and anticipated announcements. Newsworkers can prepare for the coverage of diary events. Non-dairy reports - reports of events that are not expected.)

The survey reveals a heavy dependence on diary items by both news programs with 60% of economic and business items on *Channel 9 News* and 71% on *ABC News*. The percentage of diary items is higher than the 30% of 'staged performance, scheduled events'[283] found by Tiffen and this might be partly explained by economic and business news having a greater dependence on diary items than general news, and in part by methodological differences. The *Channel 9 News* item that typically illustrates Boorstin's characteristics is the federal government's release of its energy policy (15 June). This matches the criteria in the following way: 1. John Howard's speech announcing the policy is clearly a planned event. 2. The speech and the announcement are designed to be reported. 3. The ambiguous nature of the announcement is reflected by the opposition's Shadow Family Minister Wayne Swan's comments that the government is making the announcement for political reasons ahead of an election. 4. The announcement is self-fulfilling in that the government will be able to point back to the announcement as proof that it does have an environment policy. Despite these comments it is likely the government would argue that the announcement is a legitimate event designed to inform the public on policy.

---

[283]Tiffen, R. 1989. *News & power*. North Sydney, Allen & Unwin. p. 23.

Non-diary items on *Channel 9 News* include the NSW property tax (18 June) and the federal opposition's change of policy on the Pharmaceutical Benefits Scheme (22 June). These are non-diary items because the media did not know about them ahead of time and could not plan for them.

The *ABC News* displays a predisposition to go to pre-planned and staged events with 17 reports (71%) centred around diary items. Like Channel 9, the ABC covered the federal government's announcement on transport funding (7 June). Several items stand out as reporting pseudo-events; a farmers' demonstration against imported fruit (1 June), farmers at a water conference (8 June), and the National Housing Affordability Summit (28 June). Viewed against Boorstin's four criteria, the summit does 1. lack spontaneity; 2. is designed to be reported; 3. has an ambiguous relation to reality in that the participants come from vastly different perspectives (the welfare sector and the housing industry) and that the summit is powerless to produce any real outcomes; and 4. the event is a forum for parties with vested interests who can refer back to the summit with the claim that it is an authoritative occasion.

Non-diary items on the ABC included the NSW property tax (18 June), Telstra's share price has its best one-day rise in three years (21 June), the federal opposition's sudden and unexpected policy change on the Pharmaceutical Benefits Scheme (22 June) and the decision by Southcorp to cut its workforce (28 June).

The 7:30 Report shows a very different outcome with almost three-quarters of the reports rating as non-diary items. This outcome is to be expected from a current affairs program, the very nature of which is to go beyond diary or daily news items. This aspect of current affairs is further illustrated by current affairs programs such as Channel 9's *A Current Affair* or Channel 7's *Today Tonight* both of which rarely run daily news or diary items. The difference in content, approach and style between *The 7.30 Report* and *A Current Affair* and *Today Tonight* is marked. This is highlighted by comments such as: "The term 'current affairs' in television has become confused by evening commercial 'tabloid', lifestyle, consumer-oriented programs such as *A Current Affair* and *Today Tonight*, relaying mixed messages about the definition and credibility of the genre. [284]

When *The 7:30 Report* does run diary or news items (the James Hardie inquiry (14 June), energy policy and Kemp interview (15 June), and baby bonus, 30 June) it seeks to provide viewers with extra material, interviewees and insight. For example, while *The 7.30 Report* and the *ABC News* both carried reports on the government's energy plan only Prime Minister John Howard and Don Henry, of the Australian Conservation Foundation, appear in both reports. The news report has interviews with Susan Jeanes, from Renewable Energy Generators, and Opposition Leader Mark Latham. *The 7.30 Report* has interviews with Peter Cook, Greenhouse Gas Technologies, Carl Mallon, Wind Energy Australia, and Greens Leader Bob Brown.

Researchers examining news values in relation to economic and business reports on television have a variety of criticisms. Among them are that reports are excessively market focussed, making the coverage narrow[285] and with an emphasis on earnings expectations.[286] Scandal - such as criminal activity, sex, excessive profits and salaries - is another characteristic.[287] So too is the relationship between the international and national economies and government management of the economy.[288] Television's reporting of business people and how wealth is stigmatised is considered[289] as is the manner in which it takes sides in class conflict by blaming workers for inflation.[290]

These findings are reflected in the survey period. Some examples are the market focus as illustrated by the emphasis on price moves and earnings in the nightly finance reports and

---

[284] Pearson, Mark, and Brand Jeffrey (2001). *Sources of news and current affairs*, Sydney, Australian Broadcasting Authority. p. 5.

[285] Parsons, Wayne (1990). *The power of the financial press*. New Brunswick, Rutgers University Press. pp. 207-220.

[286] Martin Dick (2004). Corporate reputation: reputational mythraking. *The Journal of Business Strategy*, Vol. 25. Iss. 6. p.39.

[287] Tumber, Howard (1993). Selling scandal: business and the media, *Media, Culture & Society*. Vol. 15. Iss. 3. p.351.

[288] Block, Stephen (1992). Free trade on television: the triumph of business rhetoric, *Canadian Journal of Communication*. No. 17. p. 75. Also see Goddard P. et. al. (1998). Economic news and the dynamics of understanding: the Liverpool project. in Gavin, Neil T. (ed.) *The economy, media and public knowledge*. London, Leicester University Press.

[289] Thomas, Sari (1992). Bad business? A re-examination of television's portrayal of businesspersons, *Journal of Communication*. 42(1). p. 95.

[290] Philo, Greg et. al. (1995). Reasonable men and responsible citizens: economic news. in Philo, Greg (ed.) *Glasgow media group reader, Vol. 2*. London, Routledge. pp. 35-36.

individual news reports such as the Telstra share price rise (ABC 21 June) and Westfield re-organisation (ABC 25 June). Scandal is seen in the inquiry into the Panthers football club and payments to CEO Roger Cowan (Channel 9 and ABC 15 June). The international and national economies are reported in the oil price rise (ABC 2 June). Government management of the economy is reflected in the reports on house prices and interest rates (4 and 9 June). Class conflict is illustrated in the report on industrial relations and summarised by Opposition Industrial Relations Spokesman Craig Emerson's comment that Australian Workplace Agreements are "... commonly used to screw poor people." (*The 7.30 Report* 8 June). Broadcasting this sentiment is in line with *The 7.30 Report* result that ranked workers/public as the second highest category among 'interviewees in economic and business reports (see Table 2.4) and is in contrast with research such as Philo that finds "Broadcasters operated hierarchies of status and importance which were informed by class assumptions."[291]

The broad range of these and other issues involved in business and economic news reporting means there is dispute over the quality of television's coverage of economic and business affairs:

> I think [the coverage we get on commercial news programs of big economic or news stories] is adequate. It is straight up and down. They kind-of report what the market is doing. They tend to be fairly focused on the stock market. The corporate stories that they do tend to be related to that in terms of what profits have been announced and so on.
>
> Alan Kohler[292]

> I think [economic news on television] is generally poorly reported. We seem to have an inordinate focus on conflict or dispute or disruption or difficulty.
>
> Mark Patterson[293]

---

[291] Philo, Greg (1995). The media in a class society. in Philo ibid. p. 183.
[292] Kohler Alan. (2000). Business and Economics Editor. *The 7.30 Report*, ABC Television. Columnist *The Australian Financial Review*. Personal interview 5 July.
[293] Patterson, Mark (2000). Chief Executive, Australian Chamber of Commerce and Industry. Personal interview 16 June.

News values can be examined from three perspectives; that of journalists, of political economy, and of cultural theory. The different perspectives emphasise structure or agency, and producers or consumers in different degrees.

The perspective of journalists is displayed by the results of a worldwide survey that found news values are shaped by clearly defined criteria employed, consciously or otherwise, by journalists. The six key criteria are: consequence, proximity, conflict, human interest, novelty and prominence.[294] These, or similar criteria, are also put forward in a survey of Australian journalists[295] and presented in guides for training journalists.[296]

The bureaucratic newswork structure of journalism considers how newsroom organisational factors - such as reporters covering specific areas known as rounds - effects what is reported.[297] This adds non-events to events and pseudo-events already examined. Non-events are those events overlooked by journalists because they fail to fit into the structural framework. Fishman gives the example of a woman who accuses the local police of corruption during a county budget hearing. But because the woman's complaint was outside "...the set of alternatives..." and " ... she represented no formally constituted group which fit into the constellation of interests appropriate to the issue" she was ignored. This was despite the woman being coherent and having a sensible argument.[298]

The political economy perspective suggests news is shaped in four different ways; by consumers in the free market model, by what media owners seeking to preserve their interests require journalists to present to the audience in the manipulative model, by the routines of news work in the bureaucratic model, and through a "broad but selective interpretation of society through a mediating ideology"[299] in the ideological consensus model. Viewers can not necessarily judge which of these influences shape story selection.

[294] Masterton, Murray and Patching, Roger (1997). *Now the news in detail. A guide to broadcast journalism in Australia*. 3rd edition. Geelong, Deakin University Press. pp. 15-18.
[295] Henningham, John (1998), *Looking at television news*. Melbourne, Longman Cheshire. pp. 156-170.
[296] Alysen, Barbara (2002). *The electronic reporter: broadcast journalism in Australia*. Sydney, UNSW Press in conjunction with Deakin University Press. p. 17. Masterton op. cit.
[297] Tuchman, Gaye (1978). *Making news: a study in the construction of reality*. New York, Free Press. pp. 29-31
[298] Fishman, Mark (1980). *Manufacturing the news*. Austin. University of Texas Press. pp.78-79.
[299] Windschuttle, Keith (1984). *The media – a new analysis of the press, television, radio and advertising in Australia*. Ringwood, Penguin Books Australia Ltd. p.270. See also Philo, Greg (1999). *Message received:*

Cultural theory considers agency via two groups: producers and audiences. News is encoded by producers such as journalists and is decoded by audiences.[300] However individuals decode material in different ways. McKee illustrates the difficulty of analysis with the suggestion that media studies, have " ... demonstrated that the interpretations produced by academics of media texts might not exist anywhere outside universities."[301]

The influence of structure and agency varies and different writers have emphasised one over the other or dialectical approaches.[302] The consideration of the different models provides valuable insights into which events and issues are reported. For example, the decision-making role of individual journalists suggests a freedom for journalists to decide what issues and events to report emphasises agency. However the identification of an internationally shared news criteria and its adoption by journalism educators[303] at a time when more and more journalists are tertiary educated[304] indicates the emergence and recognition of structure. Likewise encoding and decoding appears to emphasise agency, but the uniformity of television news - shaped by factors such as journalism education, professional values, work practices, community expectations and habits, business organisation and financing, technologies - calls for structure to be considered because these limit what can be presented in television news and current affairs programs.

Glasgow media group research, 1993-1998. Harlow, Longman. and Tiffen, Rodney (1989). *News and power.* North Sydney, Allen & Unwin.
[300] Hall op. cit.
[301] McKee, Alan. 2002. Textual analysis, in Cunningham, Stuart, and Turner, Graeme, (eds.) *The media and communications in Australia.* Crows Nest, Allen and Unwin. p.68.
[302] McAnulla, Stuart (2002). Structure and agency, in Marsh, David and Stoker Gerry (eds.) *Theory and methods in political science. 2nd edition.* Basingstoke, Palgrave Macmillan. pp. 271-291.
[303] Alysen op. cit. and Masterton and Patching op. cit.
[304] Henningham (1988). op. cit. pp.68-70

Table 2.10

News criteria for economic and business reports 1 – 30 June 2004

	Channel 9 News %		ABC News %		The 7.30 Report %	
Consequence	**1**	**70.0**	1	**62.5**	2	33.3
Proximity	-	-	-	-	-	-
Conflict	3	10.0	3	16.7	**1**	**46.7**
Human interest	-	-	-	-	3	6.7
Novelty	2	20.0	-	-	3	6.7
Prominence	-	-	2	20.8	3	6.7
	n = 10		n = 24		n.= 13	

(News criteria categories defined: Consequence - the impact of events. Proximity - generally the geographical distance between the event and the audience; the closer the event the greater the interest. However this can be extended to cultural, demographic, economic and other 'proximities'. Conflict - the differences between groups; this may be most dramatically reflected in violence such as war but includes other conflicts such as those between political opponents, business competitors, national governments and world bodies and so on. Human interest - reports that appeal to audiences because of shared cultural values. Novelty - reports about unusual events and those that deal with the '- ests' such as richest, fastest smallest and so on. Prominence - reports about well-known people or organisations and their successes and failings. The different categories are, of course, not mutually exclusive with some reports meeting a number of the criteria although for this analysis the reports have been categorised by the main criteria.)

The analysis reveals that consequence (the impact of events and how they affect audiences) is by far the most frequent dominant criteria in economic and business reports on the Channel 9 and ABC news programs. This means news producers are mostly looking for economic and business items that affect viewers in some material way. *The 7.30 Report,* on the other hand, places a greater emphasis on conflict. This may be explained by the news programs seeking to cover issues and events that impact on viewers while the current affairs program has greater latitude to explore the background to issues and events.

Reports that consider consequence include items such as oil prices, interest rates and higher drug prices. Those that look at conflict include items such as the NSW government action against the club industry (both news programs 15 June), farmers against the federal government over trade policy (*ABC News* 1 June), and workers against James Hardie over asbestos-related deaths and injury (*ABC News* 4 June). An example of novelty is the share market listing of a lingerie company (*Channel 9 News* 25 June). Prominence are those items involving famous people, such as Prime Minister John Howard meeting California Governor Arnold Schwarzenegger (*ABC News* 3 June), or the reports on large and well-known companies such as QANTAS and its plan to base workers off-shore (*ABC News* 22 June), Telstra's one-day profit rise (*ABC News* 21 June) and the Southcorp job cuts (*ABC News* 28 June).

Examining what 'triggers' television to cover a particular issue or event reveals television's preference for pre-planned events with strong visual elements. One half of *Channel 9 News's* and one third of the *ABC News's* business and economic reports were triggered by events as indicated below. *The 7.30 Report* displays a much greater commitment to summary with a majority of reports falling into this category; an event is used as a peg to explore issues.

Table 2.11
Triggers for economic and business reports 1 - 30 June 2004

	Channel 9 News %		ABC News %		The 7.30 Report %	
Event	1	**50.0**	1	**33.3**	-	-
Breaking news	2	40.0	2	29.2	3	6.7
Announcement	3	10.0	3	12.5	2	20.0
Summary	-	-	3	12.5	1	**66.7**
Data release	-	-	5	8.3	-	-
Market moves	-	-	6	4.2	-	-
Investigation	-	-	-	-	3	6.7
	n = 10		n = 24		n = 15	

(Report trigger categories defined: Event - an occurrence or happening; this could be a protest gathering, a trip by an important individual, or a special ceremony or meeting. Breaking news - events or announcements that are unexpected including accidents or disasters. Breaking news might also be the release of information that was previously only known to a few people. Announcement - changes of policy, a finding or plan of action. Such announcements are often anticipated and the accuracy, or otherwise, of the reality to the anticipation can be the focus of reports. Summary - news that is generated by a review of events with a particular theme and/or use a single current event to explore a bigger topic. Newsworkers often look for a 'peg', a current event that allows the presentation of a summary or a look-ahead with preview pieces or a review of events with follow-ups. Data release - news that is generated by the release of data such as house building or employment figures and the results of surveys or studies. Market moves - reports that are sourced from market events such as a decline in the share price Investigation - an in-depth exploration of an issue not necessarily driven by breaking news or an announcement.)

Television news requires (as considered above) and is attracted to events that can be filmed. In deciding whether or not to do a report newsworkers consider 'what will we see?' or 'what can we film?' Television news needs action in front of the camera. Events include demonstrations, inquiries, political trips, interest group meetings and set-piece political occasions.

The visual event or action has different proximities - central, close or peripheral (near or far) - to the report that is presented to viewers. This can be illustrated by looking at several of the *Channel 9 News* reports. Central is when the visual event is the core of the report content itself, such as the flight of the first privately-funded rocket into space (22 June). Close is when the visual event is part of the process being reported, such as NSW Treasurer Michael Egan's entrance and address to the Legislative Assembly in bringing down the state budget (22 June); the budget speech is only a very brief summary of the much more complex budget papers and drawn-out legislative process. Near peripheral is the visual action that surrounds the event such as the state premiers arriving for the meeting on water policy in Canberra (25 June); this gives few insights into the actual discussions that will take place in priavte. Far peripheral is visual action associated with, but not a critical part of, the event or issue, such as the champagne celebration at the share market float of the Undercoverwear lingerie company (25 June); the float would happen without the champagne celebration but the celebration provides footage for the float process that is otherwise difficult to film. In other words, television is not averse to displaying events that are removed from the actual news content. This risks emphasising unimportant activity but allows coverage of non-visual issues and actions.

The *ABC News* carried several events that appeared to be aimed at attracting media interest and so influencing policy. One was the protest by farmers over apple and pear imports from New Zealand (1 June). The other was the Housing Affordability Summit (28 June). Demonstrations, public protests and meetings can serve a number of purposes, among them the sharing of information, the reinforcement of ideas by advocates being surrounded by fellow believers and as a display of solidarity. However the mass media carries the message from a protest or a meeting far beyond its own neighbourhood and that is another, if not primary, goal of the event's organisers. To turn to Boorstin again: "It is obvious too, that the value of such ... [an event] ... depends on it being photographed and reported in newspapers, magazines, newsreel, on radio and over television."[305]

Forty per cent of the economic and business reports in the *Channel 9 News* and 29% in the *ABC News* are breaking news, or in other words unexpected happenings. These include the NSW property tax (18 June), the ALP drug backflip (22 June), no capital gains (23 June) the superannuation debate (24 June), a record rise for Telstra shares (21 June) and cuts to the workforce at wine maker Southcorp (28 June). Breaking news items and non-diary items, as considered earlier, are usually the same however this is not always the case. For example Telstra's record one-day share price rise in three years reported on the *ABC News* (21 June) is a non-diary category but is not considered breaking news because of the constant volatility of the share market.

Summary reports are those that consider the wider issue around an event. An example of a summary report on *The 7.30 Report* is the energy package item (15 June). Political Editor Michael Brissenden covered the details of the government proposal announced that day. Brissenden then went further than the news reports in examining the issues that surrounded the announcement. He examined Australia's expected energy requirements in the future, the impact of the plan on different energy industry sectors, possible future technologies, and the policy in relation to the political environment.

Bennett's Rules

A set of 'rules' that guide political journalists is put forward by Bennett. [306] These rules can also be adapted for the analysis of reports and are suitable for examining economic and business reports because of the major role played by politicians. In summary the rules are: officials dominate political news accounts, greater conflict/consensus on issues means broader coverage, journalists follow the trail of power, there are rituals and customs in political processes and volatile events give journalists a greater voice.

---

[305] Boorstin. op. cit.
[306] Bennett, Lance W. (1997). Cracking the news code, in Iyengar, Shanto, and Reeves, Richard (eds.). *Do the media govern? Politician, voters, and reporters in America.* Thousand Oakes, Sage. pp. 103-117.

Analysis using Bennett's rules displays a different emphasis by each of the three programs. *Channel 9 News* is focused on government officials (40%) while the *ABC News* is focused on conflict and consensus (42%). Those positions are then reversed for the second ranked category. *The 7.30 Report* focuses on journalists' voice (47%); this could be driven by the 'volatile' events in the uncertainty ahead of the announcement of the 9 October 2004 election and by the freedom enjoyed by current affairs programs to pursue their own agenda.

Table 2.12

Bennett's rules adapted for economic and business reports 1 - 30 June 2004

	Channel 9 News %		ABC News %		The 7.30 Report %	
Govt. officials	1	**40.0**	2	20.8	3	13.3
Conflict/Consensus	2	30.0	1	**41.7**	2	20.0
Business officials	3	20.0	5	4.2	5	6.7
Trail of power	4	10.0	4	12.5	3	13.3
Rituals + customs	-	-	3	16.7	-	-
Journalists' voice	-	-	5	4.2	1	**46.7**
	n = 10		n = 24		n = 15	

(Bennett's rules categories in economic and business reports defined: Government officials - action or announcement involving politicians or government officials. Conflict/consensus - interactions including challenges and agreements between individuals or institutions. Business officials - action or announcement involving business officials. Trail of power - passage of a proposal, policy, challenge or issue through national and/or international institutions such as proposed legislation through parliament or a case through the courts. Ritual or customs - a regular event such as the bringing down of a government's annual budget (or failure to do so) or a corporate annual report.)

The leading role of conflict and consensus on the *ABC News* illustrates the importance the ABC assigns to interplay between agents and between and within institutions.

In terms of conflict the federal government is set against the farm sector over trade policy (1 June) and water policy (8 June), the federal opposition over the US free trade policy (17 June), an alliance of the farm sector, state governments and the Australian Conservation Foundation over water policy (24 June) and another alliance that promotes housing affordability (28 June). The NSW government is pitched against the Property Council and the state opposition over property tax (18 June). Another conflict sees QANTAS pitched against the unions (22 June). In all the reports the institution is represented by an individual. For example, the federal government by Prime Minister Howard, the farm sector by John Corboy, of the Fire Blight Task Force and Peter Corish, of the National Farmers Federation, the states by their premiers and so on.

Several examples of conflict within institutions are the divisions within the ALP over the Pharmaceutical Benefits Scheme (PBS) (both news programs 22 June), the US-Australia Free Trade Agreement (FTA) (*ABC News* 25 June) and division within the Cabinet over energy policy discussed in the Kemp interview (*The 7.30 Report* 15 June). On the PBS issue, Labor leader Mark Latham reversed opposition to a rise in the cost of subsidised medicines to make funds available to pay for other policy initiatives. In the free trade report Latham and a number of members of the federal opposition voted with the government in support of the agreement while other Labor MPs refused to vote and left the chamber. In the Kemp interview presenter Kerry O'Brien repeatedly asked Environment Minister David Kemp if his desire for a higher mandatory renewable energy target had been defeated by other cabinet ministers who did not support higher targets and posed the blunt question " ... did you get rolled or not?". Dr Kemp's reply was "I'm just saying it's quite inappropriate to reveal any Cabinet discussion."

Two of the reports in the consensus group are turnarounds and resolution of topics presented on previous days as conflict. These are the agreement between the farm sector and the state governments with the federal government over water policy (*ABC News* 25 June) and the federal opposition's agreement to support the federal government over the free trade policy (*ABC News* 25 June). These reports illustrate a commitment by the ABC to follow developments in ongoing issues. Consensus comes about through agents changing their positions for reasons that are not always explained. The other consensus report saw Westfield shareholders support Chairman Frank Lowy's changes to the Westfield structure (*ABC News* 25 June).

The three consensus reports came on the same day, 25 June. The likely cause of two of the resolutions is one of parliamentary processes and structure with the government struggling, in the words of reporter Jim Middleton "to clear the decks" (*ABC News* 25 June) ahead of the mid-winter break amid speculation of an August election. The timing of the Westfield extraordinary general meeting coincides with the end of the financial year.

There can also be several layers of conflict/consensus in a single report. The report on the Labor split/ FTA vote (*ABC News* 25 June), for example, has as one theme of consensus between the government and opposition, and as another theme conflict between members of the opposition over the trade agreement. The conflict is emphasised in the news reader's introduction by a graphic with the words 'Labor Split'.

The message of conflict/consensus can be subtle and framed before the reporter approaches the issue. For example, the National Summit on Housing Affordability report (*ABC News* 23 June) carries the implicit message that housing has become unaffordable through the very fact that the summit needs to be held and in the title of the event itself. The Canberra location of the summit suggests carrying the issue to the heart of government. So conflict between the summit and the federal government is established from the first moment of the report.

Conflict is displayed in *Channel 9 News* reports such as state property tax (18 June) where the NSW opposition uses a report by the Property Council on tax flaws to attack the government. It is also displayed in no capital gains (*Channel 9 News* 23 June) where the federal government attacks the opposition over disunity on pharmaceutical benefits. Consensus is the reason behind the water agreement report (both news programs 25 June) between the states and Canberra.

Bennett's rules illuminate the different news values applied by the different programs. *Channel 9 News* rates consequence as the most important; that government officials have an effect on the community. The ABC news journalists view conflict (the term itself appears in both news values and Bennett's rules) as most important and this brings cultural theory into play with a binary approach to conflict and consensus. Other binaries include government and opposition, the coal mining industry and the alternative energy industry and QANTAS management and QANTAS workers.

Journalists' voice is the largest single category in *The 7.30 Report* and reflects the non-news and non-diary approach of current affairs television; in the current affairs genre journalists have latitude to identify issues they think are important and to explore them. Journalists' voice also offers more latitude for comment. *The 7:30 Report's* Political Editor Michael Brissenden comments "Ah, the sanctity of opposition." when reporting on Shadow Finance Minister Bob McMullan's statement that the opposition would restrict spending on advertising if it was elected (16 June). Brissenden comments "Oh, dear." when opposition MP Roger Price weakens the opposition's position by suggesting that Labor should reconsider its opposition to government legislation, and comments "Surely not?" as he reports the opposition's claim that the government is playing politics with the US-Australia FTA (23 June). Heather Ewart ends her report on Australian Workplace Agreements (8 June) with the line "As employer groups ponder their next move, they shouldn't count on a Labor back down." when employer groups had not indicated that was their expectation. The different approaches taken by the *ABC News* and *The 7.30 Report* reflect the structure of the ABC and recall the conflict between ABC news and current affairs operations.[307]

Vision, Words and Pictures and Graphics:

> I think a lot of economic news is very difficult to visualise, and that's the bread
> and butter of television isn't it? The same complaint can be made about how
> television covers general news. Unless they have pictures it ain't news. That's the
> cliché isn't it?

>   Elliot Taylor[308]

> To be perfectly honest business information and financial information isn't
> necessarily a visual thing. It can be a visual thing but I wouldn't say it is as much a
> visual thing as a big explosion in general news or a revolution or something where
> the pictures are the gripping part of it. To be honest it is tougher to make business
> and financial information into exciting television. But we think it can be done.

>   James Ross[309]

---

[307] Petersen, Neville (1999). *Whose news? Organisational conflict in the ABC, 1947-1999.* Australian Journalism Monographs. Department of Journalism. Brisbane. University of Queensland.
[308] Taylor. op. cit.

An examination of the origins of vision helps explain some of the challenges of economic and business reporting. Central to any discussion of economic and business news on television is the difficulty of finding visual issues and events and reporting those issues that are not inherently visual. Newsworkers therefore seek vision from many sources that include the footage the network camera crews shot on the day; file footage from the library; footage from news agencies such as Reuters and APTN that the networks subscribe to; handout footage provided by companies, public relations firms, government and interest groups'; footage taken from advertisements and footage shot by amateurs with home video cameras.

Economic and business coverage on television faces the same restraints as general news gathering. Television needs cameras to be at an event to record it. Crews are a limited resource although their numbers have increased somewhat[310] in the more than 30 years since Epstein found that "... 90 percent or more of the national news shown on [the US network giant NBC] evening news report actually was produced by ten film crews based in five cities ...".[311] As well much of the visual action of economic and business news is repetitive or hidden; commodity prices rise and fall without immediate visual effect on mining or manufacturing, data is released at regular intervals but a change in housing affordability does not normally force families to live on the street, and key events such as central bank meetings take place behind closed doors.

A response to this is that large amounts of file footage are found in economic and business reports. Putnis found that over 50% of domestic news reports on Brisbane's four television news programs contained file footage.[312] The percentage of reports that contain at least some file and generic footage is greater in economic and business reports as illustrated below.

---

[309] Ross, James (2000). Media Marketing Director, Bloomberg Asia-Pacific. Personal interview 12 June.
[310] In the author's experience in working for commercial television stations in Sydney and Melbourne during the 1980s and 1990s each large newsroom could call on half a dozen or more cameramen during weekdays.
[311] Epstein,Edward Jay, 1973. *News from nowhere: television and the news.* New York, Random House. p.16.
[312]Putnis, Peter (1994). *Displaced, re-cut and recycled: file-tape in television news.* Gold Coast. Centre for Journalism Research & Education, Bond University. p. 73.

Table 2.13
The origins of vision in economic and business reports 1 - 30 June 2004

	Channel 9 News %		ABC News %		The 7.30 Report %	
File/generic	1	**70.0**	1	**100.0**	1	**91.0**
Handout	2	10.0	2	16.7	2	63.6
Satellite	2	10.0	3	12.6	-	-
No extra	2	10.0	-	-	3	36.3
New footage		100.0		100.0		100.0
		n = 10		n = 24		n = 15

(Vision categories defined: File/generic - vision in the television station library that is accessed as needed or vision that looks like this, for example, vision that is not directly tied to the events in that particular report. Handout - vision prepared by organisations other than the television stations and given to the station, in the form of corporate or government videos or video press releases, for purposes of publicity. Satellite - overseas vision that is received via satellite [or recently optical cable or the internet] and often filmed by an organisation other than the television station. No extra - a report that contains only vision shot on the day [or very recently] for that particular station by its own newsworkers. New footage - vision shot on the day [or very recently] for that particular report.)

Seventy percent of the *Channel 9 News* items contain some file or generic material with examples such as footage of solar power cells in the green power report (15 June), footage of the Panthers club interior and football games in the Panthers report (15 June) and footage of apartment blocks in the State property tax report (18 June). File or generic vision, such as that of the solar power cells, is a visual shorthand, or signifier. File footage can carry different messages. On one hand the message to viewers of the solar panels is 'you recognise this image, we're talking about alternative power sources' or on the other hand it may be a visual cliché with the message 'same old vision, same old comments about alternative energy'.

All of the *ABC News* reports contain what appears to be file or generic vision and several illustrate the risk of repetition that comes with using file footage. The reports on interest rates (4 June) and home lending (9 June) contain the same file footage - flags advertising the Beechwood Estate, a second estate advertised by a man in a red shirt, and a third estate with three blue flags - which means the two reports have a similar look leading to a sense of sameness or deja-vu for people who are regular viewers of the *ABC News*. A distinctive older

Canberra-style white house with a sold sign also appears in the home lending report (9 June) and again in the housing affordability report (28 June).

New, fresh vision in two of the Channel 9 items, rocket plane (22 June) and Undercoverwear (25 June) result in visually interesting reports, interest built by the dramatic nature of a space launch and landing and the fashionable appeal of lingerie.

Action in footage can also bring freshness and a positive message about the people involved. For example in delivering the NSW budget (22 June), NSW Treasurer Michael Egan is shown bounding up the steps to a press conference, portrayed as the man in control. Similarly, state Premiers Carr, Beattie and Bracks (25 June) are shown striding purposefully - arms swinging, coats blowing back with the pace of their walk, official papers tucked under their arms, assistants walking loyally by their side - toward their meeting with John Howard on water use. The message is a strong one of unity, power and determination.

These images do not happen by accident; the NSW treasurer and the premiers decided, or were advised, to present themselves in a positive way. The cameramen obliged by being there and recording, the journalists wrote the vision into their scripts and the editors cut the vision into the report. Consciously or not, Channel 9 newsworkers took the opportunities engineered by these state politicians to present them to viewers in a positive way. This is an illustration of the process of 'distillation' that Epstein[313] identifies in which each individual in the production chain makes an effort to select the most interesting material. The outcome is that the premiers benefit from the coverage and the newsworkers gain good material in what might be described as a 'coincidence of interest'.[314] Alternatively, it is no coincidence but an illustration of the interdependence between politicians and the media considered in Chapter 5.

All of *The 7:30 Report* items examined contained at least some new vision shot specifically for that report. At times this represented considerable effort such as the re-enactment of the cross-examination of witnesses in the James Hardie inquiry report (14 June). The national nature of the program and goal of relating to viewers across Australia calls for diverse

---

[313] Epstein. op. cit. p. 176.
[314] This term was suggested by Professor Rodney Tiffen during a discussion on this chapter.

shooting locations and interview comment as illustrated in the car dealers report (15 June) with footage of car dealers and interviews in south-east Queensland, Sydney and Melbourne.

Handout vision is defined as material shot by non-news or current affairs crews and intended to promote a particular product or organisation. The 2004 government Medicare advertisements and the 1995 ALP election advertisements featuring Bill Hunter (ad spending 16 June) are two examples of advertising material used in *The 7:30 Report*. The use of advertisements in reports on *The 7:30 Report* may take advertisers' messages, such as an advertisement for bank loans (8 June) to the ABC audience, some members of which might not otherwise see advertising material.

Further consequences of using handout material are illustrated in *The 7.30 Report* item on the government's energy policy (15 June). Viewers see complicated animated graphics of pipelines running from a city to deep under the ocean without any specific explanation of what they are watching. It is not until more than three minutes into the report that the graphics are seen for a second time with the explanation that this is an illustration of a process called geosequestration, or burying coal emissions underground. The handout footage emphasised geosequestration as an environmental option. The advocates of geosequestration sought to promote their technology by making the footage available and newsworkers at the ABC, on the lookout for useful vision, obligingly presented it to their audience.

Among the *ABC News* reports that contain handout vision are children's food television commercials in costly drugs (22 June), footage from an Australian Conservation Foundation commercial in water debate (24 June), and material from a corporate video in Southcorp jobs (28 June). These examples that material prepared to promote a particular perspective is regularly finding its way into news programs. The fourth report, workplace reforms (28 June), contains amateur footage of a building collapse that has the appearance of being given to the ABC by groups seeking to support the argument for workplace reform.

As digital technologies make it cheaper and easier to film and disseminate footage, more and more material that promotes particular causes or groups is likely to be made available to television networks and be broadcast.

The two main elements of a television news report - words and vision - work best when working together. For example, the script in the apple and pear demonstration report (*ABC News* 1 June) sets out the argument by Australian farmers against the government's plan to open the Australian fruit market to New Zealand producers. The footage shows good humoured, weather-beaten farmers handing out free fresh fruit to city pedestrians in a peaceful demonstration. The demeanour of the farmers and their comments suggests they have been put upon and exasperated for a long time but only now have they made the trip to the city in a last, justified protest against a government with no sympathy or understanding of their plight. The footage of the farmers suggests they are the very model of reason and provides visual support for their case that is put forward in words.

At other times the script and vision can work against each other to make the report hard to comprehend. One example is in the *Business Sunday* report on the company Hydro Pacific (7 July). The opening words in the script are:

> The comparison between Australia's support for environmentally friendly energy generation and its international peers leaves a gap so big it's left Pacific Hydro looking elsewhere for the majority of its expansion opportunities.

The script presents a negative message about Australian policy on the environment and suggests Australia is well behind the rest of the world. The footage, of a mountain range covered with trees, however, contradicts the message in the script.

Matching words and vision can be made more difficult by the number of different topics in a script. The Labor split/FTA report (*Channel 9 News* 25 June) illustrates the number of different topics that can be contained in one television news report. The news reader's introduction tells of Prime Minister John Howard "Seizing on divisions within the Labor Party ..." over the FTA. The report itself starts: 1. with a summary of the week: " [It] hasn't been a great week for Labor Leader Mark Latham and the Labor Party.". It then moves to 2. the Labor policy change on the Pharmaceutical Benefits Scheme; and 3. internal party conflict over the FTA; then 4. carries an interview grab of Liberal MP Andrew Southcott seeking to make political capital from this. The report next considers 5. Prime Minister John Howard's and Labor MP Kim Beazley's differences over linking the FTA to Australia's support for the United States in Iraq, and there is an interview grab from both Beazley and Howard. The report next 6. considers NSW Premier Bob Carr's position in urging Labor to support the FTA with an interview grab from Carr. Reporter Jim Middleton then 7. wraps up with the government attempting to clear the decks ahead of a five-week winter break and speculation about an August election.

The vision includes Mark Latham in Parliament, MP Andrew Southcott outside Parliament, Latham in a chemist shop and a customer, John Howard and US President George Bush, interiors of Parliament, Latham and opposition members in the corridors of Parliament, Kim Beazley in Parliament, a Howard interview grab on Sky television, Howard in Iraq and Australian forces in Iraq, Beazley in Parliament, a piece-to-camera from Jim Middleton, an interview grab from NSW Premier Bob Carr, Commonwealth cars waiting for MPs to finish the session and Howard avoiding waiting journalists and entering Parliament House. The total duration of the report is 1:47.

Unlike the apple and pear demonstration report considered earlier, the footage, with one major exception discussed below, does little to complement the script. Other than needing the supers to identify the interviewees, the script would be intelligible as a radio script. It fails the television adage 'If you can watch a television news report with your eyes closed and understand the report, it is a radio story. And if you can watch a television news report with you ears blocked and understand the report half the medium has been ignored.' Neither is an effective use of television.

The vision that is used falls into two main categories. There are the mechanical shots of interview grabs that go with the audio and are necessary but do little to enhance the report. Andrew Southcott for example is seen pausing to deliver his comment as he enters Parliament, Kim Beazley is seen addressing Parliament. Then there are the visual metaphors that are familiar to viewers; the footage of ALP leader Mark Latham in Parliament to signify the whole opposition challenge to the government, footage of Australian troops in Iraq to signify the whole Australian commitment in that country and the footage of Commonwealth cars queued up outside Parliament to signify MPs working late, trying to finish the session and to leave Canberra for their electorates.

One of the few shots in the report to enhance the script is that of John Howard brushing past waiting reporters outside Parliament as the script talks of election speculation. That shot carries a message; reporters are waiting, the country is waiting, for John Howard to announce the election yet he brushes past with a laugh and throw-away line. The script concludes with a powerful combination of words and vision as Jim Middleton talks about election speculation as viewers see the prime minister make it clear he is not about to end the speculation.

Television uses graphics to illustrate and explain and to enhance reports. In the first decades of television graphics were rudimentary. Whale writes:

> The sad fact is that for many of the ideas in which television coverage of current affairs must trade there are no useful illustrations possible. The vital details of a rent bill are not made clearer by little drawings of houses. Economics defy pictures altogether.[315]

In the 37 years since that was written technological advances such as computer-generated graphics have made animated graphics a useful tool in overcoming the challenge of presenting economic and business news on television.

> I try to introduce the emphasis through graphics. I think graphics do tend to emphasise. I prefer to show something in graphics than say it. Like $2.6b [profits] – if you see it appear in the graphic there, it has much more of an impact and then compare it to the loss BHP made the last year in red. Then people go 'oh wow' that is quite spectacular.
>
> Philip Lasker[316]

> We have a lot of graphics on screen which is one way for us of making it a very busy kind of program, a busy show, lots of things happening. If you are not immediately interested in the interview which is actually on the air at the time you are watching ... there is a lot of information on the screen like news headlines,

---

[315] Whale op. cit. p.25.
[316] Lasker. op. cit.

historical information like how the currency stocks have performed. So we kind of use other methods to make the program exciting for viewers.

James Ross[317]

Forty percent of the economic and business reports on *Channel 9 News* and 50% of those on the *ABC News* have a graphic to help explain the report.

Table 2.14
Graphics in economic and business reports 1 - 30 June 2004

	Channel 9 News %		ABC News %		The 7.30 Report %	
No graphic	1	**60.0**	1	**50.0**	1	**46.7**
Moving graphic	2	30.0	3	20.8	2	40.0
Static graphic	3	10.0	2	29.2	3	13.3
		n = 10		n = 24		n = 15

(Graphic categories defined: No graphic - no illustrations or other artwork. Moving - a complex graphic or illustration with either the main data moving, for example a moving line to illustrate a trend, or a moving background, for example moving vision of manufacturing, to illustrate industrial output, behind data of output. Static - a single-frame graphic, for example a table, cut into the report. Neither the background or details move.)

Examples of reports with graphics on *Channel 9 News* are green power (15 June) where a graphic is used to set out the three main points of the government's environment plan and the superannuation debate report (24 June) where a backdrop of $50 and $100 notes float onto the screen followed by figures of a hypothetical salary, superannuation payments, the government contribution and the overall benefit.

In the nightly finance segment, running about 20 seconds, *Channel 9 News* uses two sets of full-frame graphics to illustrate share market moves, with brief comments about individual companies, and currency moves; in both sets of graphics green arrows represent a gain and red arrows a loss.

On the *ABC News* an example of static graphics are three segments of text, in bullet-point form, used in the transport funding report (7 June) to identify the locations of Federal

---

[317] Ross. op. cit.

Government expenditure on road works. More complex moving graphics are used to describe the change in spending on investment housing between April 2002 and April 2004 with spending illustrated by a moving yellow line on a date (x axis) and value (y axis) graph.

Another use for graphics is demonstrated in *The 7.30 Report* with the corporate structure of James Hardie's Australian and overseas arms displayed (14 June). A complex graphic illustrating the process of geosequestration (15 June) is also used.

Reporters' Pieces-to-camera and Gender of Reporters and Interviewees

Some US television journalists call it 'face time'. In Australia it is called a piece-to-camera or a stand-up. This is the television technique when a journalist looks into the lens of the camera and delivers their lines directly to the viewer (A piece-to-camera is recorded to be inserted into a package and is different from a two-way when the reporter is talking with the presenter.) A piece-to-camera aims to demonstrate that the journalist is on the spot with first-hand knowledge, promotes the journalist as one of the news team that viewers can identify with and trust, adds variety to interviews and overlay footage in the report and provides recognition for the journalist among sources.

Table 2.15

Reporters' pieces-to-camera (ptc) in economic and business reports 1 - 30 June 2004

	Channel 9 News %	ABC News %	The 7.30 Report %
Yes ptc	100.0	91.7	63.6
No ptc	-	8.3	36.4
	n = 10	n = 24	n = 15

(Piece-to-camera defined: The television technique when a journalist looks into the lens of the camera and delivers their lines directly to the viewer. Also called a stand-up.)

All of the *Channel 9 News* reports have a reporter piece-to-camera. In an example of one of the most interesting and useful piece-to-camera Los Angeles-based United States Correspondent Karl Stefanovic travels to the Mojave Desert for the rocket plane flight (22 June). It is an event that news presenter Jim Waley calls "A day in aviation history ... the dawn of commercial space flight ...". With their reporter on the spot in a remote location Channel 9 is able to display a commitment to news by spending the money and making the effort to be where the news is happening. It is the type of piece-to-camera that is useful for future network promotions along the lines of 'Nine was there when history was made.'

The locations selected by ABC reporters for their piece-to-camera include the sites of demonstrations, a petrol station, the White House in Washington D.C., the Reserve Bank building in Sydney, state Parliament House in Sydney, and a number of locations around Parliament House in Canberra.

The business and economic items in *The 7:30 Report* during the survey period consist of nine reporter-presented pieces, four Canberra bureau-sourced Michael Brissenden studio-based reports (consisting of studio links, voice-over and interview material), and two studio interviews. Of the nine reporter pieces, three contain pieces-to-camera and four do not. The two reports analysed off the script did not make it clear if there were pieces-to-camera or not.

A survey of Australian television journalists found that 72% of Channel 9 journalists and 73% of ABC journalists are male.[318] The study looked at total newsroom staff so comparisons with the on-air reporters measured in this project are limited. Another survey - of all media - found that 67% of finance journalists are male.[319] Again comparisons are limited because the economic and business reports considered for this project were prepared by both specialist finance journalists, such as the ABC's Philip Lasker, and non-finance journalists, such as Channel 9's Christine Spiteri. The finding from this project however - that approximately three-quarters of the reports were prepared by male journalists - is roughly in line with both of those surveys.

Table 2.16
Gender of reporters in economic and business reports 1 - 30 June 2004

	Channel 9 News %	ABC News %	The 7.30 Report %
Male	80.0	83.4	73.3
Female	20.0	16.7	26.7
	n = 10	n = 24	n = 15

---

[318] Henningham (1988). op. cit. pp.65-66.
[319] Henningham, John (1997). Characteristics and attitudes of Australia's finance journalists. *Economic Analysis and Policy*. Vol. 27. No. 1. March. p. 49.

Factors such as the knowledge, approach and workload of individuals influence news managers in assigning reporters to stories. Gender bias might be the reason Christine Spiteri was assigned to the report on the listing of Undercoverwear (Channel 9 25 June) because it is about lingerie, a 'woman's issue'. A male reporter may have handled the topic differently. Following the report Channel 9 presenter Jim Waley appeared amused. Was this because of the intimate nature of lingerie, because of the novelty of a lingerie company listing on the stock market or for some other reason? Newsreader reaction to reports - introducing light-hearted items in a good natured manner or distressing reports in an excessively sombre manner - can be problematical; newsreaders might be anticipating or cueing the audience response in the belief their values are the same as the audiences' values.

The consideration of gender reveals that female reporters are more likely to seek comment from women than are male reporters. This illustrates the important role of reporters in selecting interviewees and what perspectives are presented to the audience.

Table 2.17
Gender of reporters/interviewees in economic and business reports 1 - 30 June 2004

	Channel 9 News		ABC News		The 7.30 Report	
Males interview male/female %	88.4	11.5	92.5	7.5	74.1	25.9
Females interview male/female %	66.6	33.3	84.6	15.4	72.2	27.8
	n = 10		n = 24		n = 15	

(Note: interviews conducted by the hosts of the programs are excluded because they are not packaged reports.)

The female reporters with *Channel 9 News* selected women interviewees three times more frequently than males and the female reporters with ABC news selected women interviewees twice as often as males. The selection by gender is easily identified. This bias may be explained by females relating better to females. It may be because female reporters have a conscious or unconscious desire to give women a greater voice. It may be because female reporters are more aware of women who have expertise in a particular area. This bias by journalists illustrated by gender may also hold true in other cases such as left-leaning journalists seeking out left-leaning interviewees. However bias in ideology or other areas is much harder to detect than bias in gender.[320]

The 7.30 Report does not illustrate this same bias with the percentage of men interviewees and women interviewees about the same for both male and female reporters. (The number of women interviewees however, is boosted by the baby bonus report [30 June] that included eight interviews with mothers or mothers-to-be. These interviews feature short, sharp grabs, almost vox-pop style, and appear to be carried out in locations where there were a large number of women or 'captive' interviewees. If this is taken into consideration the results change markedly with male reporters selecting women interviewees with a frequency of 10.6% instead of 25.9% which is more in line with the other programs.)

Location

Canberra and Sydney are emphasised in both the *Channel 9 News* and the *ABC News*. *The 7.30 Report* takes a much more national perspective incorporating locations or content from different parts of the country. This is in accordance with the concept of a national nature of *The 7.30 Report* that does not emphasis one city but rather seems to float in the air somewhere over the nation.

Table 2.18
Location of economic and business reports 1 - 30 June 2004

	Channel 9 News %		ABC News %		The 7.30 Report %	
Canberra	1	**50.0**	1	**45.8**	2	33.3
Sydney	2	40.0	2	41.7	3	8.3
Foreign	3	10.0	3	8.3	-	-
National	-	-	4	4.2	1	**58.3**
Melbourne	-	-	-	-	-	-
	n = 10		n = 24		n = 15	

---

[320] US journalist A. Kent MacDougall provides an example of a journalist promoting an individual ideological perspective in the media. In three articles in the *Monthly Review*, November and December 1988 and January 1999, MacDougall recounts being " … an undeclared socialist reporter for the capitalist press …" and introducing readers of *The Wall Street Journal*, where he worked for a decade, to " … the ideas of radical historians, radical economists … in sympathetic page-one stories." MacDougall, Kent A. (1988). Boring from within the bourgeois press (part 1). *Monthly Review*, Nov. 1988 v40 n6. pp. 13-25.

(Location categories defined: Foreign - reports from outside Australia. National - reports that are drawn from a number of locations around Australia and/or where the report is clearly shot in Australia but the location of the report is not identified.)

The greatest number of economic and business reports on Channel 9 originate in the Canberra office where reporters Laurie Oakes and Nigel Blunden are based. However, even reports with a Canberra super are difficult to identify by location such as the superannuation debate (24 June). This starts with footage of Federal Parliament while the bulk of the report appears to have been filmed in Sydney. Networks like Nine attempt to give reports on national topics a national look not characterised by one city so they can be used around Australia without viewers becoming alienated because they feel the network has a bias toward a city other than the one they are in.

On the *ABC News* a majority of reports originated in Canberra and Sydney displaying the ABC's view of the central nature of these two cities. Not one report came from Melbourne, once regarded as Australia's financial capital.[321] Five journalists - Russell Barton, Greg Jennett, Craig McMurtrie, Elizabeth Byrne and Jim Middleton - reported from Canberra. In Sydney the reports are from Finance Correspondent Phillip Lasker, Adrian Raschella, Deborah Rice, David Spicer, Andrew Robertson and Simon Santow. ABC reporters usually make their location clear with either a super informing viewers of the city they are in or a tag or signoff (saying their name and location) at the end of the report. In the apple and pear demonstration report (1 June) Adrian Raschella brought together events in Sydney, Melbourne, Brisbane and Perth for a truly national report although his location was identified as Sydney. One international report came from North America Correspondent Leigh Sales.

While most viewers of *The 7:30 Report* would probably correctly assume the program is produced out of Sydney there is no indication, either by supers or voice-over, that this is the case. The majority of the reports have a national flavour and their geographical locations can be diverse or difficult to identify.[322] The location of particular reporters is not stated and is

---

[321] Note: The ABC generally runs distinct news bulletins in the capital cities and this research does not examine the Melbourne bulletin. However it is unlikely any major economic or business reports would not run in both cities.

[322] As well as aiming for national coverage *The 7.30 Report* may be aiming to deflect criticism that its focus is on Sydney, Canberra and Melbourne at the expense of Brisbane, Adelaide, Perth and Hobart that are known as the BAPH states. Price, Matt (2000). *The 7.30 Report's* sad state of affairs, *The Australian*, 16 June. and Emerson, Scott (2000). Few tears for Kerry outside the golden triangle. *The Australian*, 16 Dec.

often hard to identify in reports such as car dealers (15 June) that is filmed in a number of different states. It is therefore difficult for the viewer to get any real feel for where many of the reports come from. Political Editor Michael Brissenden appears before a graphic of Parliament House in Canberra. The location of Business and Economics Editor Tim Lester is not made clear. A production approach of *The 7:30 Report* (experienced first hand by the author) is to use reporters in several places who are not busy preparing their own reports to film interviews and locations that are then packaged by one reporter. This contributes to the difficulty in pinpointing the source of individual reports but adds to the 'national' feel of the program. The location of some of the reports however, such as Tasmanian waterfronts (30 June), is clear from their content.

CONCLUSION

Economic and business news is an established element of Australian news and serious current affairs programs even if it is no more than the daily finance segment. There are a number of considerations however that shape or distort what is presented in economic and business reports.

The need for visual material makes television prone to cover diary events, pseudo-events or to focus on peripheral visual material as a way to illustrate events. Television's need for visual material also makes it prone to use advertising or handout material. Access to personalities is also critical and politicians who make themselves readily available are a major source of news and influence what is covered. The view of 'ordinary' Australians, such as workers and other members of the public, gets only limited representation on television.

Television's attempt to explain the world of economics and business is further clouded by jargon and is also limited through scripts that contradict the visual material and through the repetitive nature of file footage. The structural demands of television news processes, such as working to deadlines, time limits and the need for drama, can also lead to excessively short interview grabs and the failure to identify interviewees that can further harm comprehension.

CHAPTER 3

SPECIALIST BUSINESS PROGRAMS ON AUSTRALIAN TELEVISION

... the business world is also very much about people, and there TV has an advantage with its ability to show and tell, especially that which can't ordinarily be seen and heard.

Geoffrey Foisie[323]

PROGRAMS AND CONTENT

This chapter will examine the economic and business reports that went to air on Channel Nine's *Business Sunday* program between 6 June and 4 July 2004[324] and on the ABC's *Inside Business* program between 6 and 27 June 2004. *Business Sunday* was selected because it is the longest-running and best known business program on commercial television and *Inside Business* because it is a similar program on the major public broadcaster.

Current Affairs and Business Programs and Topics

Definitions of a current affairs program are varied. Industry groups and expert interviewees consulted by Pearson and Brand indicate that current affairs reports are longer than news reports, interpret and comment on the news and that the coverage is deeper than news.[325] The reports on *Business Sunday* and *Inside Business* fit these criteria in that the items are longer than news reports, there is interpretation and comment, there is more detail about specific issues over a longer duration (if that is depth), and the material is often not covered on news

---

[323] Foisie, Geoffrey (1992). Television and business news: a bull market. *Television Quarterly*. Winter v. 25 n. 4. p. 74
[324] Note: 4 July was included because there was no *Business Sunday* program on 20 June due to sport.
[325] Pearson and Brand 2001 op. cit`

programs.

There is a benefit for business programs to present as similar to news or serious current affairs programs because by doing so they can benefit from the credibility established by these programs. Thus the general look of business programs - opening titles similar to a news program, an experienced and knowledgeable presenter, news segments, reports packaged in a news style, reporters with news backgrounds - is similar to news and current affairs. A key question however is if the credibility of business programs is as high as those serious news and current affairs programs.

Business Sunday on Channel 9 started in 1986 and attracts a national audience of about 135,598.[326] The program runs for one hour between 8:00am and 9:00 am on Sunday mornings although it is sometimes shortened or dropped altogether to make way for major sporting events such as cricket.

A typical program, based on those during the survey period, begins with a 6:30 minute news segment with sport and weather. There is another 1:30 minute news update toward the middle of the program. Terry McCrann and Alan Fels each have comment pieces of about 1:40 minutes. The program has four major items: two packaged reports, a location interview (both about 5:30 minutes), and a major live studio interview of about 6:00 minutes. Additional material: exchange rates, a diary for the week ahead and a web poll question and answer are included in the playoffs ahead of the commercial breaks. The program has five 2:30 minute commercial breaks for a total of 12:30 minutes and a program duration of 47:30 minutes.

Inside Business started in August 2002 and goes to air on ABC Television on Sunday mornings at 9:45 to 10:15 but is pre-recorded the day before. *Inside Business* attracts a national audience of about 83,333.[327] The program is preceded by the political program *Insiders*. *Insiders* host Barrie Cassidy throws directly to *Inside Business* and viewers first see presenter Alan Kohler welcoming them to *Inside Business* and teasing on items in the program. The program's titles then roll before Alan Kohler returns with more teasers. This is

---

[326] Average for ratings weeks 23, 24, 25, 27 of 2004. Source Seven Corporate media release. http://sevencorporate.com.au/page.asp?partid=44 and previous.
[327] This audience figure is based on evidence given by Walter Hamilton, Head of National Coverage, ABC News and Current Affairs, to the Australian Industrial Relations Commission, 7 April 2004, C2004/6560.

followed by business news headlines with viewers first seeing news vision with off-screen narration by news presenter Kate Tozer. Tozer then appears and throws to a comment piece by one of the program's three regular commentators, Tom Elliott, from fund manager MM&E, Thomas Murphy, of Deutsche Bank, or Marcus Padley, a stockbroker. Three packaged items or interviews of about 6:00 to 8:30 minutes each follow. Kohler also has a comment section that runs about 1:30 minutes.

A distinguishing feature of the program is the large number of interviews - six out of the twelve items (50%) during the survey period - conducted by Alan Kohler. The explanation for this is a desire to create the program around Kohler. This was set-out at an Australian Industrial Relations Commission hearing[328] by Walter Hamilton, head, National Programs, ABC News and Current Affairs, "... We saw (*Inside Business*) as a vehicle for Alan in a very substantial way."[329] This approach also restricts costs in that fewer staff are required with Kohler presenting the program as well as doing the major interviews. Kohler also has a comment section, in which he presents his personal views. This is in contrast to *Business Sunday* where the commentators and the presenter are different people, an approach that avoids any possible challenge to the presenter's objectivity.

Kohler is the driving force behind *Inside Business*. The program is a result of proposals Kohler presented to Hamilton. This is also an illustration that in an organisation as large as the ABC a national program can be created from the proposal of one individual of sufficient status, backed by a senior executive.[330] The program is in line with ABC finance reporter Philip Lasker's assessment of the ABC board's wish to present more economic and business information considered previously. In the 2005 commission Hamilton recalled the genesis of *Inside Business*:

I'd been in discussion with Alan Kohler for some time, who had been pressing the

---

[328] In 2004-5 Commissioner Smith in the Australian Industrial Relations Commission (C2004/6560 and C2005/1811) heard a dispute between the Media, Entertainment and Arts Alliance, on behalf of the former executive producer of *Inside Business* Neheda Barakat, and the ABC over Barakat's removal from the program. Evidence from the witnesses, including Barakat, Alan Kohler, Walter Hamilton and others, offers rare insights into the development, management, assessment and personal relationships of a television program.

[329] Hamilton, Walter. op. cit. PN5294.

[330] Kohler and Hamilton can be seen as agents bringing ideational change (for a new approach to business television) to the ABC.

idea that the ABC should embrace a current affairs business program. We decided that it would be a program that would be complementary to the *Insiders* political program on Sunday morning ... The key issue of [the] program was that we wanted it to be a stylish current affairs television program. We wanted it to showcase Alan's profile in the business community as a well-known media performer, so it would have key interviews by Alan. He was also keen, and we were keen, to use the program to showcase Australian small and medium-sized business, and we did that through a segment called First Person which is an attempt to show how, I guess, smaller-scale business in Australia deals with the day-to-day problems of making money and all the other issues of business.[331]

The four key elements of the program at its inception were 1. a market report 2. a key interview 3. a feature story and 4. the first person segment about medium and small business.[332] Two years later, during the survey period, this is generally the look of the program, although on two (13 and 27 June) out of the four weeks two interviews rather than one were carried.

Kohler's interview style is to draw information from his guests rather than to be confrontational. He seems genuinely curious to obtain information and to pass it on to the program's viewers. Kohler's style of presentation is conversational, informal and explanatory. For example, in talking about News Corporation's move to the United States (27 June) Kohler said: "Now that everyone has digested the shock, the immediate focus has shifted to the length of the transition – that is, how long local fund managers will have to get out of News."

As with that report on News Corporation, *Business Sunday* and *Inside Business* display an emphasis on the activities of big and small business unlike the emphasis on, say, fiscal issues displayed by *Channel 9 News* and *The 7.30 Report* (but not the *ABC News*). (The topics category is intended to be applied across the range of news, current affairs and business programs in the survey so a sub-division that further explores the specific interests of the

---

[331] Hamilton, Walter. Evidence before the Australian Industrial Relations Commission C2005/1811 PN5000. 6 April 2005.
[332] Hamilton, Walter, op. cit. PN5002.

business programs is displayed in table 3.1.

Table 3.1
Topics - economic and business reports 6 June - 4 July 2004

	Channel 9 Business Sunday %		ABC Inside Business %	
Business	1	**76.2**	1	**83.3**
Other	2	14.3	2	16.7
Resources	3	9.5	-	-
Fiscal	-	-	-	-
Trade	-	-	-	-
Monetary	-	-	-	-
	n = 21		n = 12	

(For category definition see Table 2.2)

Among the items in the 'other' category are the impact of e-mail on worker efficiency (*Business Sunday* 4 July), the states' agreement over biotech (*Inside Business* 6 June), medical imaging and aged care in the David Vaux interview (*Inside Business* 13 June), personal relationship issues in the Yvonne Allen report (*Inside Business* 20 June) and entertainment with the Ritz Cinema report (*Inside Business* 27 June).

Resource issues are considered in two reports; one on world oil supplies in OPEC (*Business Sunday* 6 June) and in relation to alternative energy sources in Pacific Hydro (*Business Sunday* 4 July). These items look at resources from a consumer and an investor point of view - eg. motorists in relation to OPEC and the stock market in relation to Pacific Hydro - rather than from an environmental perspective.

The impact of government decisions on business is not the main topic in any of the *Business Sunday* or *Inside Business* reports, although it is touched on in a number of items. For example the Federal Government's decision not to increase the level of mandatory renewable energy targets (MRET) is considered for its impact on operations of Pacific Hydro (*Business Sunday* 4 July). The role of regulators, in particular the Australian Competition and Consumer Commission (ACCC), is discussed briefly in relation to banking with Frank Conroy, chairman of St George Bank (*Business Sunday* 6 June) and in relation to the fruit juice industry with Terry Davis, the managing director of Coca-Cola Amatil (*Business Sunday* 13 June) and Nudie (*Business Sunday* 4 July). Trade is considered in relation to wine exports in the Fosters report (*Business Sunday* 8 June) and the Evans & Tate report (*Business Sunday* 4 July). Superannuation is examined in two items (*Inside Business* 13 June and 20 June).

The objective of many of the above reports appears to be to provide information for investors in the case of listed companies Pacific Hydro, St George Bank, Coca-Cola Amatil and Evans & Tate. *Business Sunday* presenter Ali Moore asked several questions about Nudie (4 July) being merged with the larger and listed company Signature Brands.[333]

The above categories can be further refined and this reveals banking and financial sector is the most emphasised category in both business programs. *Business Sunday* gave equal emphasis to the food/beverage category, a category that was not covered at all by *Inside Business*. Media issues ranked second on *Inside Business*.

Table 3.2
Business sub-categories in economic and business reports 6 June - 4 July 2004

	Channel 9 Business Sunday %		ABC Inside Business %	
Financial/bank	1	**25.0**	1	**33.3**
Food/beverage	1	**25.0**	-	-
Media	3	12.5	3	16.7
Investment	3	12.5	4	8.3
Manufacturing	5	6.3	4	8.3
Sport	5	6.3	-	-
Construction	5	6.3	-	-
Retail	5	6.3	-	-
Other	-	-	1	**33.3**
	n = 21		n = 12	

[333] On 13 August *The Age* reported "The price drop (of Signature Brands down 23.7% to 33 cents) comes after the company announced that its juice bars business, Pulp, would not merge with the private fruit and vegetable bottler Nudie Foods. When news of the merger plan reached the market last month , it drove Signature Brands' shares up 12.5 percent." Costa, Gabrielle (2004). Signature takes a belting after juice deal sours. *The Age*. 13 Aug. A Factiva search of major news and business publications reveals no mention of a Nudie-Signature deal or merger until 6 July so the 12.5% surge in Signature's share price may be a result of the *Business Sunday* comments and a reflection of the effect of business news on television although the contribution of other media that is not tracked by Factiva, such as radio, cannot be ruled out.

(Business sub-categories defined: Financial/banking - provision of finance and services to lenders and borrows. Food/beverage - food and beverage production and distribution. Media - print, broadcasting and telecommunications services and regulation. Investment - services to investors. Manufacturing - the transformation of materials and components into new products. Sport - individuals or services involved in sporting pursuits. Construction - construction of homes, buildings and infrastructure. Retail - sale of goods to final consumers. Other - activities outside the defined categories.)

A comparison of these results with the composition of the Australian stock market reveals the news values and content of both business programs varies with the sector weighting of the market as measured by S&P's/ASX200.[334] For example the financial/banking sector and the investment sector combined are the largest category in both *Business Sunday* (38%) and *Inside Business* (42%), which is close to the ASX200 where it is also the largest group (44%). The ASX's second largest sector however, materials (19%), is not represented by any reports on either business program. The ASX's third largest sector of consumer staples (7%) is over represented on *Business Sunday* (25%) and not represented at all on *Inside Business*.

There is, of course, no reason why the survey results and the ASX 200 sectors should run parallel but the differences indicate that news values at the business programs are driven by producers' perceptions of audience interest rather than by their economic or business importance. For example, *Business Sunday's* emphasis on consumer products such as food and beverages may reflect the consumer values of a commercial network or the personal interests of the newsworkers. News production processes also play a part in report selection. The difficulties in accessing the minerals industry for example, which is usually in remote locations, is difficult because of the time needed for crews to travel to remote locations and expensive, and may help account for the business programs' lack of coverage of the materials sector.

The finance/banking sector topics are an interview with Frank Conroy, chairman of St George Bank (*Business Sunday* 6 June), a report on the details of the Cabcharge payment system (*Business Sunday* 13 June), details of the operation of GE Money in Australia (*Business Sunday* 27 June), the corporate governance issues involving the National Australia

---

[334] Standard & Poor's, May 2004, *Understanding indices*, p.12. (data is at 31 Dec. 2003 and not the survey period of June 2004 however changes are small and unlikely to substantially effect these comments. This comparison is limited by the different categories.
www2.standardandpors.com/spf/pdf/index/A5_CMYK_UIndices.

Bank (*Business Sunday* 27 June), two superannuation items (*Inside Business* 13 and 20 June), changes to audit services (*Inside Business* 6 June), changes to the S&P indices that will change the framework for institutional investors following News Corporation's move to the United States (*Business Sunday* and *Inside Business* 27 June) and the performance of AMP (*Inside Business* 27 June).

On *Business Sunday* the food/beverage topics are the report on the opening of Coca-Cola's new distribution facility and the future directions of the company (13 June), the new CEO of Fosters, Trevor O'Hoy (13 June), the report on niche company Nudie in the fruit juice market (4 July) and the 40% earnings increase and outlook for wine company Evans & Tate (4 July).

The media category contains reports on News Corporation's plan to move to the US (*Inside Business* 13 June), the interview with Sensis CEO Andrew Day (*Inside Business* 20 June) that considers the converging media environment, and ALP Shadow Communications Minister Lindsay Tanner (*Business Sunday* 13 June) on media ownership.

The range of topics covered by *Inside Business* is illustrated by the joint number one ranking of the Other category. These reports were Joss super car (6 June), David Vaux on health care (13 June), introduction agency Yvonne Allen (20 June) and the Ritz Cinema (27 June).

Economic Terms

Both *Business Sunday* and *Inside Business* use economic, business and management terms that are not explained. *Business Sunday* presumes the greatest economic and business literacy among its audience with only a small percentage of those terms explained.

Table 3.3
Reports with economic/business terms 6 June - 4 July 2004

	Channel 9 Business Sunday %	ABC Inside Business %
Reports with eco/bus. terms	90.5	91.7
Explained	5.3	36.4
Not explained	94.7	63.6
	n = 21	n = 12

(For category definitions see Table 2.3.)

This content analysis reveals there is often little distinction between economic and business terms. Marketing terms and concepts are an additional category that can make comprehension difficult for the uninitiated viewer. The level of understanding among Australians was considered in the previous chapter and found to be low although it is likely that the two business programs assume a higher economic/business/management/marketing literacy than the news programs on Channel 9 and Channel 2 and *The 7:39 Report.*

All but two of the twenty one items on *Business Sunday* contained one or more economic/business/management/marketing terms. Some of the terms used include 'stapled entity', 'revenue synergies', 'strategic footprint', 'margin consolidation' and 'acquisition via scheme of arrangement'. It is noteworthy that those two items that did not contain such terms are the two items – Wal-Mart legal (27 June) and e-mail (4 July) prepared by CBS and CNN respectively and not by *Business Sunday.*

It may be that many of the terms are comprehensible on reflection but not necessarily when presented quickly on television. For example in the property trust report (*Business Sunday* 6 June) terms, concepts and jargon such as those under consideration are used on average once every 16.5 seconds. It is suggested that viewers need to have mastered the terms, concepts and jargon of economics, business, management and marketing for a complete comprehension of any one episode of these business program and that many viewers might not understand all the terms, particularly across different industry sectors.

Another example of a report with a large number of items that might not be immediately comprehensible to a viewer with only a general knowledge of finance is the News Corporation report (*Inside Business* 13 June). The terms used include 'institutional investors', 'indices', (harvest a) 'group of assets', '7.5% of the ASX top 300 index', 'brokers as principals', 'spread', 'short term movement', 'liquid', 'value for shareholders', 'primary revenue base', 'rich capital markets', 'preferred shares', 'ordinary shares', 'active fund manager', 'position against the market', '$74 billion market cap. company', 're-rated upwards', 'price and valuation', 'road shows', 'S&P 500', 'qualitative requirements', 'transfer of value', 'reshape their portfolios', 'earnings forecast', 'EPS', 'compound' (growth), 'depression in the price', 'co-ordinated response' (by S&P's), 'index manager', 'primary revenue sources', 'fundamentally undervalued', 'unlock value', 'greater choice of investment', and 'greater opportunity of return'. Of these 34 terms, explanations are offered for only three; for preferred and ordinary shares and for active fund manager.

The Rugby Union/Andrew Johns report (*Business Sunday* 4 July) is a reminder that specialist terms are also used in other forms of television programs (and other media), for example sport programs, that also presume knowledge of relevant terms, concepts and jargon. Both economic and business reports and sports reports suggest that attention needs to be given to the contribution of specialist language to the meaning of the text. This issue is explored by Starr (2004), among others, who considers how text is used to " ... define, codify and limit discourse to certain realms of economic knowledge ..." and how individual audiences take meaning from specific texts.[335]

Specialist programs such as business programs also have to strike a balance between providing explanations for non-expert viewers without alienating more knowledgeable viewers:

> We found if you make the stories too plain, too simple, you do get complaints
> from established viewers – by insulting their intelligence. They don't come
> tumbling in by the thousands. But every now and then you get someone ringing up

---

[335] Starr, Martha A. (2004). Reading *The Economist* on globalisation: knowledge, identity , and power. *Global Society*, vol. 18, no. 4. Oct. p.375.

and whinging about a story. You look at it and it sometimes just feels a little too simple.

Glen Dyer[336]

SOURCES

Interviewees, Interview Occasions and Different Voices

Business sources form the largest group in *Business Sunday* while politicians are the largest group in *Inside Business*. This, and the different nature of the topics of a number reports, illustrates an important difference between the two programs; *Business Sunday* is more focussed on those individuals representing companies producing consumer goods while *Inside Business* pays more attention to the individuals who shape or reflect the structure of the Australian economy.

Table 3.4
Interviewees in economic and business reports 6 June - 4 July 2004

	Channel 9 Business Sunday %		ABC Inside Business %	
Business	1	**38.1**	6	7.4
Analyst/comm.	2	20.5	2	18.5
CEO	3	13.6	2	18.5
Politician	4	9.1	1	**29.6**
Spokesman	4	9.1	4	11.1
Worker/public	6	4.5	7	3.7
Other	7	2.3	4	11.1
Lawyer	7	2.3	-	-
	n = 21		n = 12	

(For category definitions see Table 2.4.)

The business category, for interviewees identified by their employment titles, is the largest category on *Business Sunday* and illustrates the broad range of executives available for comment with four interviewees identified as managing directors, three as chairmen and one as president. CEOs are the biggest single-title group on both *Business Sunday* and *Inside*

---

[336] Dyer. op. cit.

Business, a finding that supports the notion that the CEO comes to personify the company.[337] On *Inside Business,* however, several of the CEOs are identified only by their company affiliation, not by title, so the prominent role of CEOs is partly disguised. Taken together, the business and CEO categories on *Business Sunday* make up more than half of all interviewees and suggests the program's producers and journalists believe leadership is a key factor in presenting economic and business issues.

Politicians are the largest category on *Inside Business* and these interviewees include the premiers of South Australia, Victoria, Queensland and New South Wales in state against state (6 June), Assistant Federal Treasurer Helen Coonan in superannuation (13 June) and Parliamentary Secretary to the Treasurer, Ross Cameron, former Labor Prime Minister, Paul Keating, and Shadow Financial Services spokesman Stephen Conroy all in superannuation reform (20 June). This suggests producers and journalists on the program believe politicians play a key role in economic and business issues. It might also reflect a sensitivity on the part of the ABC toward politicians; a perspective perhaps influenced by the ABC's reliance on federal funding and often difficult relationship with politicians.[338]

The critical role of superannuation in Australia's economy - which is reflected in the two reports above - is highlighted by commentators such as Trevor Sykes:

> The dominant factor in Australian business ... [in the past ten years] ... has been the rise of the superannuation funds. Since 1995 the amount of money invested in super funds has almost trebled from $230 billion to $650 billion, roughly half of which is invested in Australian equities. This treasure trove of cash, combined with falling interest rates, has fuelled massive investment.[339]

Those three reports, 25% of the reports on *Inside Business,* plus the issue of the growing demand for aged care in the interview with David Vaux, of DCA Group (13 June), display

---

[337] Hayward, Mathew L.A., Rindova, Violina P. and Pollock, Timothy G. (2004). Believing one's own press: the causes and consequences of CEO celebrity, *Strategic Management Journal*, 25. Meindl, James R. Sanford, B. Ehrlich and Dukerich, Janet M. (1985). The romance of leadership. *Administrative Science Quarterly*. 30. pp. 70-102.

[338] One of the most recent of these has been former Communications Minister Richard Alston's complaints against the ABC of bias in the coverage of the Iraq war. For example see Marr, David (2005). Static from the newsfront, *The Sydney Morning Herald*, 5 March. p. 32.

[339] Sykes, Trevor (2005). What a swell party it was. *The Australian Financial Review Magazine*, May. p. 26.

the program's interest in the future of the Australian economy.

Business Sunday, on the other hand, devotes only 14% of its reports to national issues: workplace safety in Leighton (13 June) and the interviews with federal opposition spokesmen Lindsay Tanner (13 June) and Craig Emerson (4 July). More attention is devoted to brand-name and consumer products such as Ford (6 June), Coca-Cola, Cabcharge and Fosters (all 13 June), GE Money (27 June) and Nudie and Evans & Tate (both 4 July). In making this distinction there is no intention to ignore the contribution made by companies such as these to the national economy but to draw attention to the different emphasis of the two programs.

Inside Business - reflecting the original concept of the program discussed earlier - pays more attention to smallish, individually managed or owned businesses such as Matt Thomas of Joss Supercar (6 June), Yvonne Allen, of Yvonne Allen and Associates (20 June) and George Aleksiunas, of Croydon's Ritz Cinema (27 June) than *Business Sunday* with only one report in this group, Nudie (4 July).

Both business programs have an emphasis on one-on-one interviews and this illustrates these programs seek interviewees who do not appear on other programs. The perspectives presented by these programs are therefore different from those being put forward in news programs. The low representation of press conferences in both programs again illustrates the freedom of *Business Sunday* and *Inside Business* to avoid the mainstream news agenda as defined by diary items.

Table 3.5
Interview occasions in economic and business reports 6 June - 4 July 2004

	Channel 9 Business Sunday %		ABC Inside Business %	
Interview	**1**	**75.6**	**1**	**85.1**
Studio	2	13.3	3	3.7
Set-piece	3	6.7	-	-
Press conf.	4	2.2	2	7.4
Other	4	2.2	3	3.7
Vox-pop	-	-	-	-
Dramatic	-	-	-	-
	n = 21		n = 12	

(For category definitions see Table 2.5.)

Taken together, the one-on-one interviews and studio interviews show both programs are generating unique interviews almost 90% of the time.

Business Sunday has the practice of sending reporters to do interviews in the field – for example reporter Ross Greenwood's interview with St George Bank chairman Frank Conroy, (6 June) and Adam Shand's interview with NAB Chairman Graham Kraehe (27 June). These are then aired as a question-and-answer interview without any supporting overlay vision much like a studio interview. Because these field interviews are pre-recorded however, there is the opportunity to edit the content, usually for duration, which is not the case with live studio interviews.

Live studio interviews such as those with *Business Sunday* presenter Ali Moore and Lend Lease CEO Greg Clark (6 June), Opposition Communications spokesman Lindsay Tanner (13 June) and Opposition Industrial Relations Spokesman Craig Emerson (4 July) give interviewees an opportunity to present their position direct to the audience, without edits. But at the same time live interviews present the risk of interviewees looking foolish or ill-informed on national television.[340]

---

[340] Former Labor Prime Minister Bob Hawke summed up the positives and negatives of television, although he did not refer to live television directly, when he said: "With television, they can't come between you and the voter, because television is that direct link. You've got the audience. You may bugger it up, you may not

Most CEOs are paranoid about the media. They all half know everything these days and they seem to believe that if it is edited the best bits are going to be on the floor and the worst bits are going to be on television. So their latest phobia and their big knowledge is 'if I do it live it will be fine and they can't cut it for me.' But having done a lot of television myself with my political hat on, live can be good, but it can be disastrous too because you don't get a chance to repeat anything.

Ian Kortlang[341]

A feature of *Inside Business* is the number of interviews conducted by presenter Alan Kohler in a location other than the studio, for example the David Vaux interview (13 June). This could be due to production process reasons such as the *Inside Business* set being unavailable outside the program's record time, a restraint that may be caused by limited funds.

A characteristic of both business programs is the limited number of interviewees appearing in reports. In a number of single-interviewee reports the interviewee makes comment without a contrasting perspective being put forward.

Table 3.6
Distribution of voices in economic and business reports 6 June - 4 July 2004

Number of voices	Channel 9 Business Sunday	ABC Inside Business
1	2	2
2	7	1
3	2	-
4	2	-
5	1	2
6	-	-
7	-	1
Mean is:	2.5	3.5
	n = 14	n = 6

perform well at times. But there's no one between you and [them]. That's a big plus." In Mills, Stephen (1993) *The Hawke years*. Ringwood, Viking. pp. 125-126.
[341] Kortlang, Ian (2000). Executive Vice Chairman, Gavin Anderson and Co. Former advisor and chief-of-staff to New South Wales Premier Nick Greiner. Personal interview 23 June.

(Note for above table: Studio interviews and one-on-one interviews excluded. For category definitions see Table 2.6.)

The number of interviewees appearing with the greatest frequency (in bold) is two in *Business Sunday* reports and an equal one and five interviewees on *Inside Business*. By comparison *Channel 9 News* and *ABC News* both have four interviewees and *The 7.30 Report* has six interviewees appearing with the greatest frequency.

Examples of *Business Sunday* reports that feature a single key interviewee and overlay vision of business activity are the Tom Gorman, president of Ford Australia (6 June) interview, and the Franklin Tate, CEO of winemaker Evans & Tate (4 July) interview. Other reports feature the key interviewee and a secondary interviewee, who supports the key interviewee, such as the Coca-Cola report with Coca-Cola Amatil Managing Director Terry Davis and Coca-Cola Amatil Chairman David Gonski (13 June) and the Cabcharge report with Cabcharge CEO Reginald Kermode and analyst Andrew Doherty (13 June). On *Inside Business* two reports feature only one interviewee; super cars (6 June), and Ritz Cinema (27 June). Two interviewees appear in the Yvonne Allen report (20 June) although as one of these is 'natural sound up' of a client talking in a meeting there is effectively only one interviewee, Yvonne Allen herself.

From a production point of view reports with just one or two interviewees are relatively easy to film and edit because of the limited number of interviews and locations. From an editorial point of view however, reports that contain one or two interviewees can be lacking in contrasting perspectives particularly when the two interviewees are from the same company and with the same point of view, for example in the Coca-Cola Amatil report. One interviewee reports run the risk of appearing to promote the company that is featured.

Another way of looking at the frequency of interviewees is to calculate the average interviewees per report. For *Business Sunday* this is 2.3 and for *Inside Business* 3.5. By comparison the average for *The 7.30 Report*, that runs reports of a similar duration, has 7.1 interviewees per report or at least twice as many as the business programs.

Most of those interviewees mentioned are male. Only five percent of interviewees on *Business Sunday* are female, the lowest representation of women on all of the programs surveyed.

Table 3.7
Gender of interviewees in economic and business reports 6 June - 4 July 2004

	Channel 9 Business Sunday %		ABC Inside Business %	
Male	1	**94.8**	1	**85.2**
Female	2	5.3	2	14.8
		n = 21		n = 12

The women interviewees on *Business Sunday* are Wal-Mart employee Chris Klwapnoski (27 June) and IT consultant Monica Seeley (4 July). On *Inside Business* the women interviewees are CEO of the Australian Industry Group, Heather Ridout (6 June), Assistant Treasurer Helen Coonan (13 June), matchmaker Yvonne Allen and an unidentified woman client (20 June).Of these six women only two - Ridout and Coonan - can be judged as having a significant institutional voice. Klwapnoski is prominent as an agent challenging gender bias within Wal-Martin the US. Consultants such as Seeley work outside institutions. Yvonne Allen and her client represent a niche business.

If *Business Sunday* and *Inside Business* are taken together, men represent 90% of interviewees and women 10%. This is less than the generalist programs - Channel 9 and *ABC News* and *The 7.30 Report* - in which men represent 84% of the interviewees and women 16%. This is consistent with a US Media Tenor survey that found the share of coverage of women in the specialist *Wall Street Journal* during 2004 was 11% compared to close to 20% in the generalist media of *Newsweek*, *Time* and on the *CBS Evening News* and slightly less on ABC and NBC news programs.[342]

Institutions

Business institutions receive the greatest representation on both *Business Sunday* and *Inside*

---

[342] *Women missing in media coverage* (2005). Media Tenor Institute for Media Analysis. 28 April. www.mediatenor.com

Business. However the second rank provides a contrast between the two programs with the finance category, a partner to the business category, second on *Business Sunday* while government, a regulator of business, is second on *Inside Business*. Those institutions that challenge business, such as unions, are only represented once in the Leighton safety report (*Business Sunday* 13 June). The interest groups represented on the two programs are those that represent industry groups, such as the Australian Industry Group (*Inside Business* 6 June).

Table 3.8
Institutions in economic and business reports 6 June - 4 July 2004

		Channel 9 Business Sunday %		*ABC Inside Business %*
Business	1	**52.3**	1	**37.0**
Finance	2	22.7	3	14.8
Other + non.ins	3	11.4	4	11.1
Opposition	4	4.5	6	3.7
Government	5	2.3	2	25.9
Interest groups	5	2.3	5	7.4
Union	5	2.3	-	-
National	5	2.3	-	-
Academia	-	-	-	-
		n = 21		n = 12

(For category definitions see Table 2.8.)

The institution of business accounts for more than half the representations on *Business Sunday* and includes major multi-national manufacturing companies such as Ford (6 June) and, at the sales end of that business, a local Ford dealer (27 June), property, investment management and construction company Lend Lease (6 June), beverage companies Coca-Cola Amatil and Fosters (both 13 June) and IT consultancy MESMO, rating agency Standard & Poor's (27 June), research group Aspect Huntley (13 June), drink makers Nudie and Signature Brands (4 July), advertising agency Jack Watts Currie (4 July), energy company Pacific Hydro (4 July), winemakers Evans & Tate (4 July), the NSW Rugby Union (4 July) and sports management agent John Fordham (4 July).

On *Inside Business* more than one-third of the representations are business such as auditing firm KMPG (6 June), Joss Supercar (6 June), News Corporation (13 June) and Standard and Poor's (13 and 27 June), DCA group (13 June), Rainmaker Information (20 June), Sensis (20 June), Yvonne Allen and Associates (20 June) and the Ritz Cinema (27 June).

Finance is the second largest category on *Business Sunday* with organisations including St George Bank (6 June), property investment group James Fielding, stock broker Grange Securities and investment bank Deutsche Bank-Sentinel (all 6 June), taxi payment company Cabcharge (13 June), financial services company GE Money (27 June), National Australia Bank and Macquarie Bank (both 27 June) and investment consultants Intech and Vanguard (both 27 June). Representatives of business and finance organisations together make up three-quarters of the interviewees on *Business Sunday*.

The second category on *Inside Business* is government, representing just over one-quarter of the institutions. This includes the South Australian, Victorian, Queensland and New South Wales state governments (6 June), the federal government (13 June and 20 June) and the previous Keating government (20 June). All up the non-business and non-finance institutions (national bodies, governments, oppositions, unions, interest groups, academics and others) make up almost half of institutions represented.

This can be contrasted with *Business Sunday* where the organisations, regulators and other institutions with which business interacts make up 25% of institutional appearances. In a sense then business is presented with limited representation of the dichotomies or binaries discussed in the previous chapter. Ian MacFarlane, Governor of the Reserve Bank, appears in the report on OPEC (6 June). Lindsay Tanner, opposition communications spokesman (13 June) and Craig Emerson, opposition industrial relations spokesman (4 July), both appear on the program in what is a pre-election campaign period. Opposition appearances exceeded government appearances on the program.

The interest groups that appear - the Australian Fruit Juice Association in Nudie (*Business Sunday* 4 July), the Australian Industry Group in state against state (*Inside Business* 6 June) and the Investment and Financial Services Association in superannuation reform (*Inside Business* 20 June) - represent industry and business rather than workers, consumers, tax payers or other individuals. The union movement is represented once by Ralph Edwards, an organiser with the CFMEU (*Business Sunday* 13 June). Two workers are interviewed: construction worker Mark McMillan, who witnessed the death of a workmate, for the Leighton safety report (13 June) and retail worker Chris Kwapnoski who is at the centre of the gender discrimination claim against Wal-Mart (*Business Sunday* 27 June).

Unions get a tiny two percent of coverage on *Business Sunday* and no coverage on *Inside Business*. Workers are presented through the perspective of business.[343] For example the workforce is viewed as a factor to be removed from the factory distribution process through the expansion of automation by Coca-Cola Managing Director Terry Davis (*Business Sunday* 13 June), as costs to be reduced by Evans & Tate CEO Franklin Tate (*Business Sunday* 4 July) and as a cost to be controlled through careful rostering by health care company DCA Group Managing Director David Vaux (*Inside Business* 13 June). Ford Australia President Tom Gorman acknowledges the management team but not workers in turning the company around (*Business Sunday* 6 June). Foster's CEO Trevor O'Hoy is one of the few to acknowledge the workforce when he says the employees have to be informed of change during a company turn around (*Business Sunday* 13 June).

NEWSWORKERS AND PRODUCTION PROCESS

Events, News Values and Triggers

The non-diary emphasis of the two business programs illustrates the freedom of producers and journalists on these programs to set their own agendas independently of diary events.

---

[343] Dreier, Peter (1982). Capitalists vs. the media; an analysis of an ideological mobilization among business leaders, *Media, Culture & Society*. 1982. 4, pp. 111-132, offers an examination of ideology and class issues in business reporting.

Table 3.9
Diary/non-diary items in economic and business reports 6 June - 4 July 2004

		Channel 9 Business Sunday %		ABC Inside Business %
Non-diary	1	85.7	1	100.0
Diary	2	14.3	-	-
		n = 21		n = 12

(For category definition see Table 2.9)

More than 85% of the *Business Sunday* items and all of the *Inside Business* items are non-diary and this illustrates the discretionary nature of a weekly program compared to news; the programs, unlike daily news programs, are not required to cover diary events because of competition from other media organisations. For example *Business Sunday* can run the Leighton safety report (13 June) (in which a worker was killed) some weeks after the court judgement. This is because the report is about the consequences of the judgement for business rather than the immediacy of the court ruling.

It is clear however, that the producers of both programs do have constraints dictated by events. For example, the report on Coca-Cola (*Business Sunday* 13 June) went to air two days after the company opened its new distribution centre, the Fosters report (*Business Sunday* 13 June) went to air on the Sunday following the company's announcement of a $300 million write down and the report on wine maker Evans & Tate (*Business Sunday* 4 July) went to air on the Sunday following the company's announcement of its annual results. To run reports such as these a week later would make the program look out of date.

The state against state report (*Inside Business* 6 June) is timely and went to air as four Australian state premiers travelled to San Francisco for a biotech conference. The McGrath interview on auditing independence (*Inside Business* 6 June) was conducted three weeks before a new liquidating firm headed by Tony McGrath was due to start practice. The interview with DCA Group MD David Vaux (*Inside Business* 13 June) came as his group was in the middle of a $700 million takeover. The superannuation reform report (*Inside*

Business 20 June) aired on the Sunday of the week Federal Parliament passed new disclosure laws for superannuation funds. The interview with the chairman of S&P's index committee, David Blitzer, and coverage of News Corporation and indices (*Business Sunday* and *Inside Business* 27 June) came on the Sunday of the week S&P announced News Corporation would be removed from the Australian indices. This was the only topic reported by both programs on the same day and illustrates the importance of News Corporation to the market. The news values of both programs dictated the News Corporation issue was one they had to cover on that day.

The avoidance of diary items indicates a different approach by interest groups or public relations managers and press secretaries; instead of public relations workers creating events to attract the media, as occurs in news, they offer their clients to the business programs on an individual basis. However the limited time available on the business programs makes it very competitive for the public relations workers to get their people on television:

> One of the biggest problems is to get somebody on *Business Sunday*. You have to ring up the producer and say look mate this is a great story, da da da and our guy is interesting and he is opening up a new [whatever]. Now if it is Richard Branson, who is a client of ours it's a piece of cake, they all want him. But if it's a hard sell you have to convince the producer that he should be on ... we all jockey and fight to try and get people on there.

> Ian Kortlang[344]

For their part program makers can struggle to get the interviewees they want. Corporate leaders consider the benefits of appearing on television with their board, management team or media advisors before they agree to interviews. Former *Inside Business* Executive Producer Neheda Barakat told the Industrial Relations Commission:

> ... I had set quite a high [bar] for us to finish a year strongly and I had been working on getting this interview with Don Argus, who is the chairman of BHP

---

[344] Kortlang, Ian (2000). Executive Vice Chairman, Gavin Anderson and Co. Former advisor and chief-of-staff to New South Wales Premier Nick Greiner. Personal interview 23 June.

Billiton, for almost six months. And they finally had agreed at the last board meeting. So I was very proud of the program.[345]

Persuading people to make themselves available for television can be a process of negotiation. For example, journalists generally prefer not to limit the scope of interviews by setting out the issues to be discussed or the questions to be asked. As Alan Kohler illustrates however, he was prepared to ignore this preference in order to obtain an interview with the newly-appointed CEO of Fosters Trevor O'Hoy:

> (Cross-examination by Mr M. Ryan, appearing for the Media, Entertainment and Arts Alliance MEAA) ... and in fact you were also so helpful enough to point out the areas you weren't going to be asking questions on, such as the strategy of Fosters and what he would do with the wine division?

> (Alan Kohler) Yes. Okay, well, sure. It was - I don't normally - in fact I don't normally email people the questions I'm going to ask them but the thing was - that's right; well this bloke, he'd only just been appointed. He had agreed to do the interview on the basis that we, you know, it was just a profile type interview rather than asking him questions about what he was going to do with Fosters ... this was about me agreeing with that proviso.[346]

Weekly programs have greater freedom to pursue their own agendas than daily news programs but with this freedom comes the need to define the direction of the program. Hamilton sums it up this way: "The elements of making a new program are, one, clearly, the editorial content elements. What are you going to try to say in the program week after week?"[347]

The two programs both emphasise consequence - the effect of events or information - and prominence - the stature of the individuals or companies involved. Consequence ranks highest with *Business Sunday* and second with *Inside Business* and prominence ranks highest with *Inside Business* and second with *Business Sunday*.

---

[345] Barakat, Neheda. Evidence before the Australian Industrial Relations Commission C2005/1811. PN288.
[346] Kohler, Alan. Evidence before the Australian Industrial Relations Commission C2005/1811. PN4367
[347] Hamilton, Walter. op. cit. PN5002

Table 3.10
News criteria for economic and business reports 6 June - 4 July 2004

	Channel 9 Business Sunday %		ABC Inside Business %	
Consequence	1	**38.1**	2	25.0
Prominence	2	33.3	1	**33.3**
Novelty	3	9.5	3	16.7
Conflict	3	9.5	3	16.7
Human interest	5	4.8	5	8.3
Proximity	5	4.8	-	-
		n = 21		n = 12

(For category definition see Table 2.10.)

Consequence on the business programs is illustrated by reports on events such as the OPEC meeting and the consequences for oil prices (*Business Sunday* 6 June), a court ruling on workplace safety and the effect on companies of (*Business Sunday* 13 June), News Corporation's move to the United States and the likely effect on investors (*Inside Business* 13 June), and superannuation reforms and the likely effect on investors (*Inside Business* 20 June).

Prominence is illustrated by reports on well-known and influential individuals or companies. One example is the interview with Frank Conroy, the chairman of St George Bank and former CEO of Westpac (*Business Sunday* 6 June). Well-known companies featured during the survey period are car maker Ford (*Business Sunday* 6 June), beverage producer Fosters (*Business Sunday* 13 June) and financial services company AMP (*Inside Business* 27 June). At different times individuals can be more prominent than their companies, for example former investment banker David Vaux (*Inside Business* 13 June) is probably better known to the business community than his company DCA Group. Alternatively prominent companies are better known than their managers with Ford (*Business Sunday* 6 June) better known than American newcomer President Tom Gorman, and AMP better known than managing director and CEO Andrew Mohl.

The equal third ranking categories are conflict and novelty on both programs. Conflict is represented in reports such as Australian fund managers' unhappiness over ratings agency Standard & Poor's decision to remove News Corporation from the Australian indices (both programs 27 June). Novelty is displayed in reports such as British businessman John Caudwell's decision to block staff from using e-mail because he believes it wastes time (*Business Sunday* 4 July) or the report on introduction agency Yvonne Allen (*Inside Business* 20 June).

Both *Business Sunday* and *Inside Business* seek to influence the news agenda of other organisations with one gauge the follow-up by other news programs:

> We set the agenda, *Sunday*, *Business Sunday*, some weeks we set the agenda for the following week or part of the following week. That's why Seven and Ten now have got programs of the sort that you see, interview, meet the press type programs, because they have belatedly understood it.
>
> Glen Dyer[348]

> I also want [*Inside Business*] to be agenda-setting, because there was [sic] several other business programs around and we needed to ... not be just a run of the mill business program, pedestrian ... the approach is to be innovative, to be agenda-setting, to be a headline, headline unit ... we were actually setting ourselves apart, or as, whether we had follow-ups in the print the next day. And on most weeks we did. Most weeks we did. Neheda Barakat, Former Executive Producer, *Inside Business*.[349]

A Factiva news search of newspapers for *Business Sunday* during the survey period found five hits mentioning comments made on the program and zero hits for *Inside Business*. A survey for the calendar year 2004 found 85 hits for *Business Sunday* and 25 hits for *Inside Business*.[350]

Combined with the ambition to present reports that are followed up in print, the weekly business programs often seek a topical event, or trigger as discussed in the previous chapter,

---

[348] Dyer, Glen (2000). Executive Producer, *Business Sunday*, Channel 9. Personal interview 27 July.
[349] Barakat, Neheda. op. cit. PN246 and 248.
[350] The Factiva news search was conducted on 33 May 2005 via the Sydney University Library access to Factiva and used the key words Business Sunday and Inside Business to search *The Australian*, *The Australian Financial Review*, and *The Sydney Morning Herald* for the period 1 January 2004 to 31 December 2004.

to justify why a particular report is presented in a particular week. The most prominent trigger category in both programs is summary; those reports that allow an in-depth examination of an issue based around a peg. Both business programs, like the news programs, also display an appetite for events. The difference between summary and events is one of weighting; summary reports pay limited attention to the event that is the peg while event-driven reports emphasise the event with limited attention to the background material.

Table 3.11
Triggers for economic and business reports 6 June - 4 July 2004

	Channel 9 Business Sunday %		*ABC Inside Business* %	
Summary	**1**	**52.4**	**1**	**75.0**
Event	2	33.3	2	25.0
Announcement	3	14.3	-	-
Breaking news	-	-	-	-
Data release	-	-	-	-
Market moves	-	-	-	-
Investigation	-	-	-	-
	n = 21		n = 12	

(For category definition see Table 2.11)

Summary reports account for more than half the items in *Business Sunday* and three-quarters of the items in *Inside Business*. Examples of summary reports include the current position and outlook of companies such as Ford (*Business Sunday* 6 June) with the peg of a new president being appointed and Pacific Hydro (*Business Sunday* 4 July) with the peg of the release of government policy on energy. Summaries also include policy positions such as those of the federal opposition with interviews on topics such as media ownership with Lindsay Tanner (*Business Sunday* 13 June) with the peg of the forthcoming election, and industrial relations with Craig Emerson (*Business Sunday* 4 July), with the peg of a report from the Business Council of Australia criticising ALP workplace policies.

Summary reports reflect a desire by producers to be topical and are process driven. Producers decide that a report on a particular company or policy is warranted and will look - possibly through discussion with public relations workers - to see what upcoming events can provide an opportunity for new and different vision and a peg for the report. They can then plan for that peg - including researching the report, being ready to have a crew at the event, setting up interviews and obtaining file material - and put the report to air shortly afterwards. Alternatively the producers might determine what possible event pegs are coming up and consider the suitability of that peg to justify a report on that particular company.

The second largest category in both programs for the trigger of reports is events. Examples of these include the presentations to sell the wine rescue plan for Fosters and the opening of the new distribution centre of Coca-Cola (both *Business Sunday* 13 June). The Vaux interview (*Inside Business* 13 June), considers the immediate event - a take-over proposal by the DCA Group headed by David Vaux for the medical diagnostic imaging company MIA - but also touches on government practice in funding medical areas such as imaging and the examination of aged care issues, admittedly from the perspective of one player. The report on the event of the passage of new laws that require the disclosure of fees levied by superannuation funds (*Inside Business* 20 June) also considers the differences between retail superannuation funds and industry funds. The Blitzer interview (both programs 27 June) considers the event of News Corps move to the US specifically but backgrounds this with international issues affecting indices.

Other reports, however, have no peg and are timeless. The Joss Supercar item (*Inside Business* 6 June) came several months after the car was unveiled at the Melbourne motor show and considers the progress of the car project since the show. The report on introduction agency Yvonne Allen (*Inside Business* 20 June) has no peg at all. This report could have been used months earlier or held for months. Reports such as these, with a long shelf life, smooth the workflow through the production process and allow the producers of current affairs and business programs to be confident they can fill each week's program and at the same time chase reports or interviews that might not materialise with knowledge that the program will still have sufficient material.

Bennett's Rules

As noted in Chapter 2 Bennett's rules is a set of guidelines (devised to examine political reporting but applicable to economic and business reporting) for journalists to order their daily work and help make sense of what is happening.[351] The rules show that about half the reports on both *Business Sunday* and *Inside Business* are sourced from the activities or statements of business leaders. Conflict and consensus is the second most prominent category on both programs. Trail of power, the progression of an issue through institutions, is the third most prominent category again on both programs. The top three rankings are the same on both programs, although the percentages vary. This reveals a uniformity of judgement among journalists and producers although the rules are applied to different issues.

Table 3.12
Bennett's rules adapted for economic and business reports 6 June - 4 July 2004

	Channel 9 Business Sunday %		ABC Inside Business %	
Bus. officials	**1**	**47.6**	**1**	**50.0**
Conflict/consensus	2	33.3	2	25.0
Trail of power	3	14.3	3	16.7
Journalists' voices	4	4.8	-	-
Gov. officials	-	-	4	8.3
Rituals + customs	-	-	-	-
	n = 21		n = 12	

(For category definitions see Table 2.12.)

Almost half of the reports on *Business Sunday* are focused on the comments of business leaders, for example reflecting on management approaches in St George Bank/Frank Conroy (6 June) or corporate directions in Evans & Tate/Franklin Tate (4 July). Half the items on *Inside Business* are also based on business officials. Typically these are accounts of business events through the eyes of key players such as Matt Thomas, of Joss Supercar (6 June), David Vaux, MD of the DCA Group (13 June), Andrew Day, CEO of Sensis (20 June), Yvonne Allen, of Yvonne Allen and Associates (20 June), Andrew Mohl, CEO of AMP (27 June) and George Aleksiunas, of Croydon's Ritz Cinema (27 June).

The second largest category on both programs, conflict/consensus, is demonstrated on *Business Sunday* through reports that look at the different goals and needs, or conflict, between producers and consumers of oil in OPEC (6 June), a legal challenge by workers to

---

[351] Bennett, Lance W. 1997. Cracking the news code, in Iyengar, Shato, and Reeves, Richard. *Do the media govern? Politician, voters, and reporters in America.* Thousand Oakes, Sage, pp. 103-117.

management in Wal-Mart legal (27 June), consensus among analysts over News Corporation's listing in the US in News Corporation panel (27 June), conflict between two interviewees on the merits of e-mail in the office in e-mail (4 July), conflict between the Business Council of Australia over industrial relations policy (as recounted by *Business Sunday* presenter Ali Moore) and Labor's Shadow Minister for Workplace Relations, Craig Emerson, (4 July), disagreement over government energy policy from energy company Pacific Hydro (4 July) and conflict between the Rugby League and the Rugby Union in bidding for football player Andrew Johns (4 July). On *Inside Business* conflict and consensus is detailed in the state against state report over states competing for most investment but agreeing to co-operate on bio-tech projects (6 June) and is apparent in the divisions between News Corporation and institutional investors (13 June) and retail funds and industry funds in the superannuation report (20 June).

The trail of power is exhibited in the US Securities Exchange Commission investigation into KPMG that resulted in changes to KPMG's Australian operation (*Inside Business* 6 June) and the Standard & Poor's decision to remove News Corporation from the Australian Stock Exchange indices (*Business Sunday* and *Inside Business* 27 June). The last two of these are both decisions by US-based organisations that impact on Australian institutions.

Vision and Graphics

New footage, footage shot specifically for each report, was displayed in all the reports on both programs. The amount of file footage was less than that used by the two news programs but still considerable.

Table 3.13
The origins of vision in economic and business reports 6 June - 4 July 2004

	Channel 9 Business Sunday %		ABC Inside Business %	
File/generic	1	**58.8**	1	**66.7**
Satellite	2	23.5	2	16.7
No extra	3	11.8	-	-
Handout	4	5.9	2	16.7
New footage		100.0		100.0
		n = 21		n = 12

(For category definitions see Table 2.13.)

Handout material is footage shot for promotional or advertising purposes by organisations other than the television networks and is used on both programs. Advertising from Golden Circle, a juice producer in a different market segment to Nudie, is used in the Nudie report (*Business Sunday* 13 June) and state-based advertising material is used in the state against state report (*Inside Business* 6 June).

The use of file footage of a young Rupert Murdoch in the News Corporation report (*Inside Business* 13 June) introduces institutional issues related to access and the use of file footage. Prior to 1956 cinema newsreels such as Cinesound did most of the filming of events in Australia.[352] The advent of television caused the disappearance of the newsreels. Broadcasters, particularly the ABC, have built up extensive collections of file footage. Other footage was shot by individual organisations, such as the Snowy Mountains Hydro-electricity Authority, [353] or companies seeking to record their activities and individuals. Sources of footage of Australia's economic development is therefore limited to what was deemed important by the news values of the day, what was filmed for promotional purposes and what is accessible. The ABC for example charges $30 a second for broadcast file footage and this makes historical material relatively expensive.[354] Any independent producer or journalist wishing to make a program on aspects of Australia's economic development is limited by

---

[352]King, Barrie, *Newsreels.* http://wwwmcc.murdoch.edu.au/ReadingRoom/fillm/image/King.html
[353] www.phm.gov.au/hsc/snowy/investigating.htm
[354] http://www.abccontentsales.com.au/librarysales/ratecard.htm

budget constraints and by owners of material who might not be prepared to make their material available if they do not agree with the perspective of a program. Alternatives such as re-creations and the use of still photographs might not have the same impact. It is not an exaggeration to say the telling of history on television is constrained by copyright.

Two of the reports used by *Business Sunday* were prepared by other networks. Wal-Mart legal (27 June) came from CBS and e-mail (4 July) came from CNN. It is reasonable to assume they were accessed via satellite as this is how most foreign material arrives in Australia.

The two business programs have a smaller percentage of graphics than the two news programs. This may be because the business programs do not present large amounts of numeric information, such as share and currency prices and movements, but instead concentrate on broader issues such as individuals' philosophies and approaches.

Table 3.14
Graphics in economic and business reports 6 June - 4 July 2004

	Channel 9 Business Sunday %		ABC Inside Business %	
No graphic	1	**71.4**	1	**83.3**
Static graphic	2	14.3	2	16.7
Moving graphic	2	14.3	-	-
	n = 21		n = 12	

(For category definitions see Table 2.14.)

A minority of reports on the two programs (*Business Sunday* 29% and *Inside Business* 17%) are presented with either static or moving graphics. This may reflect a desire by producers to avoid the numbers-oriented approach of some overseas business programs (such as CNBC that can have several layers of tickers running across the screen at the same time), and to indicate to viewers that the programs are about individuals, companies, products and attitudes rather than numbers.

Many of the reports on both programs take a 'big picture' view of companies and consider their goals, management approaches, market overviews and other perspectives that do not lend themselves to graphics in the way that numeric details, such as share prices or P/E ratios, lend themselves to graphics.

The most imaginative approach is in the e-mail report (*Business Sunday* 4 July) that introduces each of six different graphics with the same e-mail-style interface box. This reflects the topic of the report, e-mail, and creates a continuity between the report subject and graphics. The text in the graphic highlights interviewees' comments or adds extra information. This report came from CNN and the more imaginative graphic style may reflect different newsworker values and processes or better technological support. The e-mail style graphics connect the television images and the report topic and are far removed from Whale's criticism that " ... vital details of a rent bill are not made clearer by little drawings of houses."[355]

Two of the *Inside Business* graphics display a different approach; the graphic in News Corporation plan (13 June) is created from footage of the ASX board and in superannuation reform (20 June) from data on a computer screen. These recall the early days of television when graphics were completed by an artist on boards and then filmed; the lens rather than digital data along a wire is the link between the graphic and the screen

Presenters and Reporters, Pieces-to-camera and Gender

The websites of both programs reveal that *Business Sunday* and *Inside Business* are keen to promote their presenters and commentators. Reporters are featured on the *Business Sunday* site but not on the *Inside Business* site.

Website viewers can read of *Business Sunday* presenter Ali Moore's start as a post-graduate cadet with the ABC and 16 years of international and domestic reporting, her move to finance reporting and shift to *Business Sunday* in 1995. Cost conscious business viewers can learn: "Carrying a small Video 8 camera, Ali showed early business acumen by filming her own stories for ABC television, thereby reducing her travelling costs!" [356]

[355] Whale, John (1969). *The half-shut eye - television and politics in Britain and America*. London. Macmillan. p. 25.
[356] http://businesssunday.ninemsn.co/au/aboutus/default.aspx

Nine Network Finance Editor Ross Greenwood's print experience - editor of the *Business Review Weekly (BRW)*, *Personal Investor* and *The Age's* money section as well as the editor-in-chief and one of the founders of the UK weekly magazine *Shares* - and broadcasting experience - including the BBC, CNN, Sky News and Bloomberg - are detailed. Greenwood has also been a director of a share market listed investment company and chairman of the investment committee of the journalist and entertainers industry superannuation fund and Superannuation Trustee of the Year in 1997. Commentator Terry McCrann has an Honours degree in Economics from Monash University, became Finance Editor of the Melbourne *Sun* in 1975 and is currently Associate Editor of Business for News Limited papers the Melbourne *Herald Sun*, Sydney's *The Daily Telegraph* and Brisbane's *The Courier-Mail*. He is also a multiple journalism award winner. Reporter Oriel Morrison is a former equities trader and a dealer and advisor on the futures and foreign exchange markets. Morrison worked as a reporter in London for the Reuters Financial Television network and is a finance commentator on radio station 2UE. Adam Shand is a former reporter with *The Australian* newspaper who covered finance and business during the 1980s and has worked for *The Australian Financial Review* as an investigative reporter and now works for *The Bulletin*, Channel 9's *Sunday* program as well as *Business Sunday*. (Note: Helen McCombie who was with *Business Sunday* during the 2004 survey period is no longer with the program and was replaced by Karen Tso in 2005.)

Several observations can be made from the website biographies of the *Business Sunday* journalists. One is the multi-skilling of Greenwood, McCrann and Shand in working for both television and print. This means they bring similar news values, knowledge, experience and skills to both types of media. The other is the industry experience of Greenwood and Morrison. This means they bring first-hand knowledge to finance reporting. In general terms however, ex-industry workers are likely to share at least some of the same values and attitudes as workers in the finance sector which risks an acceptance of finance industry practices that journalists without finance industry experience might challenge.

The *Inside Business* website provides similar details for presenter Alan Kohler and commentators Tom Elliott, Thomas Murphy and Marcus Padley.[357] Website visitors can learn of Alan Kohler's 35 years as a financial journalist. Kohler has been a Chanticleer columnist in *The Australian Financial Review*. He has been the editor of *The Australian Financial Review* and *The Age*. Kohler continues to write for *The Sydney Morning Herald* and *The Age* and presents a nightly economics and business segment on *ABC News*. Like his competitors at Channel 9 Kohler is able to report in print and broadcasting. The number of multi-skilled journalists on the two programs suggests any differences between economic and business coverage on television and in print could be attributed to the structure and characteristics of the television and print industries rather than the skills and values of the journalists.

The three commentators on *Inside Business* are all from the finance sector. Tom Elliott is the Managing Director and co-founder of the Melbourne-based fund manager MM&E Capital. Thomas Murphy is the head of Deutsche Bank Investment Research. Marcus Padley is a Stock Exchange Affiliate (member). All three commentators are involved in the media outside *Inside Business* to varying degrees. Elliott is a finance commentator on Melbourne radio stations 3AW and 3RRR and Padley produces a daily web newsletter. Murphy is described as a regular commentator on financial news. The three *Inside Business* commentators bring industry knowledge to the program. There is always a risk with commentators however, that their professional interests and connections pose a threat to the impartiality of their commentary.

The *Inside Business* website offers details on fewer staff members than the *Business Sunday* site. *Business Sunday* appears to have a larger reporting staff with the description of reporter beside the names of four people - Moore, Morrison, Shand and Tso (although Finance Editor Greenwood also reports) - while *Inside Business* lists only two reporters - Michael Rowland (not on air during the survey period) and Luisa Saccotelli although Kohler also regularly goes on the road for interviews.

At the inception of the program Alan Kohler was in place as the presenter and Neherda Barakat, who had produced Alan Kohler at *The 7.30 Report*, was in place as the executive producer. The reporters on *Inside Business* were recruited to prepare specific segments for the

---

[357]http://www.abc.net.au/insidebusiness/about.htm

program; in other words the individuals were recruited to fit the processes. Those key segments were earlier identified as the market report, a key interview, a serious feature story and the first person segment about small-to-medium business. Walter Hamilton's evidence at the Industrial Relations Commission indicates that preparation of the market report was not considered complicated enough to require a full-time journalist.[358] Alan Kohler would present the program and do the interviews. A member of the newsroom staff, Zoe Daniel, would do 'first person' reports based on individuals. A contract reporter, Greg Hoy, a journalist since 1980 with domestic and international experience, was hired to do a weekly feature report. Hoy's task:

> My role, as I say, was to compile a feature report on a major financial institution per week and it was … a very stimulating enthralling subject matter, as we sort of traversed the landscape of corporate Australia and it was a very interesting time. There were some very major developments, some of which had not yet come to the public's attention, with some of the biggest financial institutions in the country.[359]

Hoy also gave evidence that another reporter, Luisa Saccotelli, was employed specifically to do a small business segment. Hiring reporters for particular tasks is an example of the routinisation of newswork.[360]

This discussion of individual reporters and the importance of having familiar faces viewers can relate to is reinforced by the finding that 100% of *Inside Business* items contain reporters' pieces-to-camera.

---

[358] Hamilton, Walter. op. cit. PN5012.
[359] Hoy, Greg. Evidence before the Australian Industrial Relations Commission C2005/1811. PN2844
[360] Bantz, Charles, R. McCorkle, Suzanne, and Baade, Roberta C. (1980). The news factory. *Communication Research*. Vol. 7, No. 1. (and others).

Table 3.15
Reporters' pieces-to-camera in economic and business reports 6 June - 4 July 2004

	Channel 9 Business Sunday %	ABC Inside Business %
No ptc	64.6	-
Yes ptc	35.5	100.0
	n = 21	n = 12

(For category definitions see Table 2.15.)

The previous chapter considered the benefits of pieces-to-camera for reporters - on the spot credibility and knowledge, an additional element for packages and recognition - and for networks - credibility and commitment. Other techniques of visually identifying reporters include reverse questions (discussed below), noddies (where the reporter's head shot is used as a cutaway during interviews), two-shots (where the reporter and interviewee are shown together) and shots that show the reporter examining an item of relevance or in a location of relevance.

More than one-third of the *Business Sunday* reports and all of the *Inside Business* reports contain pieces-to-camera. One creative piece-to-camera is Geoff Hutchison's in the Yvonne Allen report (*Inside Business* 20 June) where Hutchinson opens the report sitting in a coffee shop with a piece-to-camera that starts:

> Sunday morning, coffee, croissants and *Inside Business*. What more could you possibly want? Well how about someone to share it with? This is the story of Yvonne Allen who, in 1976, became a professional matchmaker. She had $2,000, a small Sydney terrace - her neighbours thought it was a brothel -and a database, without a single name on it. It was a pretty basic beginning to a business of love.

The piece-to-camera runs for about 23 seconds and in it Hutchison does several things. He echoes the circumstances of many viewers who, at just after 10.00 am on a Sunday morning probably are sitting over a cup of coffee. He promotes *Inside Business*. And he introduces the topic of the report in a catchy way.

A reverse question is the technique where the reporter is presented face-on to camera asking a question of the interviewee. This effect can also be achieved during an interview in a two-camera shoot. A reverse question however can be done after the interview with the interviewee present, by moving the one camera and often leaving the interviewee in frame, or after the interview when the interviewee has gone. Both illustrate the reporter on location with similar benefits to a piece-to-camera. The individual style of different reporters is illustrated with Oriel Morrison including a piece-to-camera in two of her three reports and a reverse question in one of those reports while Helen McCombie has no pieces-to-camera in her five reports but reverse questions in each of the reports.

Reverse questions are useful but can be misused by unethical journalists who change the wording or the emphasis of the question after the interviewee has departed. Reverse questions can also be mocked up in a different location but a match with the original location is usually very difficult to make (because of different light and sound qualities) and this approach poses ethical questions as well.

The analysis of the survey period reveals the majority of *Business Sunday* reports were prepared by female reporters while the majority of the *Inside Business* reports were prepared by male reporters.

Table 3.16
Gender of reporters in economic and business reports 6 June - 4 July 2004

	Channel 9 Business Sunday		ABC Inside Business	
Female	1	**73.3**	2	33.3
Male	2	26.7	1	**66.7**
	n = 21		n = 12	

Henningham found that across all forms of media 71% of finance journalists are male and 29% are female.[361] The analysis shows that *Inside Business* is close to this while *Business Sunday* is almost the reverse.

In their choice of a female presenter and a majority of female reporters *Business Sunday* might be trying to emulate CNBC where reporter and anchorwoman Maria Bartiromo is a

---

[361] Henningham. 1997, op. cit. p. 49.

significant figure in US business reporting. Bartiromo joined CNBC in 1993 and 1995 was the first journalist to regularly report live from the floor of the New York Stock Exchange. Bartiromo is nicknamed the "Money Honey ... for her Wall Street savvy, Mediterranean good looks and Mary Hart-like legs ...".[362]

Bartiromo was on a program called the *Midday Call* and Busse and Green (2002) found that a positive comment about a company from Bartiromo during her segment could move the market, a result that illustrates the influence of Bartiromo in particular but also the effect of television in the era of instant trading:

> We ... find compelling evidence that some viewers trade based on the information in the segments. Trading intensity more than doubles in the minute after the stock is first mentioned, with a significant increase in the number of buyer- [seller-] initiated trades following positive [negative] reports. Furthermore, after controlling for trading costs we find that traders who execute a trade within 15 seconds of the initial mention generate small but significant short-term profits following positive reports during the Midday Call.[363]

Women reporters working on the business programs displayed a lower frequency of interviewing women than is displayed in the news programs or on *The 7.30 Report*.

Table 3.17
Gender of reporters/interviewees in economic and business reports 6 June - 4 July 2004

	Channel 9 Business Sunday %		ABC Inside Business %	
Male interview m/w %	88.9	11.1	84.2	15.8
Female interview m/w %	96.6	3.4	100.0	-
	n = 21		n = 12	

[362]Goldblatt, Henry (1998). People: Sorry guys, she's taken. *Fortune*. 26 October. Vol. 138, Iss: 8. p. 308.
[363] Busse, Jeffrey A. and Green, T. Clifton (2002). Market efficiency in real time. *Journal of Financial Economics*. 65 iss. 3. p. 416.

The lower frequency of women seeking out women interviewees when compared to the non-business programs could be because fewer businesswomen are available to be interviewed or because business is perceived as 'a man's world' and women seeking to advance in the finance media are less willing to challenge convention than female reporters on other programs such as *The 7.30 Report.*

Location

Both *Business Sunday* and *Inside Business* make an effort to promote the national nature of their program and to avoid representing one city over another.

Table 3.18
Location of economic and business reports 6 June - 4 July 2004

		Channel 9 Business Sunday %		ABC Inside Business %
National	1	**52.4**	1	**83.3**
Melbourne	2	23.8	2	16.7
Foreign	3	19.0	-	-
Sydney	4	4.8	-	-
Canberra	-	-	-	-
		n = 21		n = 12

(For category definitions see Table 2.18.)

There is no indication of the location of the *Business Sunday* or *Inside Business* studio nor is attention drawn to the geographical location of the reports on either program unless it is unavoidable or relevant. For example in the Melbourne location of Ford's Broadmeadows stamping plant (*Business Sunday* 6 June), the West Australian origins of winemaker Evans & Tate (*Business Sunday* 4 July) and the outer-east of Melbourne's Croydon Ritz Cinema are made clear.

Inside Business has a slight Melbourne bias with five out of the six package reports having identifiable Melbourne links. Two of the six packages are clearly Victoria-based; Joss Supercar (6 June) and Ritz Cinema (27 June). The state-against-state report (6 June) features Victorian Premier Steve Bracks, with 11 interview grabs or more than any other state premier. South Australian Premier Mike Rann, has four interview grabs, Queensland Premier

Peter Beattie two interview grabs, and New South Wales Premier Bob Carr, one interview grab. The report also allows Victorian Premier Steve Bracks to make the following comment about Queensland without challenge:

> There is a stronger domestic agenda for that parochialism, [Queenslanders] vacillate on whether they feel part of the nation or separate and unique and not really part of it. Of course, Victoria's history is different, our industry structure is different, we've always been national in our characteristics. And if you look back on Federation, where was if forged? It was forged from Victoria.

However other reports such as the interview with Tom Gentile, of GE Money (*Business Sunday* 27 June) and Tony McGrath, of auditors McGrath Nicol & Partners (*Inside Business* 6 June), are without a geographical reference. This reflects the national presences of services such as GE Money, available for example at any Harvey Norman store around Australia, or the 12 city presence of McGrath Nicol & Partners. The interview with Fosters President and CEO Trevor O'Hoy (*Business Sunday* 13 June) is coded as national. Despite the Melbourne origins of the company and the presence there of the corporate headquarters, the beer is available around Australia, and the world, and there is nothing in the report specific to Melbourne.

Some of the *Business Sunday* interviewees are physically in the studio, for example Lend Lease CEO Greg Clark (6 June). However, politicians Lindsay Tanner (13 June) and Craig Emerson (4 July) are interviewed via a monitor and it is impossible to determine if they in Canberra, in their electorate, or elsewhere.

This uncertainty of location of interviewees and reports contributes to a breakdown of geographical distinctions and builds a sense of globalisation. Audiences cannot be sure of the location of the presenter and set because of the freedom of movement allowed by technology such as computer generated sets. Nor can they be sure of the location of the interviewees because of the large distances travelled by executives and the possibility of going live from just about anywhere in the world. Interviewees are sometimes foreign; for example Americans Gorman (*Business Sunday* 6 June), Gentile (Business Sunday 27 June) and Blitzer (*Business Sunday* 27 June). Location is further confused by the multiplicity of corporate offices (for example footage of News Corporation offices in Adelaide, Brisbane and Sydney, *Inside Business* 13 June) and where products in reports are distributed worldwide (for example the Fosters signage in a bottle shop could be anywhere in Australia or around the world, *Business Sunday* 13 June). The international distribution of Ikea-like furniture means an outdoor coffee shop (such as the one used as a backdrop by reporter Geoff Hutchinson in the Yvonne Allen report, *Inside Business* 20 June) could be anywhere, the sameness of shopping centres with ubiquitous logos such as Harvey Norman (*Business Sunday* 27 June), global manufacturers and logos (Ford, *Business Sunday* 6 June), and similarities in architecture and town planning, mean it is often impossible to identify where a report is set. Telecommunications, with 1800 numbers and call centres often on another continent, and web pages based in cyberspace contribute to this. The old rivalry between Melbourne and Sydney as Australia's business centre has not been won by either city; both have been eclipsed by technology and international products and services.

CONCLUSION

Business programs seek to emulate the look and style of more general news and serious current affairs programs so as to benefit from their credibility. Several characteristics of reports on the business programs however - for example the focus on single companies, the summary nature of reports, the non-diary emphasis, a reliance on business elites, and the large number of one-interviewee packages that present only one perspective - identify business programs as belonging to a unique genre without the credibility of news and current affairs programs.

Business sources are able to choose whether or nor to make themselves available and thus dictate how (and probably if) a report is prepared. It may be less likely a report will be presented if these individuals are not prepared to make themselves available. Business programs are also less likely is critical of business because to do so runs the risk of alienating potential interviewees or their target audience. The use of a single interviewee to explore issues is a feature of both programs and this approach puts a particular onus on the interviewer to ensure balance.

The use of newsworkers with backgrounds in business highlights a fundamental issue of journalism. Should journalists be experts in the methods of journalism - knowledgeable of production process - and able to turn their general knowledge, curiosity, and information collection and analytical skills to a variety of topics, or should they be practitioners in the field with some journalistic knowledge? The industry practitioners offer the benefits of greater in-depth knowledge but they might also bring an unchallenged acceptance of business-sector attitudes and values.

Taken together these points - the nature of some reports on business programs, the dependence on interviewees and an acceptance of business values - mean that while business programs are informative they are also supportive of business and lack the critical approach of serous current affairs programs. Business is presented in a generally positive light.

CHAPTER 4

HOW TELEVISION PORTRAYS BUSINESS

These money men [CEOs, analysts, brokers, fund managers] are as practiced in the art of spin as the most slippery office seeker, measuring their success not in votes but in dollars, not in campaign seasons but in minute-by-minute prices.

Howard Kurtz[364]

THE NATURE OF BUSINESS SOURCES

Visions of Capitalism and the Big End of Town

The report of the Westfield shareholder meeting at the Sydney Entertainment Centre (*ABC News* 25 June) starts with a huge, close-up shot of Westfield Executive Chairman Frank Lowy's face projected on a giant screen hanging behind the stage. The message of the powerful, Orwellian big brother image is 'you must pay attention'. Below the screen on the stage, Lowy sits at the centre of a long table flanked by 14 major Westfield executives. The image is not unlike Leonardo da Vinci's *The Last Super of Christ* with Jesus and the disciples. This sense of drama is heightened by a backdrop of red curtains and spotlights. In the auditorium are 300 unit holders who have come to vote on the merger of three Westfield trusts to create the biggest listed shopping centre property trust in the world with assets worth $34 billion. The unit holders are 'served' by scurrying attendants marked by special 'symbols' (identification badges). There is music sweeping over the gathering - the Ministry

---

[364] Kurtz, Howard (2000). *The fortune tellers: inside Wall Street's game of money, media and manipulation.* New York, The Free Press. p. xiv.

of Sound's Chill Out Session Volume 5.[365] This is a high church of capitalism where investors come to see the man who has built the company over 43 years. These are the faithful who hand Lowy their future, in the form of a vote to support the merger of the trusts. Reporter Philip Lasker uses the term "adulation" to describe their response to Lowy.

The shareholders' meeting and *The Last Supper* both feature a key figure and his disciples. Both represent a decisive moment. *The Last Supper* took four years to paint, 1400 years after the event and for centuries only visitors to the Convent of Santa Maria delle Grazie in Milan could see it. The report on the Westfield meeting however was broadcast to a national audience only hours after it took place and illustrates the immediacy and reach of modern media.

The new $30 million Coca-Cola bottling plant at Mentone in Melbourne (*Business Sunday* 13 June) is as big as a cathedral. The visitors - the board, management and observers - are wearing fluorescent green safety vests over their business clothes. As they climb the stories-high catwalks inside the plant the vests make them look like worshippers in strange raiment. Each group has their own guide who points out - with sweeping gestures reminiscent of guides in a centuries-old building in Europe - the features of the plant. A central icon is a metres-high replica bottle of Coca-Cola. Coca-Cola Amatil Chairman David Gonski and his team on the stage are in front of a red-backdrop, similar to the backdrop at the Westfield function. As at the Westfield gathering there is a giant screen for the display of the key tenets of the company. The opening and tour is an event for television; the opening was reported by two newspapers ahead of the event but the event itself was not featured in the mainstream print because its emphasis was visual.[366]

These two different visions of capitalism display how business uses symbols and narrative techniques. These business television events display some of the features of traditional iconic events; for example an elite group of people as the focus, a reverent crowd, special 'ceremonial' clothing, a giant replica of a key item, music, an order of ceremony, stage

---

[365] Supporting detail such as the name of the music tracks from Elliott, Geoff (2004). Centres of attention. *The Australian*, 24 June. p 31, and Cummins, Carolyn (2004). Lowy pledges to stay put. *The Sydney Morning Herald*, 26 June. p. 51.
[366] Mitchell, Sue (2004). Things even better with Coke. *The Australian Financial Review*. 11 June. p. 55. Market Watch (2004). *The Australian*. 11 June. p. 22.

dressing for impact to enhance the importance of the event, attendant figures, and a sense of the 'virtue' of the way. This chapter will consider how newsworkers accept and transmit these symbols and narratives.

There is nothing unusual about the above events. Many companies hold large and elaborate meetings for shareholders and many companies celebrate the opening of new buildings or facilities. These events, and their portrayal on television, are visual celebrations of capitalism. They fall within Kellner's concept of a media spectacle as a form of media culture that puts contemporary dreams, nightmares, fantasies and values on display.[367] The values of those people presented in the business reports are those of a group of people whose common bond is not religion but investment and the creation of wealth and whose shared dream is even more wealth.

The Westfield meeting and the opening of the Coca-Cola plant are presented by their organisations and portrayed by the broadcasters as important events and this is typical of business coverage on television. Business has money to spend on its image and business leaders are well paid. The self-conferred elite status business and its leaders project through buildings, signage, decoration, personal appearance, and entourage, is echoed in how business and its leaders are presented on television.

One report, Telstra (*ABC News* 21 June), offers several different examples of the powerful presence of business. An aerial shot of a big Telstra logo on the roof of a building dominates surrounding buildings. This, the shot says, is an important company. In the same report a Telstra shareholders' meeting is dominated by a dozen executives on stage with a huge screen several metres high, as at the Westfield and Coca-Cola meetings. Again the visual message is that these are important people. The visual confirmation of status is apparent even away from the office. For example, file footage of former Telstra Chairman Bob Mansfield filmed at his home in an exclusive suburb reveals a set of imposing gates, a sweeping driveway and a house hidden by trees. It is a house that few 'ordinary' Australians could afford.

Elsewhere BHP Billiton Chairman Don Argus is shown shoulder-to-shoulder with Prime Minister John Howard - access to the national leader most Australians can only imagine - as

---

[367] Kellner, Douglas, 2003. *Media spectacle*, New York, Routledge. pp. 15-17.

they promote Australian gas sales to California (*ABC News* 3 June). Another example of the differentiation of powerful and privileged business leaders is Fosters President and CEO Trevor O'Hoy (*Business Sunday* 13 June) conducting a press conference at Sydney's upmarket Intercontinental Hotel surrounded by polished wood fittings and heavy drapes. Again, an environment many Australians would rarely experience.

Insiders, Hands-On Managers, Middlemen and Outsiders

In a society that values appearances and equates success with luxury surroundings, the interview settings, backdrops and lighting[368] reveal four different groups of interviewees. These are: 1. the insiders; 2. the hands-on managers; 3. the middlemen; and 4. the outsiders. The first two of these groups are the business elite and they are presented by newsworkers in a manner that reflects this.

The insiders are presented in lavish and exclusive surrounds with careful and painstaking lighting that reflect their elite position as perceived by the journalists and camera crews. President and CEO of GE Money Australia and New Zealand Tom Gentile (*Business Sunday* 27 June) is interviewed with intimate mood lighting in an environment of modern, restrained furniture. Chairman of the National Australia Bank Graham Kraehe (*Business Sunday* 27 June) is filmed in what looks to be a well-furnished boardroom. Again the lighting is dark and moody and there is a soft-focus, presumably valuable, painting in the background. It is a look of control and power. Chief executive officer of the Investment and Financial Services Association (FSA), Richard Gilbert, (*Inside Business* 20 June) is interviewed in what also looks like a well-fitted boardroom with a view through the window that indicates the room is in a high building in a major city CBD. The view suggests an exclusive location for an important business figure. The importance of these business leaders is enhanced by the way they are presented by newsworkers.

---

[368] Numerous researchers have studied television newsgathering processes including Tuchman (1978), Schlesinger (1978) who used the phrase "stop watch culture" to describe the time critical nature of work practices and program rundowns, Harrison (2000) and Garcia Aviles and Leon (2002). These studies focus mostly on newsroom activity and fail to pay sufficient attention to the 'on the road' work of journalists and camera crews. Much of television news and current affairs footage originates 'on the road' (including the material from satellite feeds and file) so the culture, creativity and technology of, and constraints on, camera crews are a critical influence on what appears on the screen.

Interviews with the insiders - board level and senior corporate decision-makers - may take many months and extended negotiations to set up (see comments from Barakat and Kohler in the previous chapter). This means that the time and place of the interview is known well in advance and the camera crew is usually given plenty of time to set up and light the location. Corporate headquarters can offer lavish locations such as boardrooms that are unused much of the time. Mood lighting can take half an hour or longer to set-up. Crews will often move furniture or change ornaments and paintings for the most attractive backdrop. Interviewees at the insider level are likely to have busy calendars and crews might have to wait beyond the appointed time for the interview.

Corporate locations such as boardrooms are also available to senior corporate leaders such as the hands-on managers. But this group - an example is Ford Australia's Tom Gorman - opt (advised perhaps by the journalist or public relations staff who realise the value of action footage) to be filmed in the work place. This can require considerable time as the cameraman finds varied positions for shots, waits for the right back-drop of, for example, cars at a particular stage of assembly, and may often require the interviewee to repeat their actions a number of times to get the desired level of activity in the background. Active locations such as factory floors are often noisy and can require special microphone arrangements or retakes when ambient noise rises to excessive levels. Corporate executives make themselves available for these extended periods because they think the exposure is worth the effort. The time and energy invested by newsworkers in these extended filming sessions are justified by newsworkers' news values of obtaining good images of key figures.

President of Ford Australia Tom Gorman (*Business Sunday* 6 June) for example is first seen on the assembly line and says: "I feel very comfortable in the manufacturing environment." He is later seen driving a new vehicle out of the plant and demonstrating the features such as the opening door and lift tailgate. The message is this is a man who knows his business. Similarly Nudie's Tim Pethick (*Business Sunday* 4 July) is first seen in the burnt-out ruins of the fruit juice factory that was a target of arsonists. Pethick is interviewed in a food hall; in an outlet and among the consumers of his product. Again the message is here is a manager in touch with the production and sales sides of his products. CEO and managing director of Qantas, Geoff Dixon (*ABC News* 22 June), is filmed walking into a press conference in a small, ordinary meeting room. It is a weekday, yet Dixon is wearing an open-collared shirt and talking to the media without widow dressing. The message is of a no-nonsense, hands-on manager.

The middlemen are those such as analysts who are experts in their fields and may be influential but without control. The director of Policy and Research at the Association of Superannuation Funds of Australia (ASFA), Michaela Anderson (*Channel 9 News* 24 June), is pictured in her work environment, an ordinary office with plain walls, a shelf of papers and folders and a desktop computer on a work bench. Analysts Adrian Mulcahy, of Perennial Investment Partners, and Scott Maddock, of BT Financial Group (both *Inside Business* 13 June) are filmed in ordinary meeting rooms. Daniel Eakin, of Deutsche Bank, is also filmed in what appears to be a meeting room with a painting as a backdrop but without the mood light that is reserved for those with control and power such as NAB's Graham Kraehe.

These middlemen are less critical to a report. There are usually a number of analysts who are knowledgeable about a particular company or industry sector who are available for comment. This means interviews can be arranged with short lead times. Analysts are unlikely to be shown on the factory floor or other visually interesting location; their workplace is their desk and computer screen. Analysts are also less likely to have access to luxurious locations such as boardrooms so the interviews are conducted in impersonal spaces such as meeting rooms that are booked by the half-hour.

Outsiders are people with limited power in the business world. These are workers, union representatives, consumer advocates and members of the public. The very nature of outsiders means they are short of assets such as boardrooms or meeting rooms and are therefore filmed in everyday locations. Their backdrops might be alongside a freeway, Leighton safety (*Business Sunday* 13 June), or shelving in a distribution centre, industrial relations (*The 7.30 Report* 8 June). Worker Michelle Raven (*The 7.30 Report* 8 June) is seen in the yard with her children and at home in a suburban living room. The two unidentified workers in the superannuation report (*Channel 9 News* 24 June) are interviewed on the factory floor of a metal fabricating company. Matt Warburton, of the Flight Attendants' Association (FAAA), (*ABC News* 22 June) is filmed on the street. Many outsiders have little to gain by appearing on television and can be unwilling to devote extended periods of time to filming or are restricted in how much time they can offer to newsworkers because of work schedules that are outside their control.[369]

The different production deadlines of news and of current affairs also shape how interviewees are presented. A weekly deadline allows crews to light and dress interview locations. A daily deadline means that many news interviews are filmed on exterior locations to save time. For example analyst Scott Maddock, BT Financial Group, and Fiona Balzer, the Australian Shareholders Association (ASA), were both filmed in external locations in the Telstra report (*ABC News* 21 June). Maddock was previously interviewed in a meeting room for *Inside Business* (13 June) but the news crew may have been too rushed to set up their camera and lights inside for the news report.

A final note on backdrops is that the changing nature of Australian industry, with a decline in traditional manufacturing and an increase in services, is at odds with television's need for visual material. A car manufacturing plant, such as Ford, offers good visual material plus the opportunity for executives such as Tom Gorman to demonstrate the features of the company's vehicles. Reports on service industries such as finance or banking offer much less by way of footage. A trading room, a call centre, a help desk or even a newsroom can all look much the same with workers in front of screens. Industries such as aged health care (*Inside Business* 13 June) offer limited and possibly (in the eyes of producers and journalists) less appealing visual opportunities, so the coverage of these may be restricted to one-on-one interviews as is displayed in the interview with aged health care provider David Vaux.

TELEVISION AND BUSINESS ELITES

Business Elites and the Authority to Speak

The visual portrayal of the importance of the insiders and the hands-on managers - on stage, surrounded by supporters, in locations of affluence or authority - reinforce Becker's notion of a 'hierarchy of credibility' expanded by Cottle as he examines "... whose voices and

---

[369] This of course can vary; some groups of outsiders, such as the unemployed, have few time constraints so are willing to devote large amounts of time to filming that might also be a welcome novelty and/or welcome exposure.

viewpoints structure and inform news discourse ...".[370] The hierarchy of credibility suggests that the elite in any group are able to "... define the way things really are ..." and that "... credibility and the right to be heard are differently distributed through the ranks of the system ...".[371]

Authority also comes from language. Bourdieu likens language to Homer's skeptron - a staff passed to individuals that gives them authority to speak - and writes "Language at most represents this authority, manifests and symbolises it."[372] As with the similarity between business events and religious meetings, the specific language used by the interviewees gives legitimacy to their appearing on television. Bourdieu writes:

> The stylistic features which characterize the language of priests, teachers and, more generally, all institutions, like routinization, stereotyping and neutralization, all stem from the position occupied in a competitive field by these persons entrusted with delegated authority.[373]

One example of business interviewees using language to display their knowledge and authority to speak is their use of the term the 'market'. Some examples are: "all facets of the market" (Conroy), "no wild new market" (Clark), "the market needs time to understand" (Clark), "still a difficult market in Australia" (Davis), "if anybody wants to come into the market" (Kermode), "there is a market and it will be around for some time in the five to ten dollar range." (O'Hoy), "inform the market" (O'Hoy), "550,000 total credit cards in the market" (Gentile), "part of the Australian market" (Blitzer), "international exposure within the market" (Coop), "I'm sure we'll be in that market" (Duffell), "other international markets" (Harding), "the greatest part of the UK market which is wine sold under five pounds" (Tate), and "the market drove what he could deliver personally" (Neill). Reporters too use the term, for example: "stabilise the oil market" (Greenwood), and "took the market by surprise" (Morrison).

---

[370] Becker, Howard (1967). Whose side are we on? Social Problems 14. pp 239-247. in Cottle, Simon (ed.) (2003). *News, public relations and power.* London, Sage. p. 8.
[371] Cottle, Simon (ed.) (2003). *News, public relations and power.* London, Sage. p. 5.
[372] Bourdieu, Pierre, (1991). Language and symbolic power. (edited and introduced by John B. Thompson).Cambridge, Polity Press, p. 109.
[373] ibid.

The identification of the repetitive use of a term such as 'market' offers scope to use literary theory to analyse economic and business discourse.[374] Fish suggests the meaning of a term is "constrained ... in the ways in which it could ... be heard".[375] This explains why viewers do not confuse one market with another. Conroy's 'market' (for banking and finance products) is not the same as Kermode's 'market' (for methods of paying taxi fares) which is not the same as O'Hoy's 'market' (for wine in a specific niche) which is not the same as Duffell's 'market' (for fruit juice products) and so on.

The use of 'market' by presenter Ali Moore and journalists Greenwood and Morrison displays their authority to communicate with the interviewees. However, as the gatekeepers of which interviewees appear on the program and what is contained in the reports, the journalists have their own authority independent of the business community. Their ongoing credibility however, rests with that community's acceptance of what they say.

Some of the comments such as O'Hoy's "inform the market", Clark's "the market needs time to understand" and Morrison's "took the market by surprise" personify the 'market'. Budzinski suggests the personification of the market has been brought forward by the "impersonality of the neoclassical market concept".[376] An additional explanation may be a greater familiarity of different financial markets brought about by increased coverage of the markets by the media and by a greater percentage of the public holding shares. The personification of the market might also be explained by 'irrational' rises and falls without any apparent reason.

An additional way television can help maintain the authority of leaders is to re-inforce their public presence. This can be self-perpetuating as Gitlin explains:

> ... news is what is made by individuals who are certifiably newsworthy. Once an individual has been certified as newsworthy, he or she has been empowered, within limits, to make news. In the mass-mediated version of reality,

---

[374] Henderson, Willie, Dudley-Evans, Tony and Backhouse, Roger (eds.) (1993). *Economics and language.* London, Routledge. McCloskey, Donald (1985). *The rhetoric of economics.* Madison, University of Wisconsin Press.

[375] Fish, Stanley (1980). *Is there a text in this class? The authority of interpretive communities.* Cambridge, Harvard University Press. p. 307.

[376] Budzinski, Oliver (2003). *Pluralism of competition policy paradigms and the call for regulatory diversity.* Paper presented at the New York University. 10June. p. 4. (citing permission needed).

organisations, bureaucracies, movements - in fact, all larger and more enduring social formations - are reduced to personifications. [377]

Gitlin was observing radical student leaders during the 1960s in the New Left politics of the US. But his comments are appropriate to business leaders in general and in particular the high-profile business leaders in Australia in the 1980s such as Alan Bond, Peter Abeles, John Elliott and Christopher Skase:

> Those leaders elevated to celebrity were flamboyant, or knew how to impersonate flamboyance … they knew what the media would define as news, what rhetoric they would amplify. They were already *leaders* in some sense, or the media would not have noticed them; the media made them *celebrities*. [378]

In the early days of business coverage, before the 1970s, journalists had to go to great lengths to gain access to business leaders with Robert Gottliebsen describing "… the first interview with BHP [Chairman Ian McLennan] was like a summit. BHP was a shut shop."[379] Gottliebsen, the founding editor of *Business Review Weekly (BRW)*, who also had a segment each weeknight on the *Channel 10 News* during the 1980s, saw business leaders as crucial to capturing a television audience:

> We try to make business and finance interesting. And it is. The characters in business are just as interesting as the characters in sport and politics … I think that any business, small or big, is best when the people involved can look up to a leader who is guiding their way. In our journalism in Australia we have emphasised those leaders more, and the rest of the world is only starting to catch up. It's much easier for people to relate to a Brian Loton than it is for them to relate to BHP or George Herscu rather than Hooker.[380]

---

[377] Gitlin, Todd (1980). *The whole world is watching: mass media in the making and unmaking of the new left.* Berkeley, University of California Press. p.146.
[378] ibid. p. 153.
[379] Tiffen, Rodney (1989). *News & power.* North Sydney, Allen & Unwin p. 41.
[380] Packer, Steve (1989). Behind Robert Gottliebsen. *The Sydney Morning Herald Good Weekend.* 22 July. p.70.
Note: Brian Loton, held various senior positions at BHP until he stepped down as Chairman in 1997. Journalist Trevor Sykes noted that during this period, in the twenty years to 2000, "bad investment decisions" cost the

Television's need for simply-told stories and strong, readily-identified visual cues makes the representation of companies by CEOs attractive to journalists.

> [CEOs personifying the company] is the way that business is going and it is easier on television than anywhere else. I mean a print journalist can sit down and reflect upon the various responsibilities of the chairman and the board and even shareholders but on TV you need someone to grab hold of.

> Trevor Sykes[381]

The changing nature of business - including the decline of owner-managed companies, the emergence of professional managers and the more-complex and faster-moving business environment - helps make CEOs more prominent and attractive to the media.

> Absolutely the principal reason [for the emergence of the CEO] has been a revolution in business thinking. The business restructuring is now taken for granted. The idea of restructuring a business twenty years ago wasn't on anybody's agenda. Now if you are not constantly restructuring you are not in the game. There has been just an absolute revolution in business thinking about the way in which corporations are run.

> Max Walsh[382]

The roll-call of the business leaders appearing on *Business Sunday* and *Inside Business* during the survey period includes the leaders of some of Australia's biggest, most established and best known companies such as Ford Motor Company, St George Bank, Lend Lease, Coca-Cola Amatil, Fosters Group, National Australia Bank and AMP as well as newer and smaller companies such as CabCharge, Pacific Hydro, Evans & Tate and Sensis. The CEOs

---

company $13 billion. *The Australian Financial Review*, 4,5 and 6 Sept. George Herscu was the Chairman of Hooker Corporation that collapsed in 1989 owing $1.77 billion. Herscu was sentenced to five years in jail in December 1990 for giving a $100,000 bribe to Queensland politician and minister Russ Hinze. Australia's biggest jail terms for businessmen. (2005). *The Sydney Morning Herald*, 14 April.

[381] Sykes, Trevor (2000). Senior writer and Pierpont columnist, *The Australian Financial Review*. Personal interview 17 July.

[382] Walsh, Max (2000). Editor-in-Chief, *The Bulletin*. Personal interview 18 July 2000.

and other leaders are willing to go on television because they see the benefits of the publicity
and of reaching a wide market.

> ... maintaining the share price, keeping it up, is regarded as one of the prime
> responsibilities of a CEO. It used to be they did not care about the share price,
> they cared about the results; they said let the results speak for themselves. But
> now days you have to keep massaging that market. Otherwise if your share price
> drops, you are in an era of hostile takeovers. So you might have a good business
> and a lousy share price, you won't be around for long ... you look at what's
> happened with things like the Commonwealth Bank and Telstra and BHP. These
> have hundreds of thousands of shareholders, you don't get them on a road show.
> You've got to keep them happy and in line and you've got to communicate with
> them as often as possible.

> Max Walsh[383]

This view differs from that of Tiffen who writes "Publicity via the news media is irrelevant or
even harmful to companies pursuing their interests."[384] These two positions can be reconciled
by considering when business seeks publicity - to support the share price as presented by
Walsh - and when it seeks to ignore or even block publicity - when business is going about its
day-to-day activities - as presented by Tiffen. Business is therefore particularly sensitive
about what type of material is publicised and when it is publicised and puts considerable
effort into managing the flow of information. Companies are also influenced by each other
and other bodies such as regulators and as some become more transparent others follow.

One Voice in Single-Interviewee Reports

One approach that restricts what information is presented is illustrated by the focus on CEOs
in a unique, and problematical, style of report displayed on *Business Sunday* that features a
single interviewee with set-up questions and overlay of business activity. In the Tom Gorman
report (6 June) and the Evans & Tate report (4 July) Tom Gorman and Franklin Tate are the

---

[383] ibid.
[384] Tiffen. op. cit. p. 41.

key and sole interviewees. Their statements go largely uncontested and the reporter sets up the interviewee to make positive statements. For example:

> Helen McCombie: Only two months in the job, and Tom Gorman is at home in his Melbourne manufacturing plant, with its build rate of 500 cars a day ... the company in good shape after its best profit in six years.

> Tom Gorman: The basic, simple message is, to take what is a very good company and continue to make it great. Geoff Polites [former president of Ford Australia] and the team have done a phenomenal job over the last four or five years really in turning Ford around not just the business but the image in the marketplace is now in a good spot and heading in the right direction, and my job really is to accelerate the pace of improvement.

And with Franklin Tate:

> Helen McCombie: The latest move in the Evans & Tate growth strategy; the acquisition of an east coast distributor and the formation of a national distribution network.

> Franklin Tate: This is a very exciting move for us, and means that under a separate brand we will not only be marketing the wines of Evans & Tate, but we will also be marketing a number of other brands, from other like-minded producers who in turn, as our colleagues in this project, will have their brands promoted alongside ours and will get a cross benefit. But the linkage between us as producers and the consumer is going to get a lot closer, and that's a very important outcome for us.

> Helen McCombie: The company is very optimistic about its export business.

> Franklin Tate: I think there is a great opportunity in the UK. Obviously people think, well the UK buys a lot of Australian wine, does that compromise the opportunities for Australian producers? Far from it ... We are extremely encouraged by the response of key retailers in the UK, key supermarket groups

and how they've responded to our propositions, indeed we have been so busy in the months of May and June, packaging wine to send to the UK for promotions in September, we couldn't bottle all the wine they needed, such was the level of activity.

This style gives the interviewees an opportunity to promote their company. It is reminiscent of a corporate video produced to portray the subject company in the most favourable way. These reports clearly illustrate the risks of top-down reporting identified by Gans[385] by emphasising the perspective of the single interviewee, excluding other elites, bureaucracies or critics, allowing the promotion of self-interest and associating the reporter with the interviewee in the way set-up statements corroborate the interviewee.

Negatives of CEOs Personifying the Company

Business and television is a two-way exchange; television programs get access to business leaders, the leaders get access to audiences. This is an extension of Gandy's 'information subsidy' under which media organisations are willing to accept material from outside sources because of economic efficiencies.[386] The business leaders making themselves available for interviews provide accessible and free content for the programs, but the content is limited because the leaders are only going to present information from their perspective. And business leaders are unlikely to make themselves available if they expect negative coverage or hostile questions.

> We have trouble getting people on when there are problems in companies. And that to me is the great shame of business. Sometimes you see politicians running and hiding but in the end politicians can't hide. They have to explain their role in things, they have to explain their position ...or they will be caught. Business wants to be a part of Australia, business wants to participate in Australian life, business wants to influence Australian life, Australian government, they want you and I to part with our money and give them profits. That is all well and good but

---

[385] Gans, Herbert (2002). *Democracy and the news*. New York, Oxford University Press. p. 45.
[386] Gandy, O. (1980). Information in health: subsidized news, *Media, culture and society*, vol. 2, no. 2. April. Another example of this is the way some television networks install cameras in banks and use these to obtain regular economic comment from bank staff although this was not displayed in the survey material.

they should also be accountable, they should be more accountable.

Glen Dyer[387]

CEOs personifying a company carries positives and negatives for both the CEO and the company. Hayward et al indicate that journalists continue to report corporate actions and results through the CEO and extend this personification to hold the CEO responsible for outcomes:

> ... journalists celebrate a CEO whose firm takes strategic actions that are distinctive and consistent by attributing such actions and performance to the firm's CEO. In so doing, journalists over-attribute a firm's actions and outcomes to the disposition of its CEO rather than to broader situational factors. [388]

Hayward et al summarise other material to conclude that celebrity CEOs are likely to assert greater control over their firms and, because of their celebrity status, receive greater remuneration. Hayward et al add the negatives are that celebrity CEOs are likely to become overconfident, fixed on their strategies, pay higher premiums for acquisitions and underestimate the impact of competition and other external factors. These attitudes displayed by celebrity CEOs heighten the risk of poor decision making.

> It's not entirely unfair [that a CEO comes to personify a company] because the rewards that chief executives are giving themselves these days does tend to focus attention on them. If someone is going to give himself a package of $13 million, he is saying "I am the company, it relies upon me." If he is rewarding himself that handsomely I think he deserves everything he gets in the way of either praise or blame.

Trevor Sykes[389]

---

[387] Dyer, Glen (2000). Executive Producer, *Business Sunday*, Channel 9. Personal interview 27 July.
[388] Hayward, Mathew L.A. Rindova, Violina P. and Pollock, Timothy G. (2004). Believing one's own press: the causes and consequences of CEO celebrity. *Strategic Management Journal*, 25. p. 637.
[389] Sykes. op. cit.

The unwillingness of business leaders to appear on television when there are problems contributes to what Schultz and Matolcsy[390] call business boosting by the media. Another perspective, however, is offered by journalist Max Walsh:

> ... when you deal with people who fail to understand the difference between, say, the world of politics and the world of business [there is a perception problem]. [They say] you are boosting business and you are not being critical enough, you don't treat business people on television the way you treat politicians, which is perfectly true. Of course there is a huge difference. The politician has a certain obligation to appear on television, a career obligation, unless he exposes himself his political career is going to go nowhere. The businessman has no such compulsion what so ever. He can sort of say stuff it, I don't want to go there. You have to cajole them, persuade business people to come on and if you treat them in a discourteous and aggressive fashion the way you can treat a politician and get away with it, they simply will not come back. So that is a simple fact of life.

> Max Walsh[391]

The soft approach by the media to business was most evident in the 1980s coverage of the flamboyant entrepreneurs. This is scrutinised by Toohey (1993):

> ... decisions made by the media were instrumental in creating an environment in which the '80s entrepreneurs were free to operate without the usual scrutiny the fourth estate claims to provide ... Television was not exempt from the excitement generated by the boom either. Specialist new programs were introduced, generally adopting a similarly supportive stance.[392]

Toohey summarises the business reporting of the 1980s this way:

> No-one, it seemed, wanted to hear about the hard slog behind designing and manufacturing a better widget. Instead, the market for new readers lay with

---

[390] Schultz and Matolcsy (1993). op. cit. pp. 9-33.
[391] Walsh. op. cit.
[392] Toohey, Brian (1993). The entrepreneur as folk hero. Schultz, Julianne (ed.). *Reporting business*, Sydney, Australian Centre for Independent Journalism, University of Technology. p. 33 and p.36.

stirring tales about tycoons juggling billions in takeover 'plays' featuring green-mailers, white knights, poison pills and golden parachutes.[393]

The business leaders interviewed on television during the 2004 survey period however, present a different agenda. They express ambition to manufacture a better widget with quality, efficiency and growth within existing businesses among their goals. For example Ford Australia President Tom Gorman (*Business Sunday* 6 June) has these goals "Number one we are focused on improving quality and again accelerating the pace of improvement …". The CEO of Fosters, Trevor O'Hoy (*Business Sunday* 13 June) is looking at existing business for growth: "We are going to have a good hard look at ways to improve organic growth and also ways of actually getting synergies across the business." So too is the CEO of GE Money, Tom Gentile (*Business Sunday* 27 June) "… what we would like to do is to develop stronger and deeper relationships with those clients that we have." Other leaders stress efficiencies, for example the CEO of Evans & Tate, Franklin Tate (*Business Sunday* 4 July) "We also want to put more efficiencies into our wine quality centre …" and the managing director of DCA, David Vaux (*Inside Business* 13 June) "… we generate good profits [in the nursing home business] and I think that is because we are a very efficient, productive manager."

Contrasting Causal Narratives and Ideational Change

In this section several different concepts will be brought together to support the concept of causal narrative that interviewees use to present their case. Causal narrative is story telling to illustrate how an event or action causes a consequence.[394] The consequence can be intended or unintended. The examination of causal narratives requires the identification of linkages between events and actions and consequences. Causal narrative can explain or help achieve ideational change. Causal narrative can also contain a sense of crisis as an added justification for action. Causal narrative can also involve institutional disequilibrium.

The concept of causal narrative is suggested through the examination of the reports during the

---

[393] ibid. p. 34.
[394] For examples of further discussion of causal narrative see Bennett, Andrew and Elman, Colin (2006). Complex causal relations and case study methods: the example of path dependence, *Political Analysis*, 14. and Gysen, Joos, Bruyninckx, Hans and Bachus, Kris (2006). The modus narrandi - a methodology for evaluating effects of environmental policy, *Evaluation*. Vol 12 (1).

survey period. It builds on concepts put forward by Street and others. For example:

> ... focus on the narrative ... Stories create a causal chain: this happened because
> she did that, he responded by doing this. They identify notions of responsibility
> and blame; they make sense of the chaos of events 'out there', and in doing so
> steer the audience's response towards one view of the world rather than
> another.[395]

While Street is reflecting on how journalists construct stories and narratives, this author
suggests that interviewees - specifically business people and politicians for the purposes of
this project - also construct causal narratives to explain actions, events and consequences.

The examination of narrative can also draw on myth and this approach fits within the
culturalist paradigm put forward by Cottle, Bird and Dardenne and others and differentiates
between the sociological paradigm and the culturalist paradigm in news analysis.[396] The
sociological paradigm considers "... strategic and definitional power, examining patterns of
news access, routines of news production and processes of source intervention ..." while the
culturalist paradigm considers the "...textural structures of news representation - ritual, story,
narrative - and thereby contribute to and sustain wider cultural myths that resonate within
popular culture."[397]

Analysing a business report on television as a mythical story helps display the concept of
narrative in economic and business reports. In myth the hero is a figure such as a young
prince, the challenges are personal weakness, evil villains or dragons and the hero might be
assisted by items such as magic swords. In television business reports the hero might be a
CEO, the villains are business competitors and circumstances or the government, and the
magic weapons are skills such as analysis and recognition of problems and opportunities and
a good business plan. For example, in his account of his dismissal as chief executive of
Westpac (*Business Sunday* 6 June), St George Chairman Conroy identifies his slowness of
action as a flaw that saw the villain, the Packer camp, bring about his resignation. Conroy, the

---

[395] Street, John (2001). *Mass media, politics and democracy*. Houndmills, Palgrave. p. 4.
[396] Cottle, Simon (2000). Rethinking news access, *Journalism Studies*, Vol. 1. No. 3. Bird, S. Elizabeth and
Dardenne, Robert W. (1988). Myth, chronicle, and story: exploring the narrative, in Cary, James W. (ed.)
(1988). *Media, myth and narratives – television and the press*. Newbury Park, Sage.
[397] Cottle, Simon (2000). Rethinking news access, *Journalism Studies*, Vol. 1. No. 3. pp. 428-429.

hero, subsequently overcame that flaw by recognising that speed of action is important and successfully applied that during his time at St George for victory. This example using St George Bank is particularly apt because journalists regularly use the myth of St George and the dragon in business accounts.[398] For Fosters' O'Hoy, the villain is the global oversupply of wine, the magic formula is his wine rescue plan and the hero will be O'Hoy himself provided he can turn the company around. The outcome of the struggle - victory continuing employment and perhaps greater financial remuneration or dismissal - for O'Hoy is at the time of writing unresolved.

Conroy tells his story in narrative form. The sequence of events is played out over time; his slowness to react, the intervention of the Packer camp resulting in the loss of support from the Board, Conroy's forced resignation, his recognition of his slowness, and his subsequent success at St George because of this recognition. It is a condensed account of events but it is an account that is easy to understand. Bird and Dardenne see narrative as "… an entrance point into a culture … that encodes values and guides …".[399] Conroy's narrative brings viewers into the world of big business with a familiar story, of failure and redemption, that is an accepted part of western business culture. The emphasis on the need for speed of action is unique to Conroy's narrative but one viewers can recognise.

Conroy's narrative is causal in that his slowness of action caused his forced resignation. The mechanism or linkage between the cause and consequence however needs to be identified for the causal narrative to be understood. As Elster writes "To cite the cause is not enough: the causal mechanism must also be provided, or at least suggested."[400] The linkage between Conroy's slowness and his forced resignation is the Packer camp. As Conroy presents his narrative "… the Packer camp saw that (slowness) and exploited it". This linkage comes about by the human action of the Packer camp who were about to join the board of the bank. Other linkages can come about by market action - such as the OPEC announcement of

---

[398] Headline writers can not resist the mythic references suggested by the name of St George Bank. For example the headline of one report about the bank was How the dragon is slaying its rivals, Boyd, Tony (2004). *The Australian Financial Review*. 2 Nov. p. 16.
[399] Bird, S. Elizabeth and Dardenne, Robert W. (1988). Myth, chronicle and story, in Carey, J.W. (ed.) *Media, myths and narratives; television and the press*. Newbury Park, Sage Publications. p. 75.
[400] Elster, Jon (1989). *Nuts and bolts for the social sciences*. Cambridge, Cambridge University Press. p.4.

increased oil production causing oil prices to fall - or by natural events - such as the lack of rainfall causing drought.

Institutional disequilibrium and ideational change were also part of Conroy's departure from Westpac although they are not part of Conroy's account on *Business Sunday*. Conroy is recalling events and outcomes that commenced 12 years prior to his account on television. By way of background the institutional disequilibrium came about because Kerry Packer had purchased $400 million worth (8%) of Westpac shares and was about to become a director of the bank. The approach of Packer's lieutenant, Al Dunlap, who was also about to become a director, was " ... a new boss must destroy the old culture."[401] While this is not ideational change of the scale considered in recent writings such as liberalism in the United States[402] or social democracy in Europe[403] it is a significant change within a single organisation.

The characteristics of television - limited time for reports, inability of the audience to refer back to previous material, competition for the audience attention by surrounding activities, difficulty in dealing with abstract terms and a varied level of knowledge by the audience - make causal narrative a useful tool for explaining issues and actions. The mythic nature of narrative reinforces the viewers' perception of importance of business to the community. Bird and Dardenne write "Myth has meaning only in the telling ... values exist only if they are communicated ... myths must constantly be retold."[404] So Conroy's narrative - of a businessman who overcomes adversity and does well - is familiar and reinforces western business cultural values of hard work and determination bringing success. It is echoed by Nudie's Tim Pethick who has brought his company back into production after a suspicious fire (*Business Sunday* 4 July). It is echoed by Rupert Murdoch's sometimes risky climb to wealth and influence of which analyst Adrian Mulcahy (*Inside Business* 13 June) says " ... most people ... wouldn't have bet that [Murdoch and News Corporation] would get to where they are today."

---

[401] Carew, Edna (1997). Showdown behind Westpac's boardroom brawl. *The Sydney Morning Herald*, 30 Aug. p. 93.
[402] Blyth, Mark (2002). *Great transformations: the rise and decline of embedded liberalism*. Cambridge, Cambridge University Press.
[403] Berman, Sherri (1998). *The social democratic movement: ideas and politics in the making of interwar Europe*. Cambridge, Harvard University Press.
[404] Bird. op. cit. p. 337.

Causal narrative is chronologically based. Its causes can be events or actions in the past that have consequences in the past, present or future. The causes can also be current actions that have consequences in the present or the future. The causes can even be predicted events or actions in the future with consequences in the future. Or they can be all three. For example, the report on the James Hardie asbestos inquiry (*The 7.30 Report* 14 June) recounts that work practices in the past caused/are causing death and illness of workers in the past, the present and the future. The victims' illnesses are the unintended consequences of the company's decision to mine and process asbestos. The report on the inquiry also reveals that James Hardie management manipulated information on the extent of asbestos-related illnesses and the company's liability; a corporate decision in the past likely to cause a shortage of funds for compensation in the present and the future.

Some reports contain only one causal narrative while others contain several causal narratives that might or might not be competing. An example of one causal narrative is when the managing director of health care provider DCA Group David Vaux, says the capital resources and good management of his firm will cause it to become the largest player in the aged care market (*Inside Business* 13 June). No other causal narrative is presented in the report to challenge Vaux's narrative.

Several contrasting causal narratives can be put forward by different actors. An example is the report on QANTAS's plans to reduce costs by basing flight attendants overseas (*ABC News* 22 June). One causal narrative is put forward by QANTAS CEO Geoff Dixon who says action now in basing flight attendants in Britain will reduce costs in the future. An alternative narrative is put forward by ACTU President Sharan Burrow who says: "QANTAS will not sustain Australian loyalty if it continues to erode Australian jobs and wages for working families." The viewer is presented with two competing causal narratives: Dixon's narrative that the plan will keep QANTAS a profitable company in the future or Burrow's narrative that the plan will cause a reduction in support for QANTAS and the erosion of jobs and wages. Further, the two narratives emphasise different things; Dixon's profitability, Burrow's customer loyalty and jobs and wages. This creates a challenge to the cultural values of viewers who have to weigh profits against loyalty, jobs and wages.

Analysis by causal narrative can also illustrate single or multiple consequences. The example above of the growth of DCA in the aged care market is a single consequence. An example of multiple consequences is apparent in the John Singleton interview (*The 7.30 Report* 24 June). Suggestions that a fourth free-to-air commercial television licence might be issued have caused Singleton to announce he would be interested in starting a network with all-Australian content. This is the first consequence. Singleton's announcement puts other players - competitors and the government - on notice and means they will have to take him into account when the proposed licence is considered. This is the second consequence.

If a sense of crisis can be introduced into the causal narrative it can add urgency to the reason or need for action. This is most pressing when the need for action in the present is demanded to bring about a particular consequence in the future. Several of the reports warn of a crisis that would affect all Australians. For example the report water - liquid gold (*The 7.30 Report* 23 June) says current water usage will cause a crisis in the future. Scientist Dr Tim Flannery says the water shortage is "... probably the biggest threat to the southern Australian capitals that I can imagine." and West Australian Premier Geoff Gallop adds "... let's adjust, otherwise ... we're threatening the future of our civilization here in Australia."

Other suggestions of crisis affect smaller groups. The James Hardie report (*The 7.30 Report* 14 June) warns that up to 50,000 people will be affected by asbestosis, a warning delivered by asbestos victim Bernie Banton and made more dramatic by vision of him struggling to breath and needing the help of oxygen from a portable tank. The car dealers item (*The 7.30 Report* 15 June) reports the erosion of the car dealers share of the car service market by independent tuners and warns "If [car dealers] are to survive in their current form, it's a trend they have to stop." Many car owners have unwittingly contributed to that crisis by turning to the independent tuners. The energy policy report (*The 7.30 Report* 15 June) had wind energy advocate Dr Carl Mallon saying "... the wind energy industry is shocked by this announcement ... five billion dollars worth of projects stranded ... the industry will hit a brick wall...".

In summary business reports on television that make use of causal narrative present a story to viewers that is easily understood in the linear format of television. This narrative can contain un-stated mythic elements. This storytelling helps reinforce the cultural values that support the core values of western business; hard work, success and the creation of wealth. Causal narrative is also used to demand action today to avoid a crisis in the future.

BOOSTING BUSINESS

The Role of Public Relations

Business leaders and others in the glare of the media often turn to public relations and media training to help develop effective techniques of communication such as casual narrative. The work of public relations practitioners is rarely apparent from watching on-air programs because the very nature of public relations is a behind-the-scenes activity. As discussed in the previous chapter however, public relations have become an integral part of the relationship between business and the media. Zawawi illustrates the increasing role of public relations practitioners in Australia by a growth rate of 25% a year[405] to more than 8000 public relations practitioners in 1999. She estimates 65% of stories in the front news sections and almost 90% of stories in the business news section of prominent daily newspapers come from public relations sources.[406] There is a lack on agreement on this however. A survey commissioned by the GCI Group found that 80% of newsworkers believed information from PR firms was biased or irrelevant and that less than 20% of press releases were used.[407] Despite that, the ABA-Bond survey found that 85% of journalists used public relations material, most from government sources.[408] This wide variation on the influence of PR is echoed by British research that found between 20% and 80% of news output was based on public relations

[405] Zawawi, Clara (2000). A history of public relations in Australia, in Johnston, Jane, and Zawawi, Clara. *Public relations; theory and practice.* Crows Nest, Allen & Unwin. p. 32.
[406] ibid. p. 38.
[407] Fox, Catherine (1999). PR gets bad press from journalists. *The Australian Financial Review*, 5 Oct. p. 38. GCI Group is part of Grey Advertising. The survey, of 100 journalists (editors, deputy editors, news editors and sub editors) across radio, television and print, was conducted by Sweeney & Associates.
[408] Pearson, Mark, and Brand Jeffrey (2001). *Sources of news and current affairs*, Sydney, Australian Broadcasting Authority. p. 337.

material.[409] The income of PR consultancies in Australia was estimated at more than $1 billion in 2000.[410]

The relationship between public relations and the media is described as having both benefits and costs. Among the claimed benefits of using PR material are the cost reductions to media organisation through the supply of low cost material and the provision of important and newsworthy stories[411] and a voice for non-official or resource poor groups, although this may be overpowered by the louder PR voice of larger opponents.[412] The negatives associated with PR include dependence on official sources and the exclusion of those critical of those sources, efforts to avoid coverage, resistance to negative investigative reporting, attempts by states and large corporations to manage the media and the acceleration of journalists' dependence on institutions.[413]

The 1999 revelations that the Australian Bankers' Association (ABA) paid broadcaster John Laws, and the radio stations involved with him, more than $1 million to promote the image of banks clearly highlights the problem of corporate money buying positive coverage outside recognised promotional methods such as advertising. The issues are hard to pin down because of different perceptions of what is news, what is entertainment and what is information and what constitutes influence, editorial material, comment, contra deals, access and conflict of interest. Taylor, for one, summarises the problem:

> There is supposed to be a thick black dividing line between the stories or the television programming and the ads or the PR spin. In practice though the line is blurred ... that line is under pressure every day, in every media outlet. Armies of advertising executives and public relations professionals are paid to put it under pressure. Not overtly, by paying journalists to write favourable copy. And not illegally. In subtle ways they aim to influence the news to put their clients in a

[409] Davis, Aeron (2002). *Public relations democracy - public relations, politics and the mass media in Britain.* Manchester, Manchester University Press. p. 26.
[410] Crisp, Lyndall (2002). Spin specialists. *The Australian Financial Review.* 13 Sept. p. 20. Downloaded 24 June 2005. http:0-global.factiva.com.opac.library.usyd.edu.au/en/arch/display.asp
[411] Zawawi. op. cit.
[412] Davis, Aeron (2000). Public relations, news production and changing patterns of source access in the British national media. *Media, Culture & Society.* Vol. 22: 39-59.
[413] Davis, Aeron (2003). Whither mass media and power? Evidence for a critical elite theory alternative. *Media, Culture & Society,* Vol. 25. pp. 669 - 690.

more favourable light. They do it with straight information, but also by plying journalists with expensive lunches, lavish corporate entertainment and free travel, by providing "exclusives", tip-offs and top-level access for "friendly" journalists: by supplying ready-to-print articles for overworked journalists trying to produce ever-expanding advertising "supplements" and advertising-driven lifestyles sections; by directing essential advertising dollars away from critical journalists' publications; by supplying subtle pressure to section editors keen for an advertising dollar.[414]

Others do not agree that PR is a threat to independent and unbiased journalism. Kate Fry, head of the Department of Communications at the University of Technology, Sydney, says "Legitimate PR can improve the quality of the media by creating a division between journalists and companies with unfair or dodgy agendas."[415] Chulov quotes one unnamed senior broadcast journalist on the distinction between PR and journalism as saying "We all deal in information, so what does it really matter?"[416] Chulov, at the time, concluded a fall in advertising revenue had led to constraints on editorial resources with resulting changes to work-practices such as journalists writing their reports without leaving the office and informed by using PR material to drive editorial coverage. He adds:

> The point of difference - even among newsrooms - is whether this all matters. After all information is still flowing, people are still being informed and anyone, from municipal groups to large corporates, have a right to get their message out.[417]

It does matter because the message from the business world is managed and manipulated. In just one example, discussed in the previous chapter, Fosters CEO Trevor O'Hoy made it a condition of appearing on *Inside Business* that his future plans for Fosters would not be discussed and that he would see a list of questions beforehand. Journalist Alan Kohler agreed to limit the scope of the interview in order to get access to O'Hoy. PR practitioners,

---

[414] Taylor, Lenore (1999). Believe it or not. *The Australian Financial Review*, 6 Nov. p. 23.
[415] Callaghan, Greg (1999). Sultans of spin. *The Australian*. 24 June. p. 26.
[416] Chulov, Martin (2002). Hacks or flacks - media economics are blurring the lines between journalism and public relations. *The Australian*. 22 Aug. p. n/a. Downloaded 24 June 2005. http:0-global.factiva.com.opac.library.usyd.edu.au/en/arch/display.asp
[417] ibid.

communications managers or media consultants are often involved in the negotiations between the media and business leader ahead of an interview or packaged report. Ian Kortlang explains: "With somebody like me, we take the initial call, check what angle the guy is doing."[418]

The public cannot know if O'Hoy discussed those questions with his public relations team. That information is not publicly available but there is every likelihood he did so. O'Hoy has a Corporate Affairs team of at least eight people to turn to; their names and contact details are made available to journalists on the Fosters web site.[419] A further exploration of the site reveals 46 press releases for the first half of 2005 (to 22 June), most of which deal with Fosters takeover of winemaker Southcorp, and five media reports featuring O'Hoy during 2004. (The *Business Sunday* report on O'Hoy (13 June) is for some reason not included on the list; either through oversight or deliberately, perhaps because of some aspect the company judged as negative and so did not want to promote the report.) The site also includes a number of downloadable images of the Fosters executive team and a variety of images of beer, spirits and wine products for use by the media further illustrating Fosters' efforts to make positive images easily available to busy newsworkers.

A review of those key points raised at the start of this consideration of public relations indicates a substantial amount of public relations material such as that generated by Fosters, finds its way into the media. Those corporate events, such as Fosters giving *Business Sunday* access to its staff at road show events (13 June) adds to the supply of material available to the media and makes the production of a report more likely. The willingness of *Inside Business* to depart from its own journalistic norms to gain access to O'Hoy illustrates the dependence on key sources and a willingness to let those sources dictate the agenda. The language of *Business Sunday* - for example a $300 million write-down is ascribed to Fosters' management "... dozing off ..." reveals an unwillingness to engage in hard criticism. This could stem from fear of exclusion from future access and an unwillingness by journalists to alienate a company as significant as Fosters.

---

[418] Kortlang, Ian (2000). Executive Vice Chairman, Gavin Anderson and Co. Former advisor and chief-of-staff to New South Wales Premier Nick Greiner. Personal interview 23 June.
[419] http://www.fosters.com.au?corporate/news/mdia-contacts.asp

One aspect of public relations is media training. This is training for people likely to deal with the broadcast media on a regular basis and involves dummy interview sessions and press conferences with a trainer - often a television journalist - who then critiques the performance and offers advice for improvement. Media training teaches interviewees how to avoid answering difficult questions and to instead use the question to promote the point they want to make. The aspect of interviewees being able to make a personal presentation direct to the audience is one of the key differentiations between the broadcast media and print.

> In the print media your guy ... doesn't really get the exposure he does on television. On TV you have to media train the individual. You have to have done more work on questions and answers. You have got to have gone through the message. You have to say 1, 2, 3; if [the interviewer] says X you have to answer Y. So there is a lot more specific media training for it ... your bloke is it ... You can school them up, you can skill them up, but in the end they can blow it. So a lot more training for television than for print.

> Ian Kortlang[420]

The *Business Sunday* interview with NAB Chairman Graeme Kraehe (27 June) is noteworthy for a technique that is often promoted by media trainers. This technique is to hold a constant position and to repeat that position however many times a question is asked, or indeed to give the same answer to different questions. This is called 'staying on message'. In answer to Adam Shand's two questions about bank processes, Kraehe responds to the first question by talking about specific changes to the CEO and chairmanship of the company and to the second question by talking about broader board and the CEO appointments. It is apparent that the changes to processes have not been made or are something Kraehe does not want to discuss so he continues to talk about senior personnel changes. Kraehe makes seven references to senior management or board changes in an interview that runs 5:30 minutes. He also makes the point of the company looking forward or moving on and not looking back on four different occasions during the interview. It is clear that these two points, management

---

[420] Kortlang. op. cit.

and board changes and moving on, are the key points he wants to make regardless of the questions. Kraehe is on message.

The risk in this technique is that when interviewees continue to repeat themselves, viewers might recognise that there are issues the interviewee wants to avoid. That should immediately set off alarms and pose the question: What is the interviewee trying to avoid? Media training can also erase individual characteristics or attitudes and present business leaders as clones.

> It is [necessary for CEOs to have television skills], but so many of them are over trained they don't get their point of view across. They look like little glove puppets ... If [the media trainers] are good, if they can help a person, male or female, young or old, explain their position quite succinctly without using the phrase "at this point in time" and "going forward". If they can get rid of those for example, they have done a good job. But if they teach them body language and control we can tell. We can pick now and we don't come back and talk to them. Or if we do, we go out trying to get under their skin trying to get to the real person.
>
> Glen Dyer[421]

Too often though 'the real person' is too hard to reach under the media training. Lieberman writes:

> As journalism has morphed into a cog in a great public relations machine, the fundamental relationship between journalists and their subjects has changed ... where once journalists took the lead ... those being questioned now lead the way, coached precisely on how to wrest control.[422]

It is a comment on business television in Australia that few of the live interviews - where media training is particularly beneficial because the interview cannot be edited - were adversarial. *Inside Business* carried six live (or strictly speaking as-live, because the program is pre-recorded) interviews (auditor Tony McGrath, Assistant Federal Treasurer Helen

---

[421] Dyer. op. cit.
[422] Lieberman, Trudy (2004). Answer the &%$#* question! *Columbia Journalism Review.* vol. 42 issue 5. 1 Jan. p. n/a. Downloaded 15 Aug. 2006. http://www.cjr.org/issues/2004/1/question-lieberman.asp

Coonan, health care businessman David Vaux, Sensis Managing Director Andrew Day, S&P's David Blitzer and AMP's Andrew Mohl) during the survey period. None of these were adversarial. In the live interview with Lend Lease's Greg Clark, *Business Sunday* interviewer Ali Moore did challenge Clark, asking four times if he was going to lift the offer - "sweeten the pot" in Moore's language - for General Property Trust (GPT). Clark used two of the questions to promote his offer and held his ground during the other two questions.

Promoting Company Names and Visual Clichés

Public relations requirements for the promotion of company names is also satisfied in clichéd shots of interviewees walking past company reception desks and along the corridors of offices. This technique is used a number of times in reports during the survey period. The technique is used twice in the Pacific Hydro report (*Business Sunday* 4 July); first when ABN Amro analyst Jason Mabee walks along a corridor and past a strategically positioned ABN Amro name and logo and secondly when Pacific Hydro MD Jeff Harding heads straight for the reception desk, with the company name on prominent display, and is handed a envelope that has apparently been left there for him. A slight variation appears in the Leighton report (*Business Sunday* 13 June) when a young woman approaches the reception desk of the Worksafe organisation and requests information. Reception areas are generally designed to promote an up-market and affluent image of organisations. The property trust report (*Business Sunday* 6 June) takes the technique further, and removes the human element entirely, by showing the Deutsche Asset Management name displayed along a corridor wall, several paintings along another wall and then the smart timber and glass reception area before cutting to Deutsche analyst Daniel Eakin. Newsworkers may intend the names and logos of these companies to provide visual material when there is little else on offer. The names and logos however are free publicity and a return to the organisations for making their staff available.

Building exteriors and exterior corporate names and logos are also used repeatedly and again represent free publicity. These include the Cabcharge building (*Business Sunday* 13 June), the Fosters headquarters in Melbourne (*Business Sunday* 13 June), exteriors of a Wal-Mart store (*Business Sunday* 27 June), exteriors of GE Money retail outlets cutting to interiors (*Business Sunday* 27 June), exteriors and people entering and exiting the News Corporation building

(*Inside Business* 13 June and *Business Sunday* 27 June) and exteriors of the Rugby League offices (*Business Sunday* 4 July).

The Property Trust report (*Business Sunday* 6 June) also features extensive footage of buildings such as the Quay Grand building at Sydney's Circular Quay but this footage may be relevant because it represents a property trust investment. Similarly, the Leighton corporate headquarters, in Leighton safety (*Business Sunday* 13 June), is featured but this is over a script that said Leighton had declined to be interviewed for the report.

Exterior shots of buildings are there as wallpaper; vision that does not really add to the information being presented to the viewer but shows something on the screen while the reporter talks. Exteriors of buildings are often used because the material in the script is conceptual and cannot be illustrated or because the reporter has been unable to get access to particular events, such as a board meeting. This author however suggests that building exteriors are of limited use because exteriors remain the same regardless of events taking place behind the façade. Exteriors are most useful when a change within the organisation being discussed is reflected by a change in the exterior, for example when a corporate logo changes and the old logo is shown being removed and replaced by the new logo.

Ideology of Newsworkers and the Portrayal of Business

Business leaders and public relations practitioners have been presented as being in a strong position to influence television coverage. But what of the ideology of newsworkers and are their political leanings reflected in the news? On one hand there is the view that the news reflects the view of a left-leaning media elite out of touch with the mass of the population.[423] On the other hand there is the view that the media is dominated by conservatives and controlled by government and business.[424] In a recent work Kollmeyer reviews the debate and, based on content analysis of the *Los Angeles Times,* concludes:

[423] For example Lichter, Robert S. and Rothman, Stanley (1988). Media and business elites, in Hiebert, Ray Eldon and Reuss, Carol (eds.), *Impact of mass media: current issues*, New York, Longman
[424] For example Gans, Herbert J. (1979). *Deciding what's news.* New York, Pantheon Books. and (1985). Are U.S. journalists dangerously liberal? *Columbia Journalism Review.* Nov/Dec. pp. 29-33

> ...the bulk of the evidence ... strongly suggests that the news media, when
> reporting on the economy, privilege the interests of corporations and investors
> over the interests of the general workforce.[425]

Another dimension in the discussion of bias is the view that audiences' ideologies affect how they view the media with Lee concluding " ... the perception that the media are biased is [more] likely grounded in an observer's own stance rather than in manifest media content."[426]

News processes limit newsworkers' political leanings from translating into pro or anti-business bias in reports. The admission by A. Kent MacDougall's that he was an undeclared socialist during a career as a journalist for more than 20 years at *The Wall Street Journal* and the *Los Angeles Times* offers a framework to examine newsworkers' ideology and its impact on news selection. MacDougall 'outed' himself in 1989 and sparked a debate about ideology and objectivity. Reese[427] examines MacDougall's admission and concludes that journalists follow an unwritten occupational ideology that promotes objectivity and defensible standards of accuracy, balance and fairness that are reinforced through routines, shared professional values and verification of standards by journalists through comparisons with colleagues. Reese also concludes sources rather than newsworkers influence the ideology of news and concludes "News is what authorities and institutional elites say it is," and adds this is influenced by the 'information subsidy'." [428]

The account by ABC television news finance reporter Philip Lasker of his working day supports Reese's framework and offers an Australian context for this debate. Lasker starts his day reading the papers and listening to radio news and current affairs. He discusses what is happening and exchanges ideas with the national news editor. Together they decide on the issues and events he will cover. Lasker also considers feedback from his non-finance, generalist journalist colleagues and shapes his story and approach so they can understand.[429]

---

[425] Kollmeyer, Christopher J. (2004). Corporate interests: how the news media portray the economy. *Social Problems*. Vol 51, No. 3. p. 451.
[426] Lee, Tien-Tsung (2005). The liberal media myth revisited: an examination of factors influencing perceptions of media bias. *Journal of Broadcasting and Electronic Media*. March. 49(1). p. 58.
[427] Reese, Stephen D. (1990). The news paradigm and the ideology of objectivity. *Critical Studies in Mass Communication*, 1990. Vol. 7. pp. 390-409.
[428] ibid. p. 425.
[429] Lasker, Philip. (2000). Personal interview 28 July.

These actions illustrate his daily working routines and shared professional values. Lasker's monitoring of the reports in newspapers and on radio means he is monitoring the competition and also verifying his news values with others in the industry. His response to his generalist colleagues has the same effect. If a journalist such as Lasker was to present a story idea shaped by extreme ideology it would face three challenges: Lasker himself would recognise it as being at odds with what he is monitoring in the media, he would have difficulty convincing his colleagues of the merits of his idea and he would risk official rejection of the idea by his superior, the national news editor.

Australian research indicates that business journalists are more likely to be left-leaning than non-business journalists. Henningham found that 54% of finance journalists considered themselves a little or pretty far to the left compared to 38% of non-finance journalists.[430] Schultz found that while 41% of finance and economics journalists have no particular political preference, one-third said they were closer to the Labor Party while 17% favoured the Liberal and National parties.[431] What is not clear from Henningham and Schultz is how the left-leaning journalists are distributed in the media and their representation in the commercial networks such as Channel 9 or the public broadcaster the ABC.

The role of elites in shaping what is news is illustrated by business leaders making themselves available - or not - for interviews. As discussed in the previous chapter 76% of *Business Sunday* and 85% of *Inside Business* interviews are one-on-one. That means interviewees have to physically make themselves available to the business programs and are unlikely to do this if they dislike the ideology of the program or the journalist in the same way they are unwilling to make themselves available when the story is negative. This reliance on interviewees makes television more susceptible to only carrying positive stories than print and supports Tiffen's comment that "Business reporting - writing for a business audience while relying on business sources - is potentially prone to sycophancy …". [432]

---

[430] Henningham, John (1997). Characteristics and attitudes of Australia's finance journalists. *Economic Analysis and Policy*. Vol. 27. No. 1. March. pp. 52-53.

[431] Schultz, Julianne (ed.). *Reporting business*, Sydney, Australian Centre for Independent Journalism, University of Technology pp. 13-14.

[432] Tiffen (1989) op. cit. p. 46.

The difficulties presented by the need to gain access to business figures and yet avoid sycophancy is acknowledged by journalists, for example by the comment from Max Walsh, editor-in-chief of the *Bulletin*, earlier in this chapter when he compared the pressures on politicians to appear on television with the pressures on business leaders. Yet others suggest access with restrictions is better than no access at all:

> I think that [the *Business Sunday* interviews] tend to give chief executives a free kick. On the other hand that is good, that works for [*Business Sunday*] because that means the chief executives come on. And part of the reason ... why the audience watches [*Business Sunday*], is because they get, for the big stories of the week, they actually get the chief executives, the top people. And the reason they get those people is because they know they are not going to be made look stupid or foolish.

> Alan Kohler[433]

> I can hardly stomach *Business Sunday*, it is just, you know, a gossip show for business executives really. It has very dry market focused stuff. It is a service program for the business community and I guess from that standpoint as long as you recognise that that is what it is, all it is, then that's fair enough. But I don't think it even attempts to do anything wider than that. I've appeared on it once (laugh) so I suppose that is something.

> Greg Combet[434]

The business community's desire for journalism that boosts the economy or business confidence and presents an optimistic point of view is also mentioned by Tiffen[435] Negative reporting does draw criticism from business leaders. Negative reporting is also viewed by journalists as being unattractive to audiences. This helps create the optimism sought by business leaders.

---

[433] Kohler, Alan (2000). Business and Economics Editor. *The 7:30 Report*. ABC Television. Columnist *The Australian Financial Review*. Personal interview 5 July.
[434] Combet, Greg (2000). Secretary, ACTU. Personal interview 2 Oct.
[435] Tiffen (1989). p. 46.

I guess the one thing that we want to reflect is some kind of success. We always want to present a relatively positive kind of attitude. We are very objective in our coverage and very balanced, always. In order to keep viewers, you have to maintain a fairly positive outlook. And you look at successful things and successful people. So I guess that there is possibly a tendency for business television and media generally to reflect success rather than failure. James Ross[436]

CONCLUSION

There are a number of factors that influence the reporting of business on Australian television. These include an inherent respect among newsworkers for business elites, limited budgets and resources that promote one-interviewee reports or a preponderance of one-on-one interviews, a willingness to let business leaders and their supporters such as public relations workers influence how business is presented and the diminishing but still present freedom of business leaders to choose not to appear on television in difficult times.

The overall effect is that business is presented in a generally positive way. In part this is because coverage of economic and business material reflects the present economic and ideological time. Western nations like Australia are currently enjoying prosperous conditions with good economic growth and low unemployment. There are also few serious ideological challenges to western capitalism in its different national variations.

The current economic and ideological conditions also influence the evergreen subject of the effect of the ideology of newsworkers on what is presented in the media. There is a homogeneity to economic and business journalists as displayed by their ability to move between print and television and to move between commercial to public television. Although newsworkers, like the general public, are likely to hold somewhat varying attitudes to particular economic policies or business approaches it is unlikely many have radical views. Even if they do, shared newsworker values and news processes are likely to minimise the effect of these on what is reported. There is therefore a sameness in material among different media platforms. All these factors combine to present a uniform and positive image of

---

[436] Ross, James (2000). Media Marketing Director, Bloomberg Asia-Pacific. Personal interview 12 June.

business people and capitalist values on television that is in line with the values and ideology of the wider community.

CHAPTER 5

TELEVISION AS A MEDIUM FOR ECONOMIC DEBATE

The sources that fill the requirements of mass production best are ... high-government officials. They have the power and the staff to create newsworthy events (ranging from decisions and activities to ceremonies) or statements (including reports, speeches, and news conferences, among others) regularly and quickly. Their power and authority make them credible sources as well, or more credible to editors and other news executives than sources with less authority and status. Whether they are more credible to more people in the news audience remains unknown.

Herbert Gans[437]

As mentioned previously, the image of state premiers Carr, Beattie and Bracks (*Business Sunday* 25 June) striding purposefully - arms swinging, coats blowing back with the pace of their walk, official papers tucked under their arms, assistants walking loyally by their side - toward their meeting with John Howard in Canberra for the Council of Australian Governments (CoAG) meeting on water use is powerful and purposeful. Images of politicians in news and current affairs reports are frequent and familiar. Politicians, as considered previously (see Table 2.4 and 3.4 and comments), make up the largest number of interviewees in economic and business reports on the *Channel 9 News* (62%), the *ABC News* (44%), *The 7.30 Report* (32%) and ABC *Inside Business* (30%). On *Business Sunday* politicians were the fourth largest category (9%).

It comes as no surprise that politicians seek coverage. Tiffen writes: "Battles for favourable

---

[437] Gans, Herbert (2002). *Democracy and the news.* New York, Oxford University Press. pp. 50-51.

news coverage are a major arena in political conflicts, and the news provides a common reference point to which the different sides relate in their subsequent actions."[438] Audiences however may see too much of politicians; a 2002 survey in Britain found that one of the points of dissatisfaction with television news is too many politicians with 64% of respondents saying politicians appeared too frequently while 4% said they did not appear frequently enough.[439] So why does television news - with its demands for action and visual material - co-operate with politicians and devote so much time to them in its coverage of economic and business news? Related issues are how politicians accommodate television, how issues are framed, how competing players seek to project authority and emphasise individual causal narratives, and how other voices are restricted. The consequences - to be explored in this chapter - are that much of the economic debate is framed in a political context and that politicians occupy a central position that allows them to dictate the issues and nature of economic debate.

WHO MAKES NEWS? POLITICAL SOURCES, ECONOMIC DEBATE AND THE CORE DEMOCRATIC FUNCTIONS OF THE MEDIA

Examples of economic coverage and debate from the survey period can be examined using Norris's synthesis of Schumpeter and Dahl's theories of representative democracy that identifies three core functions of the media. These are: 1. Providing a civic forum through balance in time, direction and agenda; 2. Performing a watchdog function through monitoring abuses of power and public scandals and failures; 3. Acting as a mobilising agent by encouraging engagement through practical knowledge, political interest and civic activism.[440] While Norris's emphasis is on political debate, these core functions can be used equally to examine economic debate: for balance; attention to abuses of economic power; and the promotion of economic knowledge and interest.

---

[438] Tiffen, Rodney (1989). *News & power*. North Sydney, Allen & Unwin. p. 178.
[439] Hargreaves, Ian and Thomas , James (2002). *New news, old news*. UK Independent Television Commission and the Broadcasting Standards Commission. pp. 76-77.
[440] Norris, Pippa (2000). *A virtuous circle – political communications in postindustrial societies,* Cambridge, Cambridge University Press.

Providing a Civic Forum

Norris examines balance in the media and expands on McQuail[441] to define three categories of balance: stop-watch balance (the amount of coverage), directional balance (positive, negative or neutral coverage) and agenda balance (issue ownership).[442] The three major topics that were put to air during the survey period - US-Australia the Free Trade Agreement (FTA), the Pharmaceutical Benefits Scheme (PBS) and water management - can all be examined against this framework.

In the news programs two reports examined the FTA (*ABC News* 17 and 25 June) and the stop-watch measure favoured the opposition (34.9 seconds) over the government (21.9 seconds). In terms of directional balance the reports are neutral with the government and opposition positions presented in an even-handed manner. In terms of an agenda balance the reports favour the government because it is promoting the FTA. Analysis via the three-point balance framework highlights several things. The first is that while the Liberal and Labor points of view are both presented, the different Labor points of view are not equally represented. The views of the 15 Labor parliamentarians who voted with the government are presented by Kim Beazley's comments (25 June). The views of the 40 Labor members who chose not to vote however are not presented and the debate is therefore restricted. From a viewer's perspective it is impossible to say if this was because these Labor members declined to make themselves available for comment, if journalists chose not to include their point of view, or if a logistical difficulty (such as the availability of camera crews or a shortage of time) made it impossible for their comments to be incorporated. *Channel 9 News* presents the FTA debate within the restoring rivers report (25 June).

Two news reports cover Labor's decision to support higher charges in the PBS. *Channel 9 News* (22 June) gives greater coverage to Liberal interviewees (19.6 seconds) than to Labor (11.8 seconds). However, because the report covers two topics, first the PBS then schools funding, the actual stopwatch count on the PBS issue puts the two parties almost equal with Labor (11.8 seconds) to the Liberals (11.7 seconds). In terms of direction there is a negative

[441] McQuail, Denis (1992). *Mass communication and the public interest.* London, Sage.
[442] Norris, Pippa, and Sanders, David, (1998). *Does balance matter? Experiments in TV news,* paper presented at the Annual Meeting of the American Political Science Association, Boston 3-6 Sept. pp. 1-27. See also Norris, Pippa (2000). op. cit.

message of the policy turnaround, described in the *Channel 9 News* report as a "shock decision" and "an extraordinary backflip". Labor Shadow Federal Treasurer Bob McMullan however attempts to portray the change in policy in a positive light - as a move to fund other policy options - by saying "It is just a hard decision that any sensible, responsible economic manager would have to make." In terms of agenda ownership, the policy change brings Labor into line with Liberal policy so ownership would seem to rest with the government. The *Channel 9 News* report makes reference to "heated opposition from some Labor MPs" but again these MPs are not quoted, or do not choose to have, a say.

The *ABC News* (22 June) report takes a similar approach to the policy change and gives greater coverage to Labor interviewees (23.3 seconds) than Liberal (14.4 seconds). However, like the Channel 9 report, the ABC report covers two topics, first the PBS, then junk food advertising, and the actual stopwatch count on the PBS favours Labor (14.3 seconds) against the Liberals (4.9 seconds). The ABC uses the term "backflip" twice as well as the terms "backdown" and "about face". The ABC also carries comment from Bob McMullan attempting to justify the change of policy. Like *Channel 9 News*, the direction of the report is negative for Labor despite Labor's attempt to portray its move in a positive light. And, as with *Channel 9 News*, ownership of the policy rests with the government.

The third major economic debate during the survey period is over water. This is covered in one report on the *Channel 9 News* (25 June) and in three reports on the *ABC News* (8, 24 and 25 June). The key players in this debate are the Federal Government, state premiers, the National Farmers Federation (NFF) and the Australian Conservation Foundation (ACF). In the first report on the ABC (8 June), the coverage given to the Liberals (14.4 seconds) and Labor (8.1 seconds) is exceeded by the coverage given to the farmers (15.5 seconds). The direction is positive for the farmers. For example, the first line of the introduction says "Australia's farmers have demanded that the cost of changing national water policy be more fairly distributed." This suggests the current policy is unfair to farmers without presenting any evidence. This report is centred on an event, the water forum that was part of the NFF's general meeting, and an ongoing attempt to shape the debate from their perspective. In the second water report (*ABC News* 24 June) Labor (16.2 seconds) dominates the stopwatch coverage with the interest groups second (9.9 seconds divided between the ACF 6.6 seconds and the NFF 3.3 seconds) and the Federal Government last (7 seconds). The direction is neutral and the agenda favours the Federal Government as the host of the annual CoAG meeting due to take place the following day. Prime Minister Howard set the target with the ABC reporting "The prime minister says [water reform] stands as one of the biggest tests for federal cooperation in 100 years."

The final two water reports, *Channel 9 News* and *ABC News* (both 25 June) are on the day of the summit. Stopwatch coverage on *Channel 9 News* favours the state premiers (19.5 seconds) over the prime minister (6.7 seconds). The ABC also favours the state premiers (21.2 seconds) over the prime minister (13.8 seconds) and the NFF (2.7 seconds). The interviewees reflect a positive outcome for most of the parties with comments such as John Howard's "This has been a tremendous day for the future of water supply in this country." and Queensland Premier Peter Beattie's comment "The environment has won and farmers have won today." (both *Channel 9 News* and *ABC News*). West Australian Premier Geoff Gallop, who did not sign the agreement, makes a negative comment "This is just not a national agreement." This earned the response from John Howard: "I just think it is rather petty and pathetic." (both *Channel 9 News* and *ABC News*).

In terms of agenda balance the Federal Government, as mentioned above, has ownership of the issue. This is partly because of the structure of CoAG that has the prime minister as chairman of the Council with the CoAG Secretariat located within the Department of Prime Minister and Cabinet. CoAG is a national body with the prime minister providing national leadership. The framework for the water reform package was agreed on at the 2003 CoAG meeting and it may be that the progress of discussions since then, unreported in the media, made it possible for the prime minister to set water reform as a test of federal cooperation with the knowledge that goal would be met. In other words, the prime minister is able to set the benchmarks that will define his performance and then successfully meet those benchmarks to enhance his reputation as a successful leader.

The 7.30 Report examines Labor's PBS policy change and the FTA in the same report (23 June). Labor (2.03 mins.) dominates the stopwatch balance compared to Liberal interviewees (59 seconds). Labor MP Roger Price however undermines the ALP position, with comments such as "I've always had reservations about holding up the legislation." His comments increase the Labor count but present a negative message for Labor. (Another example of this is NSW Premier Bob Carr's criticism of Federal Labor MPs who are blocking the FTA [*Channel 9 News* and *ABC News* 25 June]). Although this increases Labor's stopwatch count it casts Labor in a negative light.) Like the news programs *The 7.30 Report* refers to the policy change as a backflip and includes the comment from Treasurer Peter Costello, made in Parliament, of Labor's "triple double backflip" which may indicate how 'backflip' came into currency; the media that use the term backflip are echoing the language of the government, Labor's opponent and critic. As in the news programs the government has ownership of the PBS changes and FTA because they are its initiatives.

The 7.30 Report examines the water management issue in two reports (23 and 24 June). In the first, general interviewees (scientists, farmers, conservationists etc) receive the greatest coverage (4.17 mins.)[443] with Labor interviewees (state premiers and ministers) second (2.24 mins.). There was no Liberal representation. In the second report Labor interviewees (state and local politicians) receive the greatest coverage (1.23 mins.) and general interviewees second (1.11 mins.). Again there is no Liberal representation. The state-based focus of the two reports reflects state, rather than federal, authority over water issues and Labor domination of state governments. On the other hand, both reports are timed to run ahead of the Federal Government hosted CoAG meeting with the Federal Government playing a key role.

The two water reports on *The 7.30 Report* explore the different approaches to water management taken in Western Australia and Victoria. There is no conflict from political rivals. In a social framing (based on state government data) Toorak's "bad" water saving habits (24 June) are compared unfavourably to better water saving habits in inner-city and less affluent Melbourne suburbs. A woman who is apparently a Toorak resident comments on water restrictions and higher water bills by saying in a vox-pop "I think it's a bit inconvenient some times if you're not allowed to hose something that's a mess on your drive or wash your car." Reporter Heather Ewart asks another woman, apparently from outside Toorak: "What's

---

[443] Note: these times are calculated from transcripts using the television industry accepted standard of three words a minute because the analysis for this report was undertaken from a paper transcript because of a video recording error.

more important to them?" for the response: "Nice gardens. Having friends come over and look at their nice gardens." The direction of the reports on both days was generally neutral with agenda ownership going to the state governments.

A Watchdog Role

There are a number of reports that illustrate the media in a watchdog role, defined by Norris as guarding against abuses of power, protecting civil and political (and, for the purposes of this paper, economic) liberties and protecting the interests (including economic) of minorities.[444]

Several of the issues are covered across a number of programs. For example, coverage of possible abuses of funds of the Panthers football club is presented by both *Channel 9 News* and *ABC News* (15 June). Another example is the report critical of the flawed NSW property tax on *Channel 9 News* and *ABC News* (both 18 June) that is an abuse of power in that it favours some investors over others. These reports are also educational (see mobilising balance below) in that they alert viewers to the risks of poorly-drafted legislation.

The *ABC News* (4 June) and *The 7.30 Report* (14 June) reports on James Hardie and asbestosis details the plight of those who already have the disease and warns of the on-going risks to those likely to be exposed to asbestos in the future and suggests caution in dealing with it and similar dangerous products. More broadly, the report sounds a warning about companies that seek to avoid their liabilities through actions such as moving offshore. The reports discussed above on Labor's policy change on the PBS and split on the FTA sound a cautionary note on parties that change policy. These reports perform a watchdog role in monitoring how MPs vote, or fail to vote, on issues.

The 7.30 Report demonstrated a watchdog function in a number of different reports. Two threats to minorities are illustrated by the small number of people who brew their own bio-diesel having to pay excise on their home-made fuel because of the Federal Government's energy policy (24 June) and the struggle of conservationists to block development of Ralph Bay in Tasmania (30 June). The report on Labor claims that the Federal Government uses

---

[444] Norris (2000). op. cit. pp. 25-31.

taxpayer funded advertising to present political messages (16 June) is an attempt to guard against an abuse of power through the misuse of public funds.

Mobilising Action

Other reports, such as announcements of the government's transport policy (*ABC News* 7 June) or energy policy (*Channel 9 News*, *ABC News* and *The 7.30 Report* 15 June) provide information and practical knowledge and so fall under the mobilising agent category. These reports however offer little choice of action or redress to those unhappy with the policy short of not voting for the government at some future election.

Another mobilising report is the report on pending government action on water costs (*ABC News* 8 June) aired 16 days ahead of the water meeting between the Federal and state governments. The timing of this report is dictated by a water forum organised by the National Farmers' Federation. The forum was scheduled ahead of the summit to mobilise action and to make sure the NFF's position on water costs - a determination that farmers would not carry the cost of water management reform on their own - is made public. This report however is based around a pseudo-event and the website of the NFF makes it clear that the forum was part of an on-going campaign with 17 press releases related to the issue posted on the site in the first six months of the year.[445] In other words the ABC report is a response to an on-going public relations campaign by the NFF, and the ABC coverage of the NFF's concerns on national television is an illustration of the success of the campaign.

The two reports on water on *The 7.30 Report* (23 June and 24 June) considered previously illustrate how reports can fulfil several different core functions of media. The first report, liquid gold, uses interviewees who challenge the water management policies of the West Australian and New South Wales Governments. This comes under the watchdog category because it details the public failure of some of these policies. The second report uses interviewees who praise the policies of the Victorian government so comes under the mobilising agent category in that it presents solutions to the water crisis that may be of use outside Victoria.

---

[445] http://nff.org.au

The water reports, carried by *Channel 9 News* and *ABC News* and *The 7.30 Report*, are all pegged on the CoAG meeting on 25 June. How water management became an issue is not illustrated from this survey period. That can only be understood by looking at history and the role of different agents, for example academic and natural resource researcher Professor Peter Cullen and other individuals, or institutions, for example the media, interest groups or governments, in creating interest in water resources and management.[446]

Business Sunday and *Inside Business*, have related programs, *Sunday* and *Insiders* respectively, that devote more time to politics and economic debate. The business programs' style of one-interviewee reports also challenges the concept of balance in the civic forum category. However, both programs do carry items that play a mobilising role. *Business Sunday* examined Labor's communications policy (13 June), Labor's industrial policy (4 July) and gave some consideration to government energy policy (4 July). *Inside Business* examined interstate relations in attracting business (6 June) and superannuation reforms (13 and 20 June).

The Role of Analysts and Commentators

It has already been demonstrated that politicians make up the largest voice in economic debate but what of other sources? In the following sections the roles of other sources that appeared in the survey material on economic debate - analysts and commentators, Reserve Bank figures and trade union figures - is examined.

Private sector economists started to emerge as public figures in economic debate in Australia in the mid 1980s after the economic reforms of the Hawke-Keating government caused a demand for more economic information and interpretation. Will Buttrose of Lloyds Bank NZA, John Stone of Potter Partners, John Hewson of Macquarie Bank, Don Stammer of Bain and Co and Alan Wood of Syntec were highlighted as members of "... a select band of economists who wield influence over exchange and interest rates ... they appear on radio and television, write newspaper and magazine articles, publish their own economic forecasts and

---

[446] A measure of media interest in water issues is displayed by a Factiva search for the term 'water management' in *The Australian* newspaper. In the ten years starting in 1994 the search returned 0, 0, 8, 27,17, 17, 29, 27, 50, 59 and 49 (2004) hits.

are sought for public speaking engagements."[447]

A decade later another article said of economists: "They wear smart suits. And they look authoritative. Their pithy sound bites and opinions fill the airwaves and newspaper columns."[448] Senior economists, the article added, were earning $200,000 a year or more with the top names who made regular media appearances earning $400,000. Large organisations then are willing to pay more for economists with a media profile and these economists enjoy a celebrity status outside their professional circle.

> ... nowadays we have a number of economists who have a higher profile. I always
> feel their first duty is actually to the bank. But as a fellow who is in the show and
> tell game, I am very happy that they speak out publicly. They are not always right
> of course.

> Trevor Sykes[449]

The difficulties of economic forecasting are also considered in the latter article. A Reuters survey of 32 economists interviewed a week before a rate cut by the Reserve Bank revealed more than 60% of economists forecast the next move in rates would be up, 25% forecast no change, and only 12% correctly predicted a rate cut.[450]

During the survey period in 2004 economists were in equal place (25% of the analyst/commentator category) with equity analysts in terms of comment and analysis in all five of the programs. In all cases the economists appeared in reports focused on interest rates and housing prices. The benefit for economists and other commentators appearing in the media is promotion of the companies they work for and of themselves:

> Every time my name is on the screen ... BT Funds Management is also on the
> screen. So there is a bit of subtle marketing there. That is true whether it is TV or

---

[447] Deans, Alan (1986). What the economic gurus say and how they make it happen. *Business Review Weekly*. 7 March. p. 40.
[448] Hosking, Patrick (1996). Rate fall a cruel cut for some. *The Sydney Morning Herald*. 12 Aug. p. 31.
[449] Sykes. (2000). Senior writer and Pierpont columnist, *The Australian Financial Review*. Personal interview 17 July.
[450] Hosking. op. cit.

print. I like to think also that it enables me to engage in a luxury if you like …
making at least some contribution to the debate.

Chris Caton[451]

Selecting interviewees for television is driven by production processes, such as accessibility,
and newsworker knowledge. Having a good contact book with a wide range of potential
interviewees is regarded as an asset by reporters. They may be people the reporter has
interviewed previously, has seen interviewed in other media reports, been recommended by
other contacts (who are unavailable or who feel the topic is outside their area of expertise) or
found by simply cold-calling organisations. Good interviewees are knowledgeable, able to
make their point clearly and briefly and have good reputations in their industry.

> I'll speak to the people I need to speak to for my story, experts or analysts. Usually
> they will be analysts that work for banks, investment banks as opposed to
> academics, because academics may not be aware of or across the issues of the
> story of the day, which will often be market focused.

Philip Lasker[452]

A key point is that the economists and analysts who appear in the media during the survey
period are in the employment of public companies and present a market perspective. Analysts
might have a conflict of interest or have their hands tied; an analyst asked to comment on a
particular share, such as Telstra for example, might be working for an organisation that is
interested in underwriting the float of the remaining percentage of the company held by the
government. Likewise the opinion of economists on what economic policies are being
pursued might be at odds with the government for commercial reasons or they might be
constrained in what they can say:

> You don't want to get off-side with the government of the day [as a market
> economist stepping into a political issue]. It is as simple as that. Anybody will tell

[451] Caton, Chris (2000). Chief Economist, BT Funds Management Australia. Former head of the Economic Division of the Department of Prime Minister and Cabinet. Personal interview 21 July.
[452] Lasker, Philip (2000). Finance Reporter, News, ABC Television, Sydney. Personal interview 28 July.

you that is a consideration. And sometimes you can get off-side unfairly … that can happen no matter who is in government, lets just put it that way … large organisations certainly don't want to get off-side with the government of the day. So if you have one prominent employee out there getting off-side, it is a career limiting move.

Chris Caton[453]

Muted Voices: the Reserve Bank

Politicians drown out the voices of senior bureaucrats in economic debate. Reserve Bank Governor Ian Macfarlane appeared in one report (*ABC News* 4 June) and Reserve Bank Deputy Governor Glen Stevens appeared in two reports (both *ABC News* 2 June) in the only appearances by public servants on economic and business issues during the survey period. During the same period politicians made 94 appearances, thirty times that of the two bureaucrats. (It should be noted that neither appearance was specifically for television: Ian Macfarlane was presenting a summary of the Australian economy before the House of Representatives Economic Committee and Glen Stevens was making a speech before the Queensland branch of the Committee for the Economic Development of Australia.)

Television or media appearances are not a firm measure of power or influence but they do indicate participation in the public debate. The two most important national economic institutions, the Reserve Bank and Treasury, are television bit players.

> I think they [the governor of the Reserve Bank and the head of Treasury] do practically [no television] at all to my knowledge. I don't recall seeing Macfarlane interviewed at all or Ted Evans. Ted Evans, as head of Treasury, doesn't do I think any on-the-record interviews with anyone, print or television. And I think that is also the same now for Macfarlane. He did an interview, for example earlier this year with the [UK *Financial Times*] and that was notable really because it was so unusual. Neither institution [Reserve Bank and Treasury] has for example some

---

[453] Caton. op. cit.

kind of communication person who would know about television and neither would care. And I don't know that that is necessarily a bad policy.

John Edwards[454]

The risk is that if these key figures do not change their approach then the politicians will change it for them and to the politicians' benefit. In recent years there has been a debate about the public role of the Reserve Bank governor. In March 2000 *The Australian* reported: "John Howard wants Reserve Bank of Australia Governor Ian Macfarlane to lift his personal role in explaining the central bank's sensitive interest rate decisions to the Australian public."[455] The article went on to say that, in the first period of rising official interest rates in the life of the Howard government, Howard wanted the public to understand it is the Reserve Bank, not the government that sets rates and the reasons behind the moves. The following day *The Age* published a follow-up report that said: "The government has become increasingly frustrated that it has to stand up before the TV cameras and justify interest-rate rises that are made by the Reserve Bank Board."[456] The report also said the Opposition Leader Kim Beazley said " … the government was happy to be associated with falling rates but wanted to hide when rates went up."

Howard's ambition to be associated with lower rates while associating higher rates with the Reserve Bank, or someone else, is a strategy he also employed during the 2004 election campaign. The Liberals claimed that a Labor victory would push interest rates higher with Howard saying "I will guarantee that interest rates are always going to be lower under a Coalition government."[457] Howard's strategy to be on the low side of interest rates helped the Coalition to an election victory with Costar and Browne writing "Of the economic policy issues, the evidence suggests that it was the government's assault on Labor's interest rate record that bit most deeply."[458] and Tiffen adding "[Howard's] two key campaigning

---

[454] Edwards, John (2000). Chief Economist, HSBC. Senior Advisor (Economics) to Prime Minister Paul Keating, 1991-94. Personal interview 21 July.
[455] Henderson, Ian (2000). PM passes the buck to RBA. *The Australian*, 24 March. p. 21.
[456] Hudson, Phillip (2000). Face music on rates, RBA chief urged, *The Age*. 25 March. Business p. 2.
[457] Wade, Matt (2004). Labor means rate rise, PM claims. *The Sydney Morning Herald*. 30 Aug. p. 8.
[458] Costar, Brian and Browne, Peter (2005). The aftermath. How Labor lost. in (eds.) Browne, Peter, and Thomas, Julian (2005). *A win and a prayer – scenes from the 2004 Australian election*. Sydney, University of New South Wales Press. p. 114.

achievements were the constant emphasis on interest rates, and the tactical ambush on Labor's Tasmanian forests policy in the last week."[459]

The Liberal Party approach provoked concerns within the Reserve Bank, a statutory authority, over its comments on interest rates during the 2004 election campaign. *The Sydney Morning Herald* wrote "The Reserve Bank was sufficiently concerned about the Coalition's election campaign claims about interest rates that it asked the Australian Electoral Office to investigate."[460] The report went on to say that the Reserve Bank was "deeply uneasy at the intense politicisation of rates" but feared provoking headlines such as "Reserve says PM wrong' and did not want to become the centrepiece of the campaign.

The relationship between the Reserve Bank and the Federal Government got more coverage in March, 2005, when former secretary to the Treasury, Ted Evans, criticised Treasurer Peter Costello for speaking out about interest rates close to Reserve Bank board meetings.[461] In April 2005, six months after the election, the Reserve's communications policy was again under scrutiny when two board members, ANU Professor Warwick McKibbin and Woodside Petroleum and Coca-Cola Amatil Director Jillian Broadbent, spoke out about economic conditions only hours after the Reserve announced it was not going to raise interest rates.

The debate over the election interest rate claims flared again in August 2006 when the outgoing Governor of the Reserve Bank, Ian Macfarlane, said "I mean, they make these claims, you know, 'Vote for us - you'll have low interest rates,' which obviously we found annoying."[462] Macfarlane added the Bank's leadership decided to remain silent however to avoid politicising the Bank.

Macfarlane displays a strong sensitivity to the coverage of the economic debate. In April 2006 he commented:

---

[459] Tiffen, Rodney (2005). The aftermath. Must Labor lose? in Browne, Peter, and Thomas, Julian (2005). op. cit. pp. 125-6.
[460] Hartcher, Peter and Wade, Matt (2005). Reserve feared it was used as election pawn, *The Sydney Morning Herald*. 8 April. p. 1.
[461] Murphy, Cherelle and Bassanese, David (2005). Costello under fire over rates comments. *The Australian Financial Review*, 19 Aug. p. 5.
[462] Hartcher, Peter and Wade, Matt (2006). Bank chief's parting shot at PM on rates. *The Sydney Morning Herald*. 19 Aug. 2006. p. 1.

Many people, including me, have remarked on how much economic coverage there is in Australian newspapers - not just on the business pages, but on the front page and the editorial pages. Not only are the newspapers and magazines full of economic news, television news is saturated with it, there are special television programs devoted to it and radio programs as well.[463]

Macfarlane also discussed Reserve Bank research into economic coverage in three newspapers in the US, Britain and Australia the day before, the day of and the day after monetary policy announcements over two consecutive policy meetings by the respective central banks during 2004 and 2005. In the US there were 35 articles, in Britain 46 articles and in Australia there were 131. There was one front page article in both the US and Britain and 14 in Australia.[464] On the impact of coverage Macfarlane said: "The coverage probably assists with the monetary policy transmission mechanism. If interest rates go up it is the lead item on the evening news, it is on the front page of the paper. It helps to make monetary policy more effective."[465]

Muted Voices: Workers

Workers are another group with a limited voice (See for example tables 2.4 and 3.4). Tiffen comments that "Trade unions and pressure groups outside business are rarely sources, primarily because they are seen as having little information of value ...".[466] Union leaders however do practice public relations. ACTU Secretary Greg Combet comments that ACTU staff constantly monitor media such as talkback radio and if there is an issue of union interest they issue a press release or contact the program producer offering a union figure for comment. When Combet became secretary in 2000, he upgraded the communications role from one staff member to six.

---

[463] Macfarlane, I.J. (2006). Economic news: do we get too much of it? Notes for a talk to *The Australian Financial Review* leader's luncheon. Sydney. 28 April. Downloaded 17 Aug. 2006.
http://www.rba.gov.au/Speeches/2006/sp_gov_280406.html. p. 1
[464] ibid. p. 3. The newspapers were *The Financial Times*, *The Times* and *The Independent* in Britain, *The Wall Street Journal*, *The New York Times* and *The Washington Post* in the US and *The Australian Financial Review*, *The Australian* and *The Sydney Morning Herald* in Australia.
[465] Uren, David and Korporaal, Glenda (2006). Rates drama a hit for RBA. *The Australian*. 17 Aug. p. 1.
[466] Tiffen, Rodney (1989). op. cit.. p. 41.

I'm just finding in recent months that we are far more aggressively setting the agenda for debate on things like low pay, inequality in society. The fact that a quarter of the workforce are casuals with no job security, getting it on the agenda that they deserve to have fair rights like everyone else. Issues like that we have been pushing up very hard and I can see a very discernible difference in our treatment in the media.

Greg Combet[467]

... you have to be very skilled and savvy to get an issue run in the media that is an issue that concerns workers and their families ... It is very hard to get it run ... You've got to appeal to what you know the news cycle demands. And in that regard you've got to be sensitive to what print journalists need, what radio journalists need and what TV journalists need. In some senses the principle thing is to have good pictures and you try and weave your story into the pictures ... Television is critical in my experience, absolutely critical. You have very limited opportunities and you have to be very quick about it. In my experience, providing, trying to provide an environment where the television journalists can have the opportunity of good pictures, distilling your issue down to a clear simple image, that is critical if you are going to have TV and TV itself is critical.

Greg Combet[468]

STAGING AND FRAMING THE ECONOMIC DEBATE

Economics and politics

A consequence of the central role of politicians in the economic debate is that politicians are judged by the performance of the economy.

There is no sharply defined border between [politics and economics]. Treasury, the Reserve Bank and Peter Costello and John Howard all tend to meld a bit here

---

[467] Combet, Greg (2000). Secretary, ACTU. Personal interview 2 Oct.
[468] ibid.

and there and it's a bit hard to tell who has influence over what. And where one stops the other starts. We have just seen GST, which I suppose is part of the economy, introduced as a political measure for instance ... there is a great fusion between politics and economics and I don't think you can compartmentalise them very easily.

Trevor Sykes[469]

I think that frequently you get the impression politics and economics are just synonyms. And to my way of thinking politics should be broader than [that]. I would have liked to have made a pact at some stage that I won't comment on the politics ... if the politicians won't comment on the economics. It is such an all encompassing thing I guess that it is never going to happen.

Chris Caton[470]

A lot of the debate [about the economy] is coloured by the robustness of question time when the Federal Parliament sits, whenever there is a major release of economic news.

Mark Patterson[471]

... you'd have to look at how political decisions are influenced by economic matters and vice versa. How economic decisions are influenced by politics. You see that in a crude way in some economic commentary but I don't think it is generally very well dealt with.

Greg Combet[472]

The topics the politicians commented on during the survey period range from relatively small issues, such as a flaw in the NSW property tax, to national infrastructure issues, such as

---

[469] Sykes. op. cit.
[470] Caton. op. cit.
[471] Patterson, Mark (2000). Chief Executive, Australian Chamber of Commerce and Industry. Personal interview 16 June.
[472] Combet. op. cit.

transport funding and energy policy, through to international trade relations in the US-Australia FTA. Economics and politics are intertwined as summed up by the phrase 'The economy, stupid' by James Carville, Bill Clinton's political strategist in the 1992 US election. Governments and leaders are judged on how they manage the economy. For example Nickelsburg writes:

> ...the standing of the president with the public depends, more than anything else, on their success in a key domestic area, namely the economy. Incumbents of the presidential office have proved quite aware of how much their popular standing and electoral success depend on their success as the nation's chief economist.[473]

The importance of economic news on television to governments, leaders and electoral outcomes is reinforced by Gavin who found " ... television coverage of economic news plays a decisive role in the genesis of the public's economic perceptions."[474] and "... television news is related to perceptions of government economic competence and can affect government popularity ..."[475]

Economic indicators are taken as a litmus test of the government's performance:

> ... the [Canberra] Press Gallery is very insular. Every piece of economic news was reported in the context of whether it was good news or bad news for the government. Not whether it was good news or bad news for the broader Australian community... So it was just an extension of that who is winning, who is losing?

> Elliot Taylor[476]

Part of the difficulty in separating politics and economics is that decisions and actions taken by a government can have many different consequences across different areas. For example, changes to tax policy effect government revenue. They also have a social impact with

---

[473] Nickelsburg, Michael, and Norpoth, Helmut (2000). Commander-in-chief or chief economist? The president in the eye of the public. *Electoral Studies*. 19 (2-3). p. 314.

[474] Sanders, David and Gavin, Neil (2004). Television news, economic perceptions and political preferences in Britain, 1997-2001. *The Journal of Politics*. Vol. 66, No. 4, Nov. p. 1246.

[475] Gavin, Neil T, and Sanders, David (1998). Television, economy and the public's political attitudes. Gavin, Neil T. (ed.) in *The economy, media and public knowledge*, London, Leicester University Press. p. 106

[476] Taylor, Elliott (2000). Editor, *Media*, *The Australian*. Personal interview 3 Aug.

different socio-economic groups likely to be effected to different degrees. Producers and suppliers may see demand for their products shift. If the tax is a petrol excise there may be environmental consequences as consumers' habits change.

> I doubt [whether all sides and aspects in a debate] are [sufficiently explored]. And I suspect here, the issue of pre-existing bias becomes important ... if you think of the GST, if you think of tax reform as a shift in the tax mix with income being taxed less and spending being taxed more. And that is not the only way to look at it. You could look at it as a way to tax spending more efficiently than the way we did it before. But if you look at it as a shift in the tax mix, that is an issue right or wrong, it really is a political issue rather than an economic issue. And I suppose in the issue of privatisation you could make the same point.

> Chris Caton[477]

Political spin and pseudo-events

The everyday relationship between politicians and television newsworkers benefits both groups. Television offers politicians a way to reach large audiences and politicians offer television a dependable source of material. Politicians and their staff, like other news sources, attempt to maximise the benefits of television and other media and this has given rise to spin, a term attributed to author Saul Bellow in his 1977 Jefferson Lectures.[478] The term spin doctors came into media use in *The New York Times* on October 21, 1984 in an anonymous article with the headline "The debate and the spin doctors."[479] Today the term is ubiquitous, for example being used in 191 articles or letters in four major Australian newspapers during 2004.[480]

The techniques of spin are not new with some of them, such as leaks and favouring some groups with information not given to others, are as old as politics itself. What is different

---

[477] Caton. op. cit.
[478] Ingham, Bernard (2003). *The wages of spin - a clear case of communications gone wrong*. London, John Murray. p. 121.
[479] ibid. and Tiffen, Rodney (2004). Under (spin) doctors orders, *The Age*. 21 Oct.. p. n/a.
[480] Factiva search for the term 'spin doctor' in *The Australian, The Australian Financial Review, The Daily Telegraph* and *The Sydney Morning Herald*. 1 Jan. 2004-31 Dec. 2004. http://ezproxy.library.usyd.edu.au/

today, as Tiffen writes, is " ...the intensity of the enterprise, the huge amount of resources devoted to the effort, the integrated and professional approach to it; and the capacity for speedy action and response ...".[481] This is a reflection of the demand for and supply of news, the expansion of the media, politics as a news staple, the importance of media coverage in politics, the institutional nature, size and politicisation of the bureaucracy, changes to information technology on both the input and output sides, and changing work practices of journalists.

The role of media advisors and public relations workers is reviewed by Ward and includes Chulov's estimate that about 4,000 journalists work for state or commonwealth governments in public relations capacities. Ward concludes that "... in Australia, just as in the UK, the state plays a crucial role "as a dominant source of information and imagery".[482]

Former New South Wales premier Neville Wran (1976-1986) was a pioneer in Australia in recognising the potential of television for political purposes and his approach is echoed today. Television played a limited role in Australian elections before Wran, according to his press secretary Brian Dale. Dale writes that Wran was "... attuned to the reality of television as a medium of wooing popular support ...".[483]

Wran recognised that when television covers politics it concentrates on personalities and in particular - following the US presidential style - on the leader. He understood television needs action and events; footage of people doing things. Wran mastered the 30-second grab. He befriended cameramen so they would shoot him favourably and make suggestions about the best pictures and his staff identified important passages in Wran's speeches so the cameramen could film those passages. The introduction of electronic news gathering (ENG) meant material could be beamed back live from newsworthy locations and politicians could talk directly to viewers. Rail and power disputes became drama:

> ... if a newsreader could cross live to a reporter at the scene of the negotiations
> (where success or failure, a train or a stranded passenger, a hot meal or a cold

[481]Tiffen (2004). op. cit.
[482] Ward, Ian (2003). *An Australian PR state?* Unpublished paper presented at the ANZCA03 conference in Brisbane.
[483] Dale, Brian (1985). *Ascent to power.* Sydney, Allen & Unwin. p. 8.

shower hung on the razor's edge) the drama was always increased, as was the audience and the ratings.[484]

Wran in the mid-70s provided a model for political-media relations; politicians as personalities, event-driven reports, activities tailored-for-television and issues reduced to 30 or 40 second grabs. Wran provided television with good action footage and a flow of updated material to feed the news cycle. He maximised coverage by foreshadowing events, having the event itself and providing follow-ups. He perfected the art of making the statement he wanted regardless of the question that was asked. Above all Wran understood the shared purposes of politicians and journalists. Dale writes:

> ... getting stories is what journalism is all about. And, surely, getting stories on television and radio and in the newspapers is partly what politicians, especially successful politicians, are about as well.[485]

This relationship is presented as being good for both groups. By always being able to offer a story, Wran was able to gain media attention to help win and hold office. These reliable stories provided a bigger pool of material for journalists and emphasises the importance of the political round. In the two-and-a-half years from Wran becoming leader of the opposition to his election as premier the state Press Gallery doubled to fifteen Gallery reporters.[486]

The growth of the NSW Press Gallery illustrates a greater investment in covering politics by news organisations. As the media's investment in political coverage increases, the media needs to realise a return on its investment in political newsworkers and infrastructure and becomes reliant on the material that is offered to it by the spin doctors. Political events became a staple for the media. The political round (or beat) is like that of other rounds - police, health or business - in that news managers rely on rounds reporters who are knowledgeable of developments and familiar with the major players and how to access them for a regular and dependable supply of reports.

A further illustration of how television and events became a key part of politics is the

---

[484] ibid. p. 122.
[485] ibid. p. 64.
[486] ibid. p. 117.

presidency of Ronald Reagan (1981-89). Kurtz writes that "The entire Reagan administration was a made-for-TV enterprise, a daily staging of visuals for the networks; all activity came to a halt when the 6:30 newscasts came on."[487] A story of the day was decided on by Reagan's advisers and the activity or event was generated for the cameras. Reagan's advisers believed that the television pictures were more important than what was being said by the journalists and commentators.

In the 1996 Australian federal election campaign television production deadlines and the important evening news programs helped shape Liberal candidate John Howard's campaign day. His team were careful not to overwork Howard and " .. when the TV cameras shut down for the day, so too would Howard."[488] The Liberal campaign office turned from making news to watching it; every evening the team would get together in the campaign office to watch the news " ... the room would echo with groans or laughter depending on which side was getting a 'good run' or 'a kicking' from the journalists."[489] To present the best image in the television debates Howard was coached ahead of time by his campaign team and a media consultant.

The Liberal and Labor parties both built their campaign schedules around the evening news on television. The secrecy of the campaign schedules - to avoid demonstrators creating ugly scenes that would play badly on the news - saw correspondents bussed to undisclosed locations and tested the processes of news-making with camera crews given little time to get to the locations (few television stations have enough crews and putting them on the bus would restrict them from other jobs during the day). Print journalists had to tag along through the set-piece events.

Political Elites and the Authority to Speak

Manoeuvres such as those above are part of the attempt by politicians to control what audiences see and to present themselves in the most authoritative manner. The use of images is another technique and one summary of this is presented by US senatorial press secretary Jerry Ray who was ... struck by the importance of symbols, like the Capitol dome, in

---

[487] Kurtz, Howard (1998) *Spin cycle – inside the Clinton propaganda machine*. London, Pan. p. 105.
[488] Williams, Pamela (1997). *The victory*. St Leonards, Allen & Unwin. p. 195.
[489] ibid. p. 199.

television pictures.

> That Capitol out there - that says power. You have the senator talking from the Rotunda with this great painting behind him and this white statue looking down on him, blessing him. That gives the senator a statesman's image. That is what I am trying to say with my pictures.[490]

One example of creating a statesman's image and harnessing national symbols seen during the survey period is in the use of the Australian flag as a prop in political settings and as a backdrop by politicians. In one story alone, the FTA vote (*ABC News* 25 June), the Australian flag appears five times. The Australian flag, with the US flag, appears first in the graphic behind the newsreader. In the report itself, the flag - again along with the US flag in an array of eight flags - appears as a backdrop at a press conference for John Howard and US President George Bush at the White House. The flag next appears as a backdrop for Howard seated in an office in an interview with Sky Television. It is seen fluttering from a flagpole as Howard visits Australian troops in Iraq and two Australian flags are positioned on either side of the doorway Howard uses to access Parliament House from a courtyard. In the same ABC bulletin the Australian flag is seen four more times; twice as a backdrop for Howard interview grabs, once as a backdrop for the state premiers meeting in Canberra and once as a backdrop for an interview grab with Parliamentary Secretary Trish Worth.

Politicians and Canberra journalists also use language, in line with Bourdieu as discussed previously, to maintain authority and to declare their role as Canberra insiders. The language - a code - used by Press Gallery journalists is identified by Simons and described as 'Canberra-speak' and an odd vernacular. "It is hard for an outsider to understand … politicians have done somersaults and about-turns: they have upped the ante; they have downplayed things …".[491] Simons' terms come from newspapers but those same clichés and metaphors are used on television. In the nine television reports that feature Prime Minister Howard some of the expressions in use include: a long-running crisis, cautiously optimistic, expedite the legal process, fast-track, do nothing to douse August election speculation, a

---

[490] Donovan, Robert J. and Scherer, Ray (1992). Unsilent revolution - television news and American public life, 1948-1991. Cambridge, Cambridge University Press. p. 202.
[491] Simons, Margaret (1999). *Fit to print - inside the Canberra Press Gallery*. Sydney, University of New South Wales Press Ltd. p. 62.

220

shock decision, price hike, extraordinary backflip, budget bottom line, about turn, more back-downs, about face, shock tactics, sign on to the deal, thrashed out a plan, can breath easy, delivered a broadside, bucket-load of cash, a Labor split, the backflip was the ALP somersault, and adding to the discomfort.

Simons acknowledges:

> I can hear the journalists protest it is all very well for me, who has had the time to review and to hone, to criticise them when they write to a deadline. But this is not only bad writing, it is also insidious, and dangerous. It gives the impression of communicating, while failing to do so. The shrillness, the search for false impact, in fact reduces the impact.[492]

Are the journalists copying the politicians or are the politicians copying the journalists in the use of language of this nature? It is most likely that both groups are struggling to find phrases that sum up what is happening in a catchy and brief manner. In the process explanations of what is happening are reduced to colourful but uninformative expressions. If Simons' assessment of what is wrong with political communication is correct then both politicians and journalists are responsible with journalists carrying added responsibility because their job is to cut through political obfuscation.

This examination of language provides a clear example of how the language - and therefore the perspective - of politicians is taken up by the media. In his criticism of Labor's policy change on drug prices in the PBS, Treasurer Peter Costello uses the term triple double backflip. Backflip is then taken up by both the Channel 9 and ABC news journalists and *The 7.30 Report* (all programs 22 June). The word backflip was also used in *The Daily Telegraph* and *The Australian* on the following day, 23 June. *The Sydney Morning Herald*, displayed some independence and called the move 'a surprise turnaround" and did not use backflip until the next day, 24 June.[493]

---

[492] Simons. ibid. p. 63.
[493] Metherell, Mark and Allard, Tom (2004). Labor crumbles on PBS charges. *The Sydney Morning Herald*. 23 June. The use of the term was found in a Factiva search of the words 'PBS AND backflip'.

The Effect of Television on the Canberra Press Gallery

Canberra's position as the centre of national economic policy is clearly displayed. Reports of a political/economic nature overwhelmingly originated from Canberra during the survey period; 85% on *ABC News* and 80% on *Channel 9 News*. On *The 7.30 Report* reports from Canberra accounted for 44% of reports as did national reports (those reports that combined material from different parts of Australia, including Canberra, or where the origin could not be determined).[494]

The newsworkers who prepare these reports are members of the Canberra Press Gallery. The influence of the Press Gallery structure on journalistic output has been considered by Grattan,[495] Henderson,[496] Parker,[497] Simons,[498] Tiffen,[499] Waterford[500] and others. Among the themes in this material are that the members of the Gallery - 300 people working out of Parliament House[501] - are too close to politicians and each other, favour some sources over others, use jargon and 'Canberra-speak', are too centred in Parliament House, remote from their head offices, remote from members of the public who live elsewhere than Canberra, are part of a political elite, and that while they are competitive among themselves their material is similar with some issues considered off limits. These criticisms are balanced by comments that the Gallery contains journalists with specialist knowledge, that its critical mass gives the Gallery influence, that long-term observation produces good judgements and that Gallery members are better educated and harder working than journalists elsewhere.

Television has changed the nature of political reporting in Canberra with Grattan writing: "The overwhelming change in the last 30 years in the Press Gallery has been the ascendancy

---

[494] Note these figures are higher than the origin of reports given in Chapter 2 because non-national reports such as those on state government activities have been excluded.
[495] Grattan, Michelle (1996). Sharing the same kennel; the press in Parliament House. In (eds.) Disney, Julian and Nethercote, J.R. (1996). *The house on Capital Hill - Parliament, politics and power in the national capital.* Leichhardt, The Federation Press.
[496] Henderson, Gerard (1987). The rat pack. *IPA Review.* Aug-Oct.
[497] Parker, Derek (1990). *The courtesans - the Press Gallery in the Hawke era.* North Sydney, Allen & Unwin.
[498] Simons. op. cit.
[499] Tiffen. op. cit.
[500] Waterford, Jack (2005). The media report, ABC Radio, 11/08/2005.
http://www.abc.net.au/rn/talks/8.30/mediarept/stories/s1435225
[501] ibid.

of television."[502] Television, Grattan adds, has changed both how politicians communicate with the public, how political battles are conducted and how Press Gallery journalists go about their work. Politicians can choose to communicate directly with the public through programs such as *Sunday, A Current Affair* and *The 7.30 Report*. This often excludes the Press Gallery from the political communication process and means television has taken on a major role in setting the political agenda by deciding which politicians will appear and how vigorously they will be challenged.

Politicians can also choose to conduct short press conferences; answering only in sound bites and not engaging in in-depth dialogue with journalists. Key locations in Parliament House, such as the Ministerial Entrance, are equipped with feed points so camera crews can send their material live to air if necessary.[503] Journalists can watch these conferences from their offices in Parliament House (or even in other cities) reducing the need for them to attend the press conferences and further removing politicians from questioning by journalists.

In one of the reports during the survey period, FTA (*ABC News* 25 June) a sound bite of Prime Minister John Howard taken from an interview with Sky TV is used. In another report, costly drugs (*ABC News* 22 June), a sound bite of Opposition Leader Mark Latham from an unidentified radio interview is used. If a political leader talks to one broadcaster such as Sky, that broadcaster will usually seek to promote itself by making the footage available to other networks. If a political leader is interviewed on a radio station the television networks are usually informed by the politician's office ahead of time so their cameras can record the event. This immediate and national dissemination of interviews and events is another feature of modern political (and other) reporting.

Not all the networks, however, send a camera to the radio station. Too many cameras get in the way and are an inefficient use of resources. The television networks therefore pool with each other; one will cover the radio interview so the other(s) can cover other events which are also pooled. This means more events can be covered by fewer crews. The downside is that the networks may not have a journalist at the event so the context of what is said relies on

---

[502] Grattan. op. cit. p. 224.
[503] Simons. op. cit. p. 2.

what arrives in the television station. There is also likely to be a sameness of material across the networks.

This increasing, seamless, and often instant sharing of footage has been made possible by technological advances. Co-axial cables connected Sydney, Canberra and Melbourne in the mid-1960s, Aussat introduced television pictures via satellite in the mid-1980s and optical cable now allows dedicated around-the-clock transfer of images. In the television stations themselves bulky reel-to-reel tape machines have been replaced by much smaller digital machines. It has become easier to send material within networks and between networks and to disseminate it via traditional broadcast television signals, digital television signals and internet applications. An interview with a politician in one location is quickly accessible to a myriad of newsworkers in a number of locations.

Because politicians are choosing to address the public directly via television (and radio) programs the transcripts of these programs have become important. Simons notes, for example, that one of the tasks of political correspondent Laura Tingle was to go through five or six transcripts of press conferences and radio interviews every morning. Tingle is looking for " ... a rhetorical breakthrough, a new way of saying something, that gives you an indication of what is happening under the surface." Simons interpretation is that Tingle is performing 'textual analysis'.[504] In other words the meaning of what politicians are saying when they speak directly to the public is obscured and this obscurity is not always explained by journalists because politicians and journalists are using the same code.

The need to search for hidden meaning and textual differences is reinforced by Humphries who returned to the Canberra Press Gallery after a decade working elsewhere. He found the internet has:

> ... become the chief vehicle of record. Trawling its torrent of transcripts and announcements ties Gallery journalists to their desks and screens like never before. The consequence is counter-intuitive. Rather than enhancing scrutiny, it bogs it down because it further shifts the emphasis away from what is done to

---

[504] Simons. op. cit. p. 27.

what is said.[505]

This in-depth analysis of transcripts was foreshadowed and warned against by political correspondent Paul Kelly in 1991. Kelly wrote: "The political day begins with morning television, the AM program, and continues unrelentingly through a series of radio programs until the evening television news. There is so much on the record material that the journalist must read and assess. The trap is to become a victim of it and to make exaggerated interpretations of what the politicians really mean."[506]

The size, complexity and technological sophistication of Parliament House in Canberra means that newsworkers can perform much, if not all, of their work without leaving the building and its surrounds. This is in stark contrast to the logistical difficulties faced by newsworkers in the major cities such as Sydney and Melbourne considered in earlier chapters. Tiffen writes that Press Gallery journalists comment "... [you] can go through your whole working life without ever going out of the building ..." or spend 80-90% of their working day there.[507] From a logistics point of view this means that locations are generally only ever a few minutes walk away from the Press Gallery offices. In Parliament House a press conference, an interview and a piece-to-camera can all be recorded in less time than it would take for a crew in Sydney to drive from one location to another.

Interest groups can take advantage of the Press Gallery's location in Parliament House by staging their events in Parliament House; for example the National Summit on Housing Affordability (*ABC News* 28 June) was held in Parliament House itself making it easy for journalists and camera crews to attend.[508]

The report on the event displays how television reports can be put together without the need for journalists to move far from Parliament House and its surrounds. The report contains press conference comments and grabs from speeches made by Julian Disney, summit chairman, and Ron Silberberg, from the Housing Industry Association, filmed on the day. It

---

[505] Humphries, David (2005). Scrutiny, like nostalgia, has become a thing of the past. *The Sydney Morning Herald.* 1 Oct. p. 31.
[506] Kelly, Paul (1991). Who runs Australia? The Press Gallery or the Parliament? *Gerard Henderson's Media Watch.* June-July 1991. p 23.
[507] Tiffen, op. cit. p. 34
[508] National Summit on Housing Affordability, final program, www.housingsummit.org.au

also uses file footage of a housing estate, a couple reading newspaper advertisements, for sale signs, a real estate office, a house auction and house construction. File footage of Treasurer Peter Costello is used to illustrate the government's position. The reporter does a piece-to-camera that appears to be filmed outside Parliament House. Labor Shadow Treasurer Simon Crean is shown at a press conference stating Labor's policy on the first home owner scheme. It is not stated if this was part of a general press conference, a press conference Crean held to take advantage of interest in housing generated by the summit or if he was responding to a request by the ABC or other media to comment on the summit. The report is an illustration of how news processes and logistics shape what is presented to audiences.

Framing Via Conflict and Consensus

Framing economic and political issues by way of conflict and consensus can be established even before newsworkers approach an issue. For example, the National Summit on Housing Affordability (*ABC News* 28 June), a pseudo-event as defined by Boorstin,[509] carries the implicit message that housing has become unaffordable through the very fact that the summit needs to be held and by the naming of the event itself. The Parliament House location of the summit suggests carrying the issue to the heart of government. This means conflict between the summit and the Federal Government is established from the start and the newsreader's introduction to the report makes the Federal Government the target from the opening sentence:

> The Federal Government is under pressure to reconsider the favourable tax treatment of housing investment, even though the Treasurer last week rejected the idea.

Economics correspondent Russell Barton starts his report with the extent of the problem:

> The word crisis was on many lips at the Housing Affordability Summit on every level.

---

[509] Boorstin, Daniel (1962). *The image*. Harmondsworth, Penguin. pp. 22-23.

The first interviewee, Julian Disney, summit chairman, sets out the problem, and the risks, with his grab:

> Housing debt has just gone up an extraordinary level, unprecedented here or anywhere else in the world. And that is making us enormously economically vulnerable.

Barton continues to build the causal narrative:

> And at the grass roots level there was evidence home ownership had dropped by 10% in recent years accompanied by despair among young people.

The second interviewee, Ron Silberberg, of the Housing Industry Association, puts the problem into a historical and Australian context for the audience:

> For the first time in our history a generation is faced with the prospect of never being able to afford a home of their own.

The audience has been primed to blame the Federal Government from the first line of the report's introduction. But the Federal Government is not given the chance to respond with Barton briefly summing up the government's position over file footage of Treasurer Peter Costello:

> Peter Costello just last week rejected the Productivity Commission call for an inquiry into those political hot potatoes, arguing house prices were already coming down.

Julian Disney's response to the Treasurer is butt-edited (an editing technique in which one interviewee is presented immediately after another) for impact:

> If he really believes that [a house price fall] is going to solve the situation, then he's living in fantasy land.

Barton's next piece of voice-over suggests that unlike the conflict with the government over the issue, there is consensus with the alternative government, Labor:

> *But* [italics added] Labor has already picked up two other summit recommendations promising a minister for housing in the Latham government and a cap on the first home owner's grant.

Disney, Silberberg and another interviewee, Labor's Simon Crean, are clearly lined-up against the government. The report did not tell viewers who is behind the summit. Its sponsors include the Australian Council of Social Service (ACOSS), the Housing Industry Association (HIA) and the Australian Council of Trade Unions (ACTU). Julian Disney is a former president of ACOSS, Ron Silberberg is the managing director of the Housing Industry Association and the ACTU is linked to the ALP opposition and Simon Crean. These are all important Australian institutions. But the report illustrates how an organisation can stage an event, gain media coverage of that event and have the perspective of the organisation and its sponsors put forward without any real challenge. (Interestingly the public relations-nature and pseudo-event of the summit was recognised by *The Australian Financial Review* journalist Cherelle Murphy who reported " … lobbyists …. descended on Canberra …" in her account of the summit.[510])

File footage in the summit report highlights how the meanings of footage displayed in television news and current affairs reports are varied and contradictory. In the above report housing construction is used as a backdrop for comment on Labor's housing policy. In a report on interest rates (*ABC News* 2 June) footage of workers building houses is used - rather strangely - to illustrate a housing sector slowdown. In another report, property and borrowing (*The 7.30 Report* 8 June), footage of houses under construction is used for discussion of an overheated housing market.

Contrasting Causal Narratives

Politicians, just like business leaders, seek to impose their preferred causal narrative to strengthen their arguments. Political debate presented by the media is in part the battle between contrasting causal narratives and it is emphasised when the players are from the same political party. Shadow Health Minister Julia Gillard (*Channel 9 News* 22 June)

---

[510] Murphy, Cherelle (2004). Labor promise on housing. *The Australian Financial Review*. 29 June. p. 1 Downloaded 13 June 2006. http://global.factiva.com.ezproxy.library.usyd.edu.au/aa/default.aspx?

presented the causal narrative that allowing a rise in PBS charges would have the consequences of " … people going off their blood pressure medication because they can no longer afford the scripts." What made the Labor change, the backflip, so dramatic was that Labor abandoned that narrative to replace it with another; Bob McMullan's causal narrative that support for the price rise would have the consequence of allowing Labor to fund its election policies.

Causal narrative was present in the debate over water management. Prime Minister Howard's narrative is that there is a need for those from different states to consider the national picture: "If the premiers come as Queenslanders or New South Welshmen and as Victorians and not as Australians we won't get a good outcome." (*ABC News* 24 June). Howard argued that attitudes held for more than 100 years had to change. The consequence of changing those attitudes resulted in the adoption of a water management policy that the prime minister described as " … a tremendous day for the future security of water supply in this country." (*ABC News* 25 June).

Crisis adds urgency to causal narrative and is used by another player in the water issue. Peter Corish, president of the National Farmer's Federation, says "It is crunch time." (*ABC News* 24 June). As with business reports, a sense of crisis underlines the need for action. John Edwards, a former advisor to Paul Keating, recalls crisis was used by Keating to achieve outcomes:

> In both print and television, there is a great reluctance to play down a story. Alternately put, there is always encouragement to hype it up. And very often this suited the purposes of Treasury and the Treasurer in that period because it was a way of alarming the public and creating momentum for change. The most vivid example of that was of course the $A crisis in 1985-86 which motivated a lot of change. But that was actually played up by the political actors in order to terrify Cabinet into cuts in spending or to extract concessions from the ACTU. All of which had a laudable purpose and achieved its intention of motivating further

reform, from which we now benefit.

John Edwards[511]

That comment also supports the view put earlier that elites use the media to communicate among themselves. Keating may have expressed his concerns personally to the other political actors, but to see those concerns displayed prominently in the media reinforces the need to take action.

Longer reports, such as those in the business programs, allow interviewees to develop more complex causal narratives. Lindsay Tanner, Shadow Communications Minister, presents his case for more competition in the media sector to the *Business Sunday* audience (*Business Sunday* 13 June). Tanner argues that Australia has the same number of commercial television networks as it had in the 1960s and that transition to digital television has stalled. The consequence of this is that: " … [in] the communications sector, a sector that underpins the entire modern economy, we've got inadequate competition, lack of innovation, lack of advancement and that's a major drag on our economy."

The politicians themselves recognise narrative and story telling. Two examples, drawn from outside the survey period, illustrate this. Peter Costello, Treasurer, spoke about economic views in a press conference broadcast on ABC Radio in March 2005:

> You've got two pieces of economic news today. You've got a statement from the Reserve Bank Governor, who sees a very strong economy with capacity constraints, unsustainable wage growth, and you've got a statistician who sees a slowing economy with 1.5 per cent growth which is subdued. And you want to know my view? I think the truth lies somewhere in the middle. You've got two very, very interesting economic stories today."[512]

In October 2005 Prime Minister Howard announced some details of his proposed industrial relations changes. Howard was challenged in Federal Parliament to guarantee no individual

---

[511] Edwards. op. cit.
[512] Yaxley, Louise (2005). Costello says economic figures not 'totally consistent'. *ABC Radio, The World Today.* 2 March. http://www.abc.net.au/worldtoday/content/2005/s1314233.htm

Australian employee would be worse off. As Howard commenced his response that his government had a nine-and-a-half year record of boosting jobs and wages, he was cut off by interjections from the floor of Parliament. Moments later the Speaker called on the prime minister to continue. Howard re-started "Mr Speaker, I continue the narrative ...".[513] This indicates Howard's awareness of the importance of narrative in presenting political argument.

CONCLUSION

The material presented in this chapter provides a framework for understanding economic debate and the relationship between politicians and television newsworkers. A key point is shared interest: the major players - politicians and television newsworkers - have a shared interest in maximising media performances. This is because politicians are partly judged on their media appearance and newsworkers are partly evaluated on the amount and regularity of the reports they provide.

Another key point is the interdependence between political players and television newsworkers. Television delivers an audience for politicians and politicians deliver a dependable supply of content for television news and current affairs programs. Politicians and other political players rely on television newsworkers to package their messages in the best way possible. Television newsworkers make an effort to do this because effective presentation earns them regard among their employers and colleagues and assists their programs in retaining audience attention. Political players and television newsworkers are united in seeking to maximise audiences.

Economic debate, like other public debate, is carried out by competing players who attempt to present their perspectives and arguments in a manner that gives them greater weight and authority than their rivals. Political players are aware of the requirements of television and attempt to shape their messages to fit. The techniques of doing this on television include events and pseudo-events, short catchy interview grabs and causal narrative.

---

[513] McGrath, Catherine (2005). PM - Trust my record: Howard's IR guarantee. *ABC Radio PM*, 10 Oct. http://www.abc.net.au/pm/content/2005/s1478936.htm

Television's contribution to economic debate is mixed. In part this is caused by a lack of variety with different television outlets displaying uniformity in their selection of the issues they report and the terms they use to describe political actions. The presentation of issues is hampered by verbal and visual clichés. Television's contribution to vigorous debate is also limited because, on most occasions, political players and newsworkers seek to avoid alienating each other because of their interdependence. When politicians step away from this tacit agreement and fail to co-operate with television newsworkers it is because they believe the benefits of doing so - for example to create a public perception of strength - justify this or because they have underestimated or are not concerned about the public reaction. When television newsworkers step away from this agreement and are critical of or attack politicians, part of their motivation may be that they believe the benefits - such as the drama of a confrontation and the follow-up publicity - justify doing so.

CHAPTER 6

ECONOMIC AND BUSINESS REPORTING IN THE NEW MEDIA ENVIRONMENT

Television took 30 years to reach a mass market - broadband has taken three.

Jane Martinson[514]

GOING GLOBAL

New Faces/New Television

There is a new look to presenters on a screen near you. CNBC Asia features Amanda Drury, Christine Tan, Fauziah Ibrahim, Keith Liu, Lisa Oake, Mark Laudi, Martin Soong, Sabrina Kanga, and Sri Jegarajah.[515] Bloomberg Asia Pacific features Catherine Yang and Bernard Lo. The profiles of the presenters reveal that most have undergraduate degrees (from universities in Australia, Canada, England, Malaysia, New Zealand and Singapore,) and several have postgraduate degrees. The languages they speak, other than English, include Japanese, French, Cantonese and Bahasa Malaysia. Their origins include Australia, Canada, Singapore and the Philippines. Their media experience is broad with print and radio backgrounds as well as television.

The names of the presenters provide some clue to their ethnic origins but only a clue; migration from China to other parts of the region has been underway for centuries, decolonisation has seen many Asians resettle in the West, upheavals such as war have dispersed other ethnic groups. Equally the greater availability of higher education and foreign student programs means the place of education is no guide to origin nor is English necessarily

---

[514] Martinson, Jane (2005). Television took 30 years to reach a mass market - broadband took three. *The Guardian*. 14 July. 2005. (note: broadband in Britain).

[515] Downloaded 25 March 2006. http://www.cnbcasia.com/about_cnbcasia/about_anchor_correspondents.aspx

the newsworkers native language. The world of transnational television and the need to appeal to a broad multi-national audience demands newsworkers with cross-cultural backgrounds and experiences to match those of their audiences.

The presenters on these finance channels reflect a transnational journalism culture that has grown up as transnational television has developed. The presenters named above and the entire global team of networks such as CNBC or Bloomberg are available to international audiences on satellite and cable delivered pay television and increasingly on to computer screens in homes and offices and portable devices such as mobile phones and personal digital assistants (PDAs). The effects of these new media outlets need to be examined.

The focus of this book so far has been mostly on Australia. Satellite and cable television and the internet, however, have breached national borders. Australian audiences can now receive news coverage, including economic and business news, from around the world. This informs Australians about international developments and invites comparison of Australian policies, practices, institutions and culture with those elsewhere. Global media has also seen Australian media organisations forge links with foreign groups such as the Channel 9 partnership with Microsoft in ninemsn, an association that provides an Australian gateway to services from both companies. Pay television provider Foxtel is an association between Telstra, Channel 9 owner Publishing and Broadcasting Limited (PBL) and News Corporation that provides foreign and local content to Australian audiences. This chapter will review recent technological developments as a guide to future directions in television news and to the supply of economic and business material.

A major technological development is the coming together, or convergence, of television and the internet with television-style programming being delivered over broadband. This 'tvnet' sees television being reshaped with adjuncts such as interactivity, audience access to additional stored material, news on request, news programs containing only those items that an individual has expressed interest in, video podcasting, news programs shaped by feedback from audiences, and new models of advertising and revenue raising.

The scope of this research is economic and business reporting on television. However it is already clear that while television is likely to remain a major supplier of news and entertainment for the foreseeable future, the nature of television itself is changing and that television is being used in conjunction with other media technologies. Free-to-air television in Australia is presently moving from analog to digital transmission with about 15% of Australians able to access digital in early 2006.[516] The government has recently introduced reforms to media ownership.

Transnational Television

Australia is more of a consumer than a producer of global news and current affairs television. Tunstall comments:

> When a government allows news importation it is in effect importing a piece of another country's politics - which is true of no other import … and because the media deal in ideas, their influence can be unpredictable in form and strength.[517]

Australia imports a much greater amount of news and current affairs television material than it exports. The international satellite news feeds used by the ABC, SBS and the commercial channels are part of this. The non-Australian sourced channels that are available to Australian pay television viewers are another part. Among the foreign TV channels offered by Foxtel for example are dedicated news channels including Fox News, CNN, BBC World and the dedicated finance channels CNBC and Bloomberg Television.

Chalaby comments that transnational television networks play a role in shaping the new global order and writes:

> Their cross-border coverage, multinational audience and international production operations tear apart the relationship between place and television and challenge the traditional relationship between broadcasting and the nation state. Transnational television has not simply adapted to globalisation but helps to fashion the new global order. Cross-border channels help sustain the globalising

---

[516] Fels, Alan and Brenchley, Fred (2006). Digital TV rules a farce. *The Australian Financial Review*. 7 March. p. 62. Downloaded 9 March 2006. http://global.factiva.com.ezproxy.library.usyd.edu.au/ha/default.aspx
[517] Tunstall, J (1997). The media are American. London. Constable. in Appleton, Gillian (1988). How Australia sees itself: the role of commercial television. in *The price of being Australian*. North Sydney, Australian Broadcasting Tribunal. p.200.

processes shaping areas as diverse as culture, finance and politics. They add to the flow of information, providing networks of communication and systems of exchange that drive the integration of these fields on a world scale.[518]

The two dedicated finance channels, CNBC and Bloomberg Television, are both United States-based and owned and have international coverage. The expansion of finance television is illustrated by CNBC Europe that grew from 12.6 million homes in 1997 to 42 million homes in 2002. This three-fold growth was almost double the average growth of pan-European television channels over the same period.[519] The economic downturn that started in 2000 slowed the growth of pay television and finance channels. However, and looking regionally, Kagan Research forecast in 2004 that pay television in Asia Pacific would almost double from 188 million subscribers in 2004 to 356 million in 2015.[520]

CNBC (originally the Consumer News and Business Channel) was launched in 1989 as a cable channel by NBC. The channel prospered as more Americans became interested in finance and investment through retirement funds and/or mutual funds. Kurtz writes:

> For the first time in history, cable networks and web sites were giving small investors access to the kind of real-time information - analyst's reports, quarterly earnings, executive pitches, [Wall] Street chatter - that had only been available to Wall Street brokers. As the bull market took off, fuelled by technology stocks such as Microsoft and Intel, the media began celebrating the notion that this was a game anyone could play - and win.[521]

The channel was able to keep costs down because of the relative cheapness of content. Gunther writes that the cost of the stock information was several million dollars a year and CNBC personalities such as Sue Herera and Joe Kernen earned much less than network news stars. Gunther adds "All told the annual tab for programming at CNBC comes to about $100

---

[518] Chalaby, Jean K. (2003). Television for a new global order: transnational television networks and the formation of global systems. *Gazette: the international journal for communication studies*. Vol 65(6). pp. 457-458.
[519] ibid. p. 459.
[520] Downloaded 25 March 2006. http://www.kagan.com/APMM112205
[521] Kurtz, Howard (2002). On CNBC, boosters for the boom. *The Washington Post*. 12 Nov. p. AO1. Downloaded 16 March 2006. http://global.factiva.com.ezproxy.library.usyd.edu.au/ha/default.aspx

million, roughly what it costs ESPN to put on four NFL games or what NBC pays to license eight episodes of ER."[522] CNBC ratings in the United States dropped as the market slumped from its 2000 peak, falling by 44% in 2002. Today CNBC claims a worldwide distribution of about 360 million homes, with 140 million of those in Asia Pacific.[523]

In 2001 CNBC announced the launch of a separate Australian channel with Mark Froude, CNBC Asia vice president of advertising sales, commenting "Australia warrants a separate market (product) because culturally and geographically it is distinct from the rest of Asia. Increasingly, the Australian product will diverge from Asia products." Australia-specific programs such as *The Source*, *CEO Australia* and *Business Centre Australia* were foreshadowed.[524] However a review of typical weekday programming for CNBC Australia during 2006 indicates a line-up of US, Asia, Europe and Worldwide material with no Australia specific programs.[525]

Bloomberg, founded by Michael Bloomberg (now mayor of New York City), began supplying financial information to finance market traders in 1980 and expanded into television in the early 1990s. Bloomberg promotional material says the network currently broadcasts in seven languages via ten individual channels around the world. There are 1,600 reporters and editors in 87 news bureaux and the channel has cameras in more than 200 banks and financial institutions. The channel reaches 200 million households internationally.[526]

CNBC and Bloomberg both present 24-hour coverage of finance and business. Their coverage moves around the globe as time zones shift and markets open and close. CNBC Asia is headquartered in Singapore. Bloomberg, according to the Bloomberg Television website, has "… full broadcast facilities in Singapore and Hong Kong as well as its regional

---

[522] Gunther, Marc (1999). There's no business like business show business: how CNBC grew from an ugly duckling into a network to make a peacock proud. *Fortune*. 24 May. Downloaded 25 April 2000. http://web4.infotrac.galegroup.com.itw.i..._EIM_0_A54570374&dyn+28!ar_fmt?sw_aep+uq
[523] About CNBC Asia Pacific. Downloaded 22 March 2006. http://www.cnbcasia.com/about_cnbcasia/about_introduction. aspx
[524] Mah, Sadie (2001). CNBC local drive kicks off with Aussie launch. *Media*. 16 Feb. Downloaded 24 March 2006. http://global.factiva.com.ezproxy.library.usyd.edu.au/ha/default.aspx
[525] Downloaded 25 March 2006. http://www.cnbcasia.com/tv_guide/tv_this_week_schedule_query.aspx?ID=2&Schedule_Name_ID=3&Day=Wednesday
[526] about.bloomberg.com/about/media/advertise/btveurop.pdf

production headquarters in Tokyo."[527] Transnational channels such as CNBC and Bloomberg switch effortlessly between news studios in one location after another with crosses to news bureaux and reporters in the field to create a sense of television from cyberspace.

The relationship between transnational television and audiences is reflected in Robins and Aksoy's examination of the media use of Turkish-speaking communities in London. They wrote "Transnational audiences are involved in a complex process of negotiating a position between familiar national moorings and new transnational connections."[528] This comment on audiences straddling local and international media could equally apply to the global audiences for CNBC and Bloomberg. Networks such as these are information sources for global business culture in a period of intense change as globalisation continues to spread and speed up. Television is part of the process of transnationalisation that Beck describes as " … a new way of doing business and working, a new kind of identity and politics as well as a new kind of everyday space-time experience and of human sociability …".[529]

Because CNBC and Bloomberg are both pay television channels that require access via (relatively) expensive cable or satellite their audiences are affluent and, by the nature of the programs, interested in investing. CNBC advertising material claims:

> CNBC's viewers are influential opinion leaders, managers, and high-level business decision-makers who play significant roles in shaping their company's destinies. They are frequent travellers for business and pleasure, have high disposable incomes and they enjoy a good quality lifestyle, high-end goods and services, and fine living.[530]

Bloomberg claims an:

> … upscale affluent audience [that] has a higher concentration of senior management and decision-makers than viewers of any other international business

---

[527] Downloaded 25 March 2006. http://www.bloomberg.com/tv/
[528] Robins, Kevin and Aksoy, Asu (2005). Whoever looks always finds: transnational viewing and knowledge-experience. in Chalaby, Jean K. (ed.). *Transnational television worldwide – towards a new media order*. London, I.B. Tauris & Co. Ltd. p. 15.
[529] Beck, Ulrich (2002). The cosmopolitan society and its enemies. *Theory, Culture & Society*. Vol. 19(1-2). p. 30.
[530] Downloaded 25 March 2006http://www.cnbcasia.com/index.aspx

or news network. Viewers to Bloomberg Television have the highest household income, have greater disposable incomes, and are more likely to acquire high-end luxury goods than viewers to any other international network ... [viewers] also travel more frequently on business, and for leisure. ... [viewers] are also more likely to be in the financial industry and active in the investment markets. [531]

The presenters on the two financial networks are well-known to elite audiences across much of the region. The reach of these transnational channels dwarfs that of many national broadcasters. Equally the interviewees on the programs are celebrities too. Bloomberg highlights this with an index of guests who have appeared on its different programs.[532]

The projected growth of pay television in Asia and the expansion of transnational and finance news and information is likely to bring an increased participation in investment in the same way that CNBC boosted the US internet boom. This boom in transnational television however has its critics. Herman and McChesney make three criticisms. They draw on the work of Habermas and others to comment "... the public sphere works most effectively for democracy when it is institutionally independent of the state and society's dominant economic forces.[533] The economic debate being presented on CNBC is heavily influenced by interviewees from major economic institutions. Secondly they comment that commercialisation is a US goal and write "The globalisation of the commercial model has come about partly by plan and partly by simple natural processes as profit-seeking companies seek out business opportunities across borders."[534] The consequence of this is Herman and McChesney's third point that advertising - and both CNBC and Bloomberg promote their demographic to advertisers - is promoting consumption and individual freedom to choose which they say strengthens materialism and diminishes the spirit of communities, displaces the public sphere with entertainment, strengthens conservative political forces and erodes local cultures.

---

[531] Downloaded 25 March 2006. http://about.bloomberg.com/about/media/advertise/btvasia.pdf
[532] Downloaded 25 March 2006. http://www.bloomberg.com/media/tv/guests_us.html
[533] Herman, Edward S. and McChesney, Robert W. (1997). *The global media; the new missionaries of corporate capitalism.* London, Cassell. p. 3.
[534] ibid. p.149-150.

DIGITAL DEBATE

Online News

Digital technologies are re-shaping the media environment. The change of pace is rapid. Rupert Murdoch, chairman and chief executive of News Corporation, may have marked a turning point in old media attitudes toward new media in April 2005 when he told the American Society of Newspaper Editors:

> Scarcely a day goes by without some claim that new technologies are fast writing newsprint's obituary. Yet as an industry, many of us have been remarkably, unaccountably complacent. Certainly I didn't do as much as I should have after all the excitement of the late 1990s. I suspect many of you in this room did the same, quietly hoping that this thing called the digital revolution would just limp along. Well it hasn't, it won't. And it's a fast developing reality we should grasp as a huge opportunity to improve our journalism and expand our reach.[535]

Almost one year later, in March 2006, Rupert Murdoch was again talking about digital opportunities and challenges when he told the Worshipful Company of Stationers and Newspaper Makers in London:

> Power is moving away form the old elite in our industry - the editors, the chief executives, and lets face it, the proprietors. A new generation of media consumers has risen demanding content delivered when they want it, how they want it, and very much as they want it. This new media audience - and we are talking here of tens of millions of young people around the world - is already using technology, especially the web, to inform, entertain and above all to educate themselves.[536]

New media and the internet are developing so quickly - it is not much more than a decade since the first news websites were set up - that research in online journalism is still taking

---

[535] Downloaded 29 March 2006. http://www.newscorp.com/news/news_247.html
[536] Downloaded 29 March 2006. http://www.newscorp.com/news/news_285.html

shape.[537] However some of those same categories used previously in this book - newsworkers, audiences, news organisations and news content - can be used to examine news in the new media. Among the key themes are the changing roles of newsworkers, the new options for audiences, the challenges and opportunities for news organisations and the changing nature of news when it is presented via new media. The importance of news on the internet is illustrated in research by the University of California, Los Angles, (UCLA) Centre for Communication Policy that found news the third most popular online activity (52%) behind e-mail (88%) and general web surfing (76%).[538]

The internet and online journalism offer a huge and constantly expanding variety of sites. Deuze[539] (who draws on Odlyzko[540]) suggests these fall into four main categories. These are mainstream news (mostly the sites of large media organisations); index and categories (that link visitors to other sites); meta-and comment sites (that examine the news media and media); and share and discussion sites (that allow unhindered connection between visitors). The mainstream sites have the greatest concentration on editorial content while the share sites have the greatest concentration of public connectivity. Thus the mainstream sites are likely to be those with the most traditional journalistic values and gatekeeper roles for newsworkers. The more alternative a site the more those values and roles are abandoned.

The involvement of traditional media companies with the internet reached one plateau in 2000 with the $150 billion dollar merger between Time Warner and America Online (AOL). The deal was intended to merge Time Warner's print, television and movie output to AOL's huge base of internet subscribers. The technology bubble burst in that same year and two years later the merger was considered to be an enormous failure. In recent years, however, the internet has been returning to favour as illustrated by comments such as those above from Rupert Murdoch. Murdoch spent $1.4 billion in 2005 buying three young internet companies to add to News Corporation's existing businesses. The Time Warner-AOL merger and Rupert

---

[537] Domingo, David (2005). *The difficult shift from utopia to realism in the internet era.* Paper from the First European Communication Conference – Amsterdam 2005. Downloaded 30 March 2006.
http://racocatala.com/dutopia/docs/domingo_amsterdam2005.pdf

[538] UCLA Centre for Communication Policy (2003). *Surveying The Digital Future – Year Three.* p. 28

[539] Deuze, Mark (2003). The web and its journalisms; considering the consequences of different types of news media online. *New Media & Society.* Vol. 5(2).

[540] Odlyzko, A. (2001). Content is not king. *First Monday.* 2(6).
http://www.firstmonday.dk/issues/issue6_2/odlyzko/index.html

Murdoch's comments clearly indicate that big media want to commercialise the internet and dispense with the "information wants to be free"[541] approach of the internet's early years. Further evidence that technology is back in favour with investors is illustrated by the success of the Google search company that was the brainwave of postgraduate students, Sergey Brin and Larry Page. Google went public in 2004 its market capitalisation peaked at $US138 billion in January 2006.[542]

One of the main themes of research into online journalism is the relationship between existing and new media interests. Some researchers believe the online media is a threat to the old with Meyer predicting that the last daily newspaper reader will disappear in April 2040.[543] Others however, for example Alhers, suggest the internet threat to traditional newspapers and television news programs is overstated and that the internet will instead complement print and broadcast news.[544]

The development of online news sites by existing media organisations is largely motivated by the desire to maintain or increase revenue with another motive the ambition to have an online presence. Flew points to declining newspaper circulations (and falling ratings for mainstream news and current affairs programs can be added to this) and the impact on classified advertising as driving media organisations to set up online sites.[545] At the same time however he comments on the mixed success of newspaper organisations in developing online sites with one cause of failure the inability to break away from conventional 24-hour publishing traditions. Those organisations that are familiar with round-the-clock news gathering and transmission - such as CNN - are more likely to be successful. Boczkowski summarises that print news organisations adapt to digital delivery in three ways; repurpose (use print output

---

[541] This is widely attributed to futurist Stewart Brand. Downloaded 13 March 2006. http://www.anu.edu.au/people/Roger.Clarke/II/IWtbF.html

[542] Gurgle - enthusiasm for Google drains away as doubts set in (2006). *The Economist*. 16 Feb. Downloaded 28 Aug. 2006. http://www.economist.com/

[543] Meyer, Philip (2004). *The vanishing newspaper: saving journalism in the information age*. Columbia. University of Missouri Press. eBook. p. 16.

[544] Alhers, Douglas (2006). News consumption and the new electronic media. *The Harvard International Journal of Press/Politics* 11(1). pp. 25-52.

[545] Flew, Terry (2002). *New media: an introduction*. South Melbourne, Oxford University Press.

online), recombine (provide in-depth extensions and links to news reports) and recreate (generate digital media using old values).[546]

News organisations are still developing approaches to putting news online and revenue models. The options include free access, free access for a restricted period (for example the previous 24 hours or the previous seven days), free access for registered visitors or access for subscribers only. Some organisations have selected hybrid models; the *New York Times* charges a subscription for US resident visitors but, in 1999, eliminated international subscription charges for visitors outside the US with the revenue loss made up by higher advertising rates.[547] Advertising on the internet - often on online news sites - also poses a threat to traditional media revenues with the *Guardian* reporting in March 2006 that internet advertising revenue in the UK is poised to overtake press advertising revenues within the next 12 months.[548]

Old media and new media adopt the visual approaches of each other with Cooke observing that the modular layout of print and the composite graphics of television converged for scannable design that was later adopted by web designers.[549] An example of innovation moving the other way is the news ticker style popularised by websites being adopted by television.

The approaches to online news developed by news organisations are reflected in the tasks performed by newsworkers. Flew comments that news media outlets are increasingly demanding " ... journalists who possess media multi-literacies, and are able to develop stories in formats that include short online pieces, online video, television broadcasts, edited stories, and longer feature articles."[550] A first-hand account of working in an online newsroom is provided by Houston. Based on his experience with Fox News Online, Houston notes the emphasis is "... on short, more frequent stories." The newsworkers draw heavily on

---

[546] Boczkowski, Pablo J. (2004). *Digitizing the news – innovation in online newspapers*. Cambridge, The MIT Press. pp. 51-64.

[547] Pavlik, John V. (1999). New media and news – implications for the future of journalism. *New Media & Society*. 1(1). p. 58.

[548] Sweney, Mark (2006). Internet ads close gap on press. *Guardian*. 29 March. Downloaded 30 March. http://media. guardian.co.uk/print/0,,329445144-105235,00.html

[549] Cooke, Lynne (2005). A visual convergence of print, television and the internet: charting 40 years of design presentation in news presentation. *New Media & Society*. vol 7(1). pp. 22-46.

[550] Flew, Terry (2002). *New media: an introduction*. South Melbourne, Oxford University Press. p. 104.

wire services for the latest information and are constantly watching television news to gain material for their online reports. Houston adds "I am seeing web journalism for what it is becoming: a machine moving at the speed of the wires, in terms of content, and in the direction of television, in terms of form."[551] Arant and Anderson highlight concerns over the small staff numbers in online newsrooms and the risk to accuracy from constant updates.[552] Singer et al comment that:

> ... the perception among online editors that they and their staff are seen as second-class citizens demands immediate management attention before the challenge and excitement of doing something new devolves into a routine of overwork laced with bitterness and, before long, burnout.[553]

In Australia big media and commercialisation largely dominate internet sites. Burton wrote:

> Community journalism may be the next big thing but, as the Productivity Commission found in 2000, most of the so-called "new media" were, and still are controlled by the same companies which own the "old media" -newspapers, television and radio. Indeed, 10 years after the internet emerged as a significant media form, there is no major Australian site which is not controlled by one of the established media players.[554]

Burton's report appeared in *The Sydney Morning Herald* and illustrates how old media is promoting new media and supports Rheingold's view that journalists were:

> ... among the first marathon swimmers in the new currents of the online information streams ... journalists tend to attract other journalists and the purpose of journalists is to attract everybody else: most people have to use an old medium

[551] Houston, Frank (1999). What I saw in the digital sea. *Columbia Journalism Review*. July. 38.2. p. 36. Downloaded 28 March 2006. http://archives.cjr.org/year/99/4/index.asp
[552] Arant M.D. and Anderson J.Q. (2001) Newspaper online editors support traditional standards. *Newspaper Research Journal*. 22(4). pp, 57-70.
[553] Singer, Jane B., Tharp, Martha P., and Haruta, Amon (1999). Online staffers: superstars or second-class citizens? *Newspaper Research Journal*. 20(3). p. 45. Downloaded 3 April 2006. http://find.galegroup.com.ezproxy.library.usyd.edu.au/itx
[554] Burton, Tom (2006). Turn on, tune in, read on. *The Sydney Morning Herald*. 17 Feb. p. 14. Downloaded 9 March. http://global.factiva.com.ezproxy.library.usyd.edu.au/ha/default.aspx

to hear news about the arrival of a new medium.[555]

That account of how news of the internet is disseminated suggests a demarcation between the net savvy and others. It distinguishes between those people who read about internet advances in print rather than those who do so online. Another variation of this (heard in a newsroom by the author) is between those people who look for telephone numbers in the telephone book and those who look on the web (although most mobile users now probably turn to directory assistance). In 2005 Rupert Murdoch highlighted the distinction between digital natives (those people who have only known a world with broadband internet access) and digital immigrants (late comers to broadband access).[556]

In Australia, as in most of the world, the established media players dominate online news as displayed by the list below of sites Australians use for news.

Table 6.1
News-only sites visited in the last four weeks

Site	Visitors
Fairfax	1,198,000
News Ltd.	1,160,000
ninemsn	918,000
abc.net.au/news	785,000
Yahoo!news	290,000
crikey.com	190,000
Bigpond News	85,000

(Source Roy Morgan 2005)[557]

The sixth site on the list, crikey.com (started in 2000, the year of the Productivity Commission report mentioned above), is the only site that is not part of a major media or IT organisation. The site was started by Stephen Mayne, a business journalist and former political media advisor, and covers politics, media, business, sport and opinion. Mayne said "The whole rationale for crikey.com is that what you're getting in the press is too distorted by

---

[555] Rheingold, Howard (2000). *The virtual community: homesteading on the electronic frontier*. Cambridge, MIT Press. p. 37.
[556] This distinction was first made by Prensky, Mark (2001). Digital natives, digital immigrants. *On The Horizon*. Vol.9. No. 5. Oct.
[557] Downloaded 14 March 2006. http://roymorgan.com/news/pressreleses/2006/464/index.cfm?printversion=yes

three things - spin doctoring, squeezed editorial resources and the agendas of the owners."[558] By 2004 crikey.com was going to 5400 people a day, who each paid an annual subscription of $100, with about 140 of them at a Parliament House, Canberra e-mail address. Mayne adds the subscribers are "rich red raggers"; many with incomes over $120,000 a year, 70% of them in managerial/professional positions and 75% of them Labor voters.[559] In 2004 the annual income for the site was $500,000 from subscribers, advertising, and payments from Google. One clash between new media and old media is illustrated by Channel 9 blocking its staff from accessing crikey.com. Mayne believes this was because the site was too critical of the network but a Channel 9 spokesman said the block is to prevent staff from wasting time.[560]

Crikey.com is supported by contributors who pass on titbits of news and gossip. Simons commented of crikey.com and other independent sites: "Mayne is fond of referring to his "Crikey army", to whom he often appeals for leads. But none of the independent internet outlets pays their contributors anything like industry standard rates and most pay nothing." [561] Mayne himself said he employs seven people but pays less than standard rates: "If we suddenly started paying commercial rates, we'd be back in the red."[562]

In early 2005 independent publishers Eric Beecher, a former editor of *The Sydney Morning Herald*, and Di Gribble bought crikey.com for $1 million and retained Mayne as business editor. Simons called the move "… a significant event. For the first time in this country an internet-based news service, crikey.com, changed hands for real money."[563] The buyout and new management prompted a report in *The Australian* written by journalist Hugo Kelly with the headline "Website jettisons the larrikin 'who put noses out of joint'". Kelly writes that crikey.com had become " …more reactive to the news cycle rather than seeking to break

[558] Gare, Shelley (2000). Independent news keeps us honest. *The Australian*. 12 Feb. p. 20. Downloaded 14 March 2006. http://global.factiva.com.ezproxy.library.usyd.edu.au/ha/default.aspx
[559] Day, Mark (2004). Online players come of age. *The Australian*. 21 Oct. p. 20. Downloaded 15 March. http://global.factiva.com.ezproxy.library.usyd.edu.au/ha/default.aspx
[560] Leys, Nick (2004). Strewth. *The Australian*. 22 Nov. p. 10. Downloaded 15 March 2006. http://global.factiva.com.ezproxy.library.usyd.edu.au/ha/default.aspx
[561] Simons, Margaret (2005). The underground news is a going concern. *The Sydney Morning Herald*. 5 Feb. p. 27. Downloaded 8 March 2006. http://global.factiva.com.ezproxy.library.usyd.edu.au/ha/default.aspx
[562] Day, Mark (2004). Online players come of age. *The Australian*. p. 20. 21 Oct. Downloaded 15 March. http://global.factiva.com.ezproxy.library.usyd.edu.au/ha/default.aspx
[563] Simons. (2005). op. cit.

news ... more cautious ... The daily email has a sober, over-edited feel about it."[564] Publisher Eric Beecher responded that Kelly had been let go because of unprofessionalism in reporting a private, off-the-record conversation. Beecher also invited readers to judge the site for themselves.[565]

The two accounts illustrate a clash of values as the site matures. Crikey.com is in transition from an alternative site to a more mainstream site and the differing perspectives of Kelly and Beecher reflect Cohen's warning "... given the potential for democratic forms of internet communication, it is imperative that online journalism seriously interrogates whether commercial interests are unduly influencing online content."[566] If Kelly's account is correct the site took on a more serious approach when 'real' money became involved.

This brief account of crikey.com and its sale illustrates that crikey.com had several clear points of difference from existing media. Among them are crikey.com's declared intention to make inside information available to outsiders, irreverence, lack of overheads, non-standard pay rates, large use of contributor material, and the ability to use e-mail addresses to partially identify subscribers. Crikey.com subscribers appear to have a particular interest in politics, media and business and the obvious access to computers.

The difficulties faced by independent internet news sites are further illustrated by other Australian news sites that were in existence at the same time crikey.com was founded. Among them were the satirical *The Chaser*, *Zeitgeist Gazette* and *Media Flash*. *The Chaser* web site remains today, buoyed by the television success of The Chaser comedy team and programs such as *CNNN*, but it is limited in content and very satirical. *Zeitgeist Gazette* closed six months after it went online. *Media Flash*, compiled by Ash Long, was incorporated into crikey.com in 2000.[567] Another high-profile site was *Webdiary*, founded by Margo Kingston, a political journalist, for *The Sydney Morning Herald* in July 2000.

---

[564] Kelly, Hugo (2006). Website jettisons the larrikin 'who put noses out of joint'. *The Australian*. 16 Feb. p. 15. Downloaded 8 March 2006. http://global.factiva.com.ezproxy.library.usyd.edu.au/ha/default.aspx
[565] Beecher, Eric (2006). Publishers right of reply. *The Australian*. 16 Feb. p. 16. Downloaded 8 March 2006. http://global.factiva.com.ezproxy.library.usyd.edu.au/ha/default.aspx
[566] Cohen, Elisia L. (2002). Online journalism as market-drive journalism. *Journal of Broadcasting & Electronic Media*. Dec. 46(4). p. 545.
[567] Day, Mark (2000). Crikey! It's a stuff-up! *The Australian*. Media. 13 July 2000. Downloaded 14 March 2006. http://global.factiva.com.ezproxy.library.usyd.edu.au/ha/default.aspx

Kingston left the *Herald* in August 2005 with the intention of continuing *Webdiary* as an independent site. However Kingston closed the site in December commenting "Unfortunately I couldn't get funding in time to stop me going broke, and certain events have proved to me that my skin is not thick enough to survive in this game." and announced her departure from journalism.[568] Other internet news sites that have received coverage in the mainstream press are *Online Opinion* and *New Matilda*.[569]

Another challenge to online integrity is the way some internet firms appear to have placed commercial interests above other values. Globally, several major internet and media companies and organisations have displayed their willingness to accede to China rather than risk access to Chinese markets by offending the government. In early 2006 the House of Representatives International Relations Committee of the United States Congress criticised Yahoo, Microsoft, Google and Cisco for their actions in relation to China. Yahoo cooperated with Chinese authorities in providing information that linked internet postings to dissident Shi Tao leading to his 2005 arrest and sentence of 10 years jail. Microsoft blocks China-based searchers looking for words such as democracy, freedom and Falun Gong. Google also blocks searchers on its google.cn site looking for information restricted by Chinese authorities. Cisco has sold Chinese authorities equipment to monitor electronic communications and routers for its surveillance systems.[570] The BBC also attracted coverage for its recently launched site www.BBCChina.com.cn that the *Guardian* commented appeared to focus on less controversial news reports than the main Chinese-language BBC website www.BBCChinese.com. That latter site is blocked by the Chinese government.[571] The BBC's response is that the recently launched site is an English-language education site and not a news site.[572]

---

[568] Webdiary. Downloaded 15 March 2006
http://margokingston.typepad.com/harry_version_2/margo_kingston/index.html
[569] Simons. (2005). op. cit.
[570] Goldenberg, Suzanne (2006). A moral minefield for corporate America. *Guardian*. 20 Feb. Downloaded 21 Feb. 2006. http://media.guardian.co.uk/print/
[571] Dickie, Mure and Edgecliffe-Johnson, Andrew (2006). BBC tones down news on new China website. *Guardian*. 4 Feb. Downloaded 8 Feb. 2006. http://media.guardian.co.uk/print/
[572] Chapman, Nigel (2006). BBC's new China website is for language teaching and is not designed to appease Beijing authorities. *Guardian*. 7 Feb. Downloaded 8 Feb. http://media.guardian.co.uk/print/

What audiences want from online news has been examined by Tewksbury,[573] Van Heekeren[574] and others. Tewksbury found sport pages (26%) were the most popular of online news views among US users followed by business and money (13%), arts and entertainment (11%), features (11%) and US national news (10%).

In Australia the most viewed reports relate to entertainment (39%), crime (20%), Australian politics (14%), science and technology (8%) and business (6%) according to Van Heekeren's survey of the reports accessed by visitors to web pages of *The Sydney Morning Herald,* smh.com.au, between 16 August and 12 November in 2004. Visitors are automatically tracked and the results posted on the site in a 'Top Viewings' listing. The 'Top 5' sites were entertainment (26%), crime (21%), Australian politics (15%), business (6%) and science and technology (8%).[575] (Website technology that allows visitors to be tracked and the production of 'top viewings' lists pose questions about if and how newsworkers use this feedback to reshape news values. This author was unable to find research on this issue. However Knobloch-Westerwick et al found that audiences exposed to such lists spent longer on those reports than on other reports.)[576]

The role of the internet in by-passing corporate, commercialised big media to give citizens a voice and promote cyberprotest is explored by writers such as Carroll and Hackett[577] and van de Donk.[578] Jordan warns of the risk of information overload and the use of filters and restrictive searches to overcome this[579] and Tewksbury[580] who found that audiences tended to

---

[573] Tewksbury, David (2003). What do American really want to know? Tracking the behaviour of news readers on the internet. *Journal of Communications.* 53(4).
[574] Van Heekeren, Margaret (2005). What the web news reader wants. paper presented at the Annual Meeting of the Australian and New Zealand Communication Association, Christchurch, New Zealand, 4-7 July 2005. Downloaded 28 March 2006.
http://www.mang.canterbury.ac.nz/ANZCA/FullPapers/05MedSocNewmediaFINAL.pdf
[575] Van Heekeren. op. cit. p. 5.
[576] Knobloch-Westerwick, Silvia; Sharma, Nikhil; Hansen, Derek L. and Alter, Scott (2005). Impact of popularity indications on readers' selective exposure to online news. *Journal of Broadcasting and Electronic Media.* Sept. 49(3).
[577] Carroll, William K. and Hackett, Robert A (2006). Democratic media activism through a lens of social movement theory. *Media, Culture & Society.* Vol. 28 (1).
[578] van de Donk, Wim, Loader, Brian D., Nixon, Paul G., and Rucht, Dieter (eds.) (2004). *Cyberprotest – new media, citizens and social movements.* London, Routledge.
[579] Jordan, Tim (1999). Cyberpower: the culture and politics of cyberspace and the Internet. London, Routledge.
[580] Tewksbury. op. cit.

seek out only the news they want at the risk of fragmenting their knowledge with the result of weakening attention to political issues.

Financial websites

The role of technology in the growth of global markets and the expansion of television news and current affairs has been considered in previous chapters. Technology in the form of computers and the internet has also changed the way private individuals collect financial news and information. More than a decade ago the US *Fortune* magazine commented:

> If you want to track the value of your portfolio, buy 100 shares of stock, talk shop with other investors, or find a mutual fund that will help put your kids through college you can do it with a personal computer and a modem. In fact, financial research is fast becoming one of the main reasons people log on to cyberspace.[581]

Five years later in 2000 *Fortune* again looked at financial websites and named six (morning.star.com; mfea.com; www.quicken.com; www.fundz.com; findafund.com and fundalarm.com) that it considered provided in-depth and timely information for investors.[582] Reporters Diba and Stein commented "For small investors, the internet has become the great equaliser. We finally have access to the "inside" information that brokers and investment gurus have been using for years." Diba and Stein discovered that when they entered the term 'mutual funds' into the Lycos search engine it returned 60,209 matches.[583] A repeat of the search for 'mutual funds' via the Google search engine in March 2006 returned 97,200,000 results.

Australians have embraced the internet as a source of financial information. One Australian financial site that has been reported in the mainstream press is the online investment journal the *Eureka Report*. James Kirby, editor of the *Eureka Report*, says the online journal can

---

[581] Himowitz, Michael J. (1995). Cyberspace: the investor's new edge. *Fortune*. 25 Dec. Downloaded 21 March 2006. http://money.cnn.com/magazines.fortune.fortune_archive/1995/12/25/208771index.h
[582] Diba, Ahmad and Stein, Nicholas (2000). We came. We clicked. We conquered. *Fortune*. 20 March. Downloaded 21 March 2003.
http://money.cnn.com/magazines.fortune.fortune_archive/2000/03/20/276355/index
[583] ibid.

cover stories that television networks do not have time to do.[584] The site is owned by financial journalist Alan Kohler (mentioned in previous chapters for his television work), Melbourne investment bank Carnegie Wylie & Company and Eric Beecher, who bought crikey.com.[585] Among the featured reports on the *Eureka* site during March 2006 were investing for growth in Australian companies, do-it-yourself superannuation, investing in tree-growing plantations, investing in the retail sector and the prospects for CSL in the world flu vaccine market. Columns by Alan Kohler and Elizabeth Knight, both of *The Sydney Morning Herald*, Kenneth Davidson and Stephen Bartholomeusz, both of *The Age*, and Alan Wood, of *The Australian*, were also reproduced on the page. Some of the *Eureka Report* material can be downloaded and podcast for later listening. Subscribers to the site pay $240 a year and it carries advertising from companies such as ANZ, Virgin credit cards, Qantas and Telstra's Big Pond.

Financial information and news is being provided by financial institutions themselves and so side-stepping journalists as the gatekeepers of news. Pavlik comments:

> … news sources are increasingly viewing themselves as content providers who can publish their own content, without relying on a traditional journalistic publisher or gateway. The NBA.com, for example, publishes extensive news about its basketball games, and even includes video clips. Why go to CNN and ESPN when you can get it straight from the source? Perhaps this is good for basketball, but what are the implications for political campaigns and for democracy?[586]

Traditional news gateways are being displaced as economic and financial news is provided by financial institutions. *The Sydney Morning Herald* reported in 2003 that the Commonwealth Bank website, www.commbank.com.au, is listed as Australia's top financial

---

[584] Gray, Patrick (2005). New media hands power to the people. *The Age*.18 Oct. p. 4. Downloaded 15 March 2006.

[585] Gluyas, Richard (2005). Business whiz ventures afield. *The Age*. 17 March. p. 18. Downloaded 8 March 2006. http://global.factiva.com.ezproxy.library.usyd.edu.au/ha/default.aspx

[586] Pavlik, J (1999). New media and news: implications for the future of journalism. *New Media & Society* 1(3) . p. 58.

website by Nielsen/Netratings.[587] An inspection of that site in March 2006 displays a home page that gives visitors a choice of a personal banking centre, a business centre, institutional banking, information about the bank and a shareholder centre. Registered users can log on for banking (using their accounts), commsec (the bank's share trading service) and corporate facilities. The home page also features a promotion to win a World Cup trip by using the banks MasterCard facility, an education savings plan and home loan package. The site index displays 272 separate pages and some of these open even more pages; for example the useful tools section displays another 17 pages most of which allow users to interact by making calculations on individual items such as home loan repayments.

The Commonwealth Bank site includes displays of news and information on stock movements, commodity prices and economic data. There are forecasts and comment on coming economic news. There are daily streaming audio and video feeds including television-news style market reports of about 1.30 minutes duration. The site also features archived audio interviews with business leaders such as Brendan Crotty, CEO of Australand, and Stephen Allen, CEO of Macquarie Infrastructure Group. Crotty is interviewed by the bank's Chief Equities Economist Craig James, a non-newsworker in an illustration of newsworkers being removed from the provision of information on the internet.

Australians are increasingly using sites such as the Commonwealth Bank site. According to Nielsen/Netratings more than 4 million people visited a banking and finance website in the 12 months to May 2003.[588] This represents a growth of almost 24% in 12 months. Another survey, by Citibank/ACNielsen, indicates that 86% of Australians have used internet banking at least once, making Australians the second highest users of internet banking in the Asia Pacific region after South Korea.[589] Illustrating convergence within banking James Meldrum, of ACNielsen.consult said "Banks are not seeing online [banking] in isolation any more. Where they used to create separate online divisions, now they have reintegrated it into the bank's operations."[590]

---

[587] Derkley, Karin (2003). Banks go with the new flow. *The Sydney Morning Herald*. 5 Aug. p. 5. Downloaded 21 March 2006. http://global.factiva.com.ezproxy.library.usyd.edu.au/ha/default.aspx
[588] ibid.
[589] ibid.
[590] ibid.

The global nature of the internet means users are not limited by national borders when they seek information. Halavais demonstrates that on the internet, as in global television, the American voice is dominant. The United States hosts about 70% of all internet sites with Germany second at 3% and Australia fifth at about 2%. About 50% of Australian sites are linked to international sites; 40% of these linked to US sites and 10% to other nations.[591] This research relates to general internet sites and the implications for financial sites are unknown. Most Australians are likely to carry out their financial activities with Australian domiciled institutions; banking with Australian banks and investing on the Australian stock market. However, they are also likely to seek, and take an interest in, news and information from other non-Australian sites.

Blogs

The consideration of blogs is relevant because they are another indication of how technology is changing or by-passing journalism and how some issues and perspectives are underreported or overlooked by mainstream journalism. A blog, or weblog, is a diary and commentary kept on the internet and written or edited by one person and/or by contributors. The most recent comment is usually displayed at the top of the page. Blogs can vary from the model put forward by *Webdiary* that brings together expert contributors and public comment on news and current issues, to an internet-based web page for people who share an interest or an individual presenting their comments. The web service Technorati, that monitors the content of weblogs, counted 31.5 million weblogs in March 2006.[592] This is an almost tenfold increase on the over three million sites Drezner and Farrell reported on Technorati less than two years previously.[593] It is estimated that there are more than 300,000 blogs in Australia.[594] Blogs are giving ordinary people an opportunity to have their say and this may also mean newsworkers are losing their role as gatekeepers.

---

[591] Halavais, Alexander (2000). National borders on the world wide web. *New Media & Society*. Vol 1(3). p. 14 and p. 17.
[592] Downloaded 28 March 2006. http://www.technorati.com/
[593] Drezner, Daniel W., and Farrell, Harry (2004-1). *The power and politics of blogs.* Paper presented to the August 2004 American Political Science Association. Downloaded 4 April 2006. http://www.henryfarrell.net/blogpaperapsa.pdf
[594] Canning, Simon (2005). Blogs and banners strive to coexist. *The Australian*. 19 May. p. 17. Downloaded 15 March. http://global.factiva.com.ezproxy.library.usyd.edu.au/ha/default.aspx

Newsworkers may be responding to this loss in two ways. The first is by blogging themselves. Robinson suggests that j-blogs (blogs written by journalists) are a response to public or non-journalist blogs and an attempt by journalists to recapture their role as gatekeepers.[595] She adds that the internet has redefined journalism by freeing j-bloggers from the values and constraints of traditional journalism such as the need for objectivity and verifiable facts and limited first person presence and replaced these with new values such as casual presentation of facts, non-attributable sources and a strong individual presence. A second response is that the role of newsworkers on online news or blogs is changing. Bruns suggests that gatekeepers are becoming gatewatchers; instead of deciding what material is let through gatewatchers publish almost everything and give some material greater emphasis than other material.[596]

One highlight of blog history is Salam Pax's (a pseudonym for a 29-year-old Baghdad architect) "Where is Raed?" blog that commenced in September 2002 and continued during the first stage of the Iraq War. Media coverage of that stage of the Iraq conflict was dominated by big media organisations and embedded journalists. Salam Pax's blog earned comments such as Allan's "Salam's posts offered readers a stronger sense of immediacy, an emotional feel for life on the ground, than more traditional news sites."[597] Another highlight was the coverage of the bombings in London on 7 July 2005. The proliferation of relatively cheap mobile phones with cameras for stills and video footage and an immediate way of transmitting those images saw much of that material displayed on blog sites. Gibson commented"... blogging may come to be seen as the new news essential as of last week ..." because the bombings took place in office hours with people at work on computers and because blogs have become accepted.[598] Technorati reported a 30% increase in blogging activity on the day of the bombing. Mainstream news organisations also used material provided by 'citizen journalists' on the scene.

---

[595] Robinson, Susan (2006). The mission of the j-blog: recapturing journalistic authority online. *Journalism*. Vol. 7(1).

[596] Bruns, Axel (2003). Gatewatching not gatekeeping: collaborative online news. *Media International Australia incorporating Culture and Policy*. No. 107.

[597] Allan, Stuart (2004). The culture of distance. in (eds.) Allan, Stuart and Zelizer, Barbie. *Reporting war – journalism in wartime*. Abingdon, Routledge. p. 361.

[598] Gibson, Owen (2005). We had 50 images within an hour. Blogs. *Guardian*. 11 July. Downloaded 12 July 2005. htt://media.guardian..co.uk/print0,3858,5235536-105337,00.html

The impact of blogs in economic and business debate is difficult to gauge because there is so little academic material and yet so much internet material. A search for 'economic blogs' on the CSA database via the University of Sydney Library reveals only three references, the most useful of which lead to several co-authored articles by academics Daniel Drezner and Henry Farrell. A search on Google for 'economic blogs' however returns 44,000,000 results. These two results say much about economic blogs; the limited scholarly study of this recent and hard to identify genre and the scattered and overwhelming nature of information on the web. The focus of Drezner and Farrell's work in a related conference paper and article is on political blogs. They comment that while only 4% of online Americans visited blogs in 2003, blogs are:

> ... already influencing U.S. politics ... [blogs are] becoming more influential because they affect the content of international media coverage ... under specific circumstances - when key weblogs focus on a new or neglected issue - blogs can act as a focal point for the mainstream media and exert formidable agenda-setting power.[599]

Examples of how bloggers focus the attention of the mainstream media provided by Drezner and Farrell include the comments by Trent Lott, US Senate majority leader that led to his resignation in December 2002, the exposure of CIA agent Valerie Plame's identity, and bribery allegations at the United Nations.[600] Bloggers are also credited with playing a major role in exposing the forged documents relating to George W. Bush's military service presented on CBS television by Dan Rather ahead of the November 2004 election.[601]

Other examples of the growing political role of the internet include US presidential candidate Howard Dean's use of the Blog for America site to build support during the 2004 campaign. Korean presidential candidate Roh Moo-hyun's use of his internet fan club Nosamo that "... is credited with helping to propel him to his come-from-behind victory in the 2002

---

[599] Drezner, Daniel W., and Farrell, Harry (2004). Web of influence. *Foreign Policy*. Nov./Dec. p. 34. Downloaded 4 April 2006. http://www.foreignpolicy.com/story/cms.php?story_id=2707
[600] ibid.
[601] Gibson, Owen (2005). The bloggers have all the best news. *Guardian*. 6 June. Downloaded 7 June 2005.http://media.guardian.co.uk/print/0,3858,5208852-105337,00html

presidential election."[602] In France blogs influenced public opinion against Europe's constitutional treaty with two-thirds of web sites devoted to the referendum supporting the No vote in May 2005.[603]

The first result in the Google search for economic blogs discussed previously is a page on the best economic blogs as selected by the readers of *Forbes* business magazine in March 2003. Forbes introduces the site this way:

> It's an old joke that if you ask the same question of ten different economists you'll get ten different answers. The diversity of opinion on the state of the economy and what - if anything - to do about it makes economics perfect fodder for personal weblogs, or blogs. In the argot of blogging, it's called "econoblogging".[604]

The top five blogs on *Forbes* were econlog.econlib.org; argmax.com, knowledgeproblem, winterspeak.com and institutional-economics.com. The five top articles on econlog.econlib.org are on housing bubbles (from *The New York Times*), revealed preferences vs. happiness, immigration, a Harvard economics lecturer making his introductory class notes available and accreditation of colleges (from *Inside Higher Education*). The *Forbes* website biography on the blogs co-writers reveal Arnold Kling has a Ph.D. in economics from MIT and launched one of the internet's first commercial ventures Homefair.com.

Drezner and Farrell comment that "… there are formidable obstacles to the influence of blogs." These include limited resources, a dependence on traditional media for information, success causing bloggers to be hired by (and integrated into) mainstream media, and the loss of novelty and immediacy. On the other hand they say "… as more web diarists come online, the blogosphere's influence will more likely grow than collapse."[605]

---

[602] Lee, Joo-hee (2005). Internet a key playing field for politicians, but has pitfalls. *The Korea Herald*. 11 Feb. Downloaded 28 March 2006. http://www.asiamedia.ucla.edu/article.asp?parentid=20688.
[603] Thornhill, John (2005). Internet study warns politicians on power of blogs. *Financial Times*. 13 July. Downloaded 14 July 2005.
[604] Downloaded 4 March 2006. http://www.forbes.com/home/2003/03/19/cx_ah_0319econoblogs.html
[605] Drezner, Daniel W., and Farrell, Harry. op. cit. p. 40.

CONVERGING MEDIA

Convergence

Media convergence is defined by Neuchterlein and Weiser as "… the competitive offering of familiar telecommunications services through unconventional technologies, such as the provision of telephone services over high-speed cable connections to the internet."[606] In terms of telephony and television, residents of developed countries are long familiar with the former being carried over copper cables and the latter over the airwaves. The internet (and broadband in particular) however is changing that with digital content - telephony, video, and audio - being delivered via computers.

The telecom industry's embrace of new technology is driven by competition between fixed-line telephony providers, cable companies and mobile telephony providers. The degree of competition is shaped by national regulators and so varies from country to country. However, as *The Economist* reports, fixed-line operators see offering television services as a way to combat the challenge from cable television companies that can offer the 'triple play' of television, broadband internet and telephony. Mobile operators also see putting television on mobile phones as an added inducement to customers.[607]

In Australia the government media reforms emphasise existing media rather than new media. At the announcement of the government's reform proposals in March 2006, Boyd wrote:

> Australia will continue to lag behind the world in the trend toward convergence of voice, data and video services despite the government's efforts to formulate a more forward-looking digital reform package, analysts and commentators said yesterday. They said Australia was being left behind because of government media policy, the country's poor broadband internet penetration and the

---

[606] Neuchterlein, Jonathan E. and Weiser, Philip J. (2005). *Digital crossroads – American telecommunications policy in the internet age*. Cambridge, The MIT Press. p. 3.
[607] Digital convergence – TV on your phone. *The Economist*. 13 Jan. 2005. Downloaded 5 April 2006. http://www.economist.com/PrinterFriendly.cfm?story_id=3566995.

constraints imposed by Telstra's 50 per cent ownership of pay TV company Foxtel.[608]

Telstra, the owner of Australia's copper wire network, is a major mobile service provider as well as a 50% owner of Foxtel. This means the effects of the competitive pressures that exist in other countries as discussed above are reduced in Australia. The government is also a part owner of Telstra and therefore unlikely to introduce any reforms that will erode Telstra's value.

Video news and current affairs are increasingly available online. A full survey of what is available is beyond the scope of this chapter. A few examples however indicate some aspects - how much news is made available, the nature of the content, the timeliness of the material, viewer control and the revenue raising approaches - of the online services. There are several gateway sites that offer access to streaming video such as The Resource Shelf with more than 30 links to online video[609] and Blinx.tv that is a streaming video search engine. [610] Blinx.tv offers a choice of news headlines and reports from news organisations such as CNN, Euronews, Fox, BBC and ITN. The reports are displayed in a 12-by-8 centimetre window. The reports are all a number of hours old, but depending on the region they are coming from, may not be older than the international material Australians see on the evening news. Blinx.tv is free to viewers and supported by advertising; selected reports are preceded by advertisements that cannot be avoided or fast-forwarded.

The mainstream media organisations - accessed through The Resource Shelf, Blinx.tv or via a Google search - display a variety of approaches to video online.[611] Reuters offers a range of streaming video reports including brief news headlines (1.30 mins.), a summary of major US reports (1.00 min.), brief business updates (2.00 mins.), a feature report (3.00 mins.) and an entertainment summary (2.00 mins.).[612] These reports appear to have been produced

---

[608] Boyd, Tony (2006). Policies hold Australia back. *The Australian Financial Review*. 15 March. p. 50.
[609] Downloaded 6April 2006. http://www.freepint.com/gary/audio.htm
[610] Downloaded 5 April 2006. http://www.blinkx.tv/
[611] Among the other innovative broadband offerings are Information TV; Yes TV; See Me TV (with UK mobile phone group 3); and even MTV Overdrive that, on 8 April 2006 included extensive material on the events in Darfur, Sudan (five items totalling about 11 minutes) and the earthquake in Pakistan (eight items totalling about 30 minutes).
[612] Downloaded 6April 2006. http://reuters.feedroom.com/

specifically for the online service from Reuters's sources. The Reuters site carries television-style advertising. CNN, which also carries television-style advertising, offers a choice of five reports on its main news page including a 'most watched' video.[613] The reports were mostly standard news length (1.10 to 1.35 mins) and appear to be taken from mainstream CNN productions. One item, an interview with Congresswoman Cynthia McKinney, about a scuffle with a police officer, ran for almost 11.00 minutes. CNN also offers the CNN Pipeline service that allows viewers to watch up to four live streams at once as a subscription service for $US.99 cents a day, $2.95 a month or $24.95 a year. The service acknowledges that advertising can be a negative for viewers by promoting "… commercial free access to video content on demand."[614] The US free-to-air network CBS offers audiences a choice of 20 video news reports, again of standard news length and apparently taken from free-to-air news programs.[615] This site, with video advertising, allows visitors to select a number of reports they are interested in and to nominate the running order; in other words a do-it-yourself news bulletin that removes viewers from a newsworker ordering items and the linear tyranny of free-to-air bulletins. The BBC offers a subscription-only service to international viewers for its 24-hour BBC World news and information service.[616]

In Australia (not that national boundaries matter on the internet) the ABC, to take the largest public broadcaster, offers almost 50 different programs from the video link on the ABC news online page.[617] These appear in compressed video in a 10-by-6 centimetre window. News is featured with a ten minute bulletin updated three times a day, a one-minute news in brief segment and 20 individual reports from the previous 24 hours. The site also offers material from the programs *Lateline*, *The 7.30 Report*, *Insiders*, *Media Watch*, *Four Corners* and *Australian Story*. As well, there are compilations for the web page *Australia Wide* (ten items), *Rural Watch* (a five-minute program), *ABC Business* (three minutes) and *ABC Sport* (two minutes). Programs taken from ABC free-to-air television, such as *Lateline* or *The 7.30 Report* appear to be offered in a stripped-down version with no opening titles. *The 7.30 Report* page, for example, offers just two reports - on 5 April 2006 these were hospitals crisis

---

[613] Downloaded 6April 2006. javascript:cnnVideo('browse','/mostwatched');
[614] Downloaded 6April 2006. http://www.cnn.com/pipeline/
[615] Downloaded 6April 2006. http://www.cbsnews.com/sections/i_video/main500251.shtml
[616] Downloaded 6April 2006. javascript:loadlink('http://europe.real.com/smil/bbc_world_news.smil','yes')
[617] Downloaded 5 April 2006. http://www.abc.net.au/vod/news

(9.33 mins) and Westpoint rescue (6.52 mins) - that would not be enough for a complete program. No explanation is offered to web viewers as to what reports have been omitted or why.

The penetration of the internet in Australia was 5.98 million subscribers in March 2005 with 56% of Australian households having home internet access and 52% of Australians accessing the internet from home during 2004-5 according to the Australian Bureau of Statistics.[618] Internet access from home in 2004-5 was up by 3% over the previous 12 months and up by more than 300% over the seven years before. Figures for internet access from the workplace are not available but are probably substantial. Other measures of the growth of the internet indicate its impact. Kim Williams, chief executive of Foxtel, points out that broadband internet subscribers increased seven-times faster than pay television subscribers during 2005.[619] A 2005 survey of senior business executives found that 88% said they read newspapers on an average business day, 80% accessed the internet for banking and personal finance and news websites, and 70% watched commercial television.[620] In Britain the *Guardian* reported a survey by Google that found the internet had eclipsed television with the average person online for 164 minutes every day and 148 minutes watching television.[621] That finding however is disputed with the same newspaper reporting less than three weeks later that another survey found television watching accounted for 3.9 hours a day compared to 0.8 hours for the internet.[622]

Despite the conflicting nature of those claims, the overall trend is clear; more and more people are accessing the internet, there is more and more political, economic and business material available and markets are being shaped by the internet. Convergence is increasing.

---

[618] 8153.0 Internet Activity, Australia, Mar 2005 and 8146.0 *Household use of Information Technology* 2004-5. Australian Bureau of Statistics. Downloaded 7 March 2006. http://www.abs.gov.au/
[619] Lehmann, John (2006). Internet 'threat to pay-TV. *The Australian*. 10 March. Downloaded 7 April. http://global.factiva.com.ezproxy.library.usyd.edu.au/ha/default.aspx
[620] MacLean, Sheena (2005). Papers deliver at the big end of town. *The Australian*. 24 Nov. Downloaded 7 April. http://global.factiva.com.ezproxy.library.usyd.edu.au/ha/default.aspx
[621] Johnson, Bobbie (2006). Britain turns off - and logs on. *Guardian*. 8 March. Downloaded 9 March. http://media.guardian.co.uk/print/0,,3299429230-105236,00.html
[622] Brook, Stephen and Brown, Maggie (2006). More people watch the TV than use the net, listen to the radio or read newspapers. *Guardian*. 27 March. Downloaded 28 March. http://media.guardian.co.uk/print/0,,329443377-105337,00.html

New technologies are making new services - such as access to the internet via mobile devices and the provision of television on mobile phones - possible.

Changing Technology/Changing Media

A number of key strands discussed above - technological change, changes to newswork, the diffusion of economic and business news, the commercial interests of media organisations, and regulation - are reshaping the global delivery of news with consequences for the shaping of markets and for audience behaviour and belief.

Greater and greater numbers of the world's population will consume news, information and political, economic and social comment as the technologies considered above - transnational television, broadband and mobile devices - continue to spread. On the production side devices such as camera phones and other technologies and software are making it easier and easier for non-newsworkers to capture material for media organisations (that are increasingly seeking out material from citizen journalists) or for display on non-mainstream or individual websites.

The internet is becoming more and more accessible to audiences beyond developed nations. This is partly due to development in nations such as China. Efforts are also being made to include developing nations with initiatives such as micro loans for computers and mobile phones and projects such as the $US100 laptop being developed by the Massachusetts Institute of Technology (MIT) Media Lab and announced at the World Economic Forum in Davos, Switzerland, in January 2005. This will connect more and more people and help give them access to political and economic debate, business information and markets.

Technology is changing the nature of newswork with the growth of online journalism and new outlets such as streaming video. The pace of online journalism is fast with the traditional 24-hour news cycle of newspapers and a main evening television news bulletin being replaced in the online news environment by constant deadlines. The re-purposing of news material across different outlets means newsworkers are becoming multi-skilled. However re-purposing means more journalists will work away from the 'coal face' of news gathering. The interactive nature of online journalism is illustrated by audience feedback features such as surveys and 'top five' news lists that are generated automatically. The opportunity for newsworkers to engage directly with audiences via an e-mail address included in reports has not been widely taken up by large news organisations because of work pressures. Online sites such as blogs allow non-newsworkers to report events, offer comments or draw attention to other reports and these sites are already having an impact on political debate. The lack of organisational structure and institutional values mean the risks to credible online journalism include inaccuracy, incompleteness and bias.

Economic and business information holds a central place in western capitalist countries and it occupies a significant place in the expanding media environment. In part this is because economic and business information on television attracts an audience that advertisers seek. The internet offers organisations, such as financial organisations, access to a relatively low cost platform to promote their activities. News and information can be easily added to online frameworks already in place for other financial activities, such as account transactions and record keeping. The large pool of individuals with specialised economic and business knowledge offers a ready source of economic and business information for blogs and the western emphasis on wealth has created an even larger pool keen to learn and profit. This means information on, for example, the most complex issues facing central banks or the management of a giant company to running a lemonade stand[623] is instantly available around the world.

The willingness of large organisations in the expanding media world to put their commercial interests ahead of moral interests has been displayed by several of the world's major media organisations - News Corporation and the BBC - and the world's major information technology companies - Google, Microsoft and Yahoo! The example of Google and crikey.com also illustrates that as small and new media and IT companies mature and grow larger they may be prepared to sacrifice some of their values for commercial interests.

Regulatory authorities, such as national governments, play a crucial role in allocating bandwidth, deciding what type of material can be transmitted, deciding legislation and funding for public broadcasters, controlling locally domiciled internet providers and setting

---

[623] An example of how to run a lemonade stand is found at http://www.lemonadegame.com/ Lemonade stands are an entry-level approach to US-style capitalism.

ownership restrictions. In Australia, as considered previously, government legislation favours the existing large media players. The Australian government is also currently restricting digital development. Government relations with media organisations are complex because while the government can influence the media environment the media can influence public perceptions of the government. Australian governments have displayed a desire to shape what appears on the public broadcasters and also to influence the messages that are transmitted from Australia to audiences overseas.

Transnational media issues are also complex because national governments have limited direct control over transnational media organisations. Technological advances put regulatory frameworks under threat by allowing media organisations to broadcast or to present internet material from cyberspace which may be outside the reach of governments. Governments can attempt to control this in a variety of ways, including by appeal to international regulatory authorities, by blocking or restricting material with filters or competing transmissions, by commercial pressures such as restricting revenue raising or other commercial activities within their territories, and by restricting the use of reception devices. Raboy comments that the issues of global media require global solutions and adds " … [this] is in some respects so overwhelming that it is not even easy to bring it up, let alone address it seriously." and further "There are no precedents, no traditions for dealing with media policy outside the political frameworks of national states."[624]

The global organisations that are the key players identified by Raboy are the United Nations, multilateral exclusive "clubs" such as the Organisation for Economic Co-operation and Development (OECD), regional multi-state groupings such as the European Union (EU), national states, transnational private sector groups such as the Global Business Dialogue for e-commerce (GBDe), civil society organisations such as international umbrella groups like the Cultural Environment Movement, and "transversal" groups such as the Internet Corporation for Assigned Names and Numbers (ICANN). Raboy adds "At this point, the only actor successful at pursuing an agenda with anything approaching consistency is the

---

[624] Raboy, Marc (2002). Media policy in the new communications environments, in Raboy, Marc (ed.) *Global media policy in the new millennium*. Luton, University of Luton Press. p. 5.

transnational private sector ... concrete media policy developments at every level are clearly being driven by economic concerns."[625]

New media has already displayed a major influence on financial markets. The technology and new economy boom that developed in the late 1990s before the crash in 2000 was driven by market expectations for information and communication technology companies. Brock quotes from the *Wall Street Journal* that "the Great Internet Bubble ... ranks among history's biggest bubbles."[626] The online trading site eBay has taken the local market stall global and provides the structure for more than ten million auctions a day.[627] eBay has become a clearing house for world prices of many items. The internet has made it possible for consumers to compare specifications and prices and to read about the experience of other consumers with specific products. Kuwabara quotes from *The Economist* that "... [the] internet cuts costs, increases competition and improves the functioning of the price mechanism. It thus moves the economy closer to the textbook model of perfect competition."[628]

New media also informs audiences around the world about the structure and performance of economic and business institutions and models. The US style of capitalism is presented as the preferred model because of the media reach of the United States. Debate over the spread of US economic and business culture, however, has been much more muted than long-running concerns that US popular culture presented in film, television and music is driving out other cultures. Concerns over US dominance of technical culture however are illustrated by Franco-German efforts to counter dominance of the Google and Yahoo search engines by developing their own search engine called Quaero. Jacques Chirac, the president of France, said:

> We must take up the global challenge of the American giants Yahoo! and Google
> ... Culture is not merchandise and cannot be left to blind market forces ... We

---

[625] ibid pp. 7-9.
[626] Brock, Gerald W. (2002). *The second information revolution.* Cambridge, Harvard University Press. p. 280.
[627] Kuwabara, Ko (2005). Affective attachment in electronic markets : a sociological study of eBay. in Nee, Victor and Swedberg, Richard (eds.) *The economic sociology of capitalism.* Princeton, Princeton University Press.
[628] ibid. p 268.

must staunchly defend the world's cultural diversity against the looming threat of uniformity.[629]

It is also worth noting that France plans to create a French-language international television news service to balance the perspective presented by CNN.

The internet bubble was fuelled by the flow of information from the general media, specialist print and television outlets, such as CNBC, and new media such as online finance sites. Some of these sources, such as CNBC, suffered a dramatic drop in audiences after the crash but have since returned to prominence. New media - through online information and online trading - has opened up financial markets to many people in the West who were previously excluded. As transnational television and new media reaches more people in more nations - particularly the huge populations of China and India - the effect on participation in markets is likely to be dramatic. The outcomes of greater access to media in developing nations is both driven by, and driving, other economic and social changes. Transnational and new media are informing global audiences - in both developed and developing nations - about conditions, including political and economic conditions, beyond their national borders. The internet is a growing tool for international activism.[630]

The possible negatives of global media are reviewed by Chalaby who examines fears that global media will bring about deterritorialisation (the loss of the relationship between culture and territory), disembed social relationships and disconnect familiarity and place. Chalaby comments "Through the media, people … learn about the performances of stock exchanges around the world and worry about events that take place thousands of miles away from their homes."[631] Tewksbury presents another possible negative which is the specialisation of media (fragmentation of information) resulting from technologies that allow individuals to select only those reports of interest to them, say on economics and business, but that might also

---

[629] Attack of the Eurogoogle. *The Economist*. 9 March 2006. Downloaded 12 April 2006. http://www.economist.com/research/articles
[630] For example see Cleaver, Harry M. (1998). The Zapatista effect: the internet and the rise of an alternative political fabric. *Journal of International Affairs*. Spring. 51. no. 2.
[631] Chalaby Jean K (2005). Towards an understanding of media transnationalism. in Chalaby op. cit. p. 8.

blinker them to reports on associated issues, say human rights and the environment.[632]

CONCLUSION

This and previous chapters have examined the development of economic and business coverage on Australian television and considered the current nature of this genre of journalism. But what of the future? Many of the key themes - such as technology, content, newswork, institutions and production processes - are undergoing dramatic change. Technological developments - in the delivery of television and the internet - are the major forces influencing newswork and what is presented to audiences. At the same time related technological developments - such as internet blogs and mobile camera phones - are empowering non-newsworkers and eroding the gatekeeper role of newsworkers. Media and information technology organisations are having to develop and embrace new production and revenue models. Governments and regulatory authorities are clinging to old media approaches while the technology outpaces them. Citizen journalists, civic organisations and activists can reach out to world audiences but it is uncertain how long this power will exist in the face of regulation, commercial interests and embedded weaknesses.

We are witnessing the transformation of news. The television programs that have emerged as a response to new technologies, such as round-the-clock transnational business channels, the involvement of non-newsworkers, and the ease of presenting material via the internet is altering what is presented to audiences as news. The six key criteria for news are consequence, proximity, conflict, human interest, novelty and prominence. Transnational business channels such as CNBC present large amounts of material that involve relatively small changes in prices on markets that may be on the other side of the world and may be driven by innocuous and probably regular events (such as the release of data). This satisfies none of the above criteria for news. What audiences are receiving is information.

What is presented online also fails to satisfy what has been considered as news for at least most of the 20th century. During that century news was something gathered, selected and ordered by professional newsworkers, meeting consistent values and presented within

---

[632] Tewksbury, David (2005). The seeds of fragmentation: specialization in the use of online news sites. *Journal of Broadcasting and Electronic Media*. September 2005.

institutional frameworks. What is available online can be - to take the example mentioned previously in this chapter of a bank economist interviewing a corporate leader for the bank's website - presented by a non-newsworker, without consistency because the segment is an occasional one without context, and presented on a site promoting commercial interests. Online blogs are prepared by non-newsworkers far from the source, with varied values and with no institutional framework. Again this material fails to meet the criteria for news so audiences are receiving information. The proliferation of web sites from news organisations, commercial organisations, civic groups, governments and the ever increasing number of blogs listed on Technorati demand new approaches to media use.

Here are two responses. Kevin Kelly, the founding editor of techno-alternative *Wired* magazine, writes:

> What happens when everyone is uploading far more than they download? If everyone is busy making, altering, mixing and mashing, who will have time to sit back and veg out? No one. And that's just fine ... what matters is the network of social creation, the community of collaborative interaction that futurist Alvin Toffler called prosumption ... The producers are the audience, the act of making is the act of watching, and every link is both a point of departure and a destination.[633]

Albert Borgmann, a philosopher who specialises in technology and culture, writes:

> The internet in its presently free-flowing luxuriance cannot survive. The selfless enthusiasm of hackers[634] and the high-minded support of public institutions, so crucial to the first flowering of the internet, will both decline. Hackers are getting tired, institutions will get stingy. Commerce will step into the breach, drain the swamps, channel the current, erect dikes, build reservoirs, and install locks. All users will become customers and will have to pay either with money or with attention paid to commercials ... individuals will come to realise that it is beyond

---

[633] Kelly, Kevin (2005). Unto us the machine is born. *The Sydney Morning Herald*. 15 Nov. Downloaded 18 Nov. 2005. http://smh.com.au/articles/2005/11/14/1131816858554.html? page=3
[634] Note: Hackers is used in this sense in the original meaning of those amateurs with IT interests and skills used creatively and positively, not the destructive definition often used in the mainstream media.

their capacity to spot and evaluate information ... media organisations that have earned our trust in collecting, editing, and warranting information will survive or re-emerge.[635]

---

[635] Borgmann, Albert (1999). Holding onto reality: the nature of information at the turn of the millennium. Chicago, University of Chicago Press. p. 214.

CONCLUSION

The central conundrum of this project is that television is the most important source of news for people in western societies and yet has been regarded as having great obstacles in covering economic and business material. A variety of developments mean television today is very different to that of 50 years ago and while many of the traditional difficulties have been overcome new obstacles pose a different set of challenges.

The first evening news bulletins in 1956 were just 15 minutes. Now they are twice that duration and have expanded to early morning, midday, evening and late night slots as well as 24 hour news channels on pay television. Only one decade after its introduction television was judged by 31% of a national survey group as "presenting the fairest, most unbiased news" compared to 20% each for newspapers and radio.[636]

The first Australian television newsworkers adopted the techniques of news and current affairs mostly from their experiences in the US or the UK, by instruction from practitioners from these countries or by their own observation of programs. This external influence continues to this day. Australia, therefore, has no unique style of news and current affairs programming. However these imported techniques provide Australians with a way of exploring local issues and events.

Overseas news on Australian television was at first limited to international footage that arrived by air and was days old and restricted in content. From the late 1960s, however, satellites allowed world events to be broadcast live to Australian audiences. Technological improvements subsequently reduced the cost of satellite footage. International news on television in Australia increased from a trickle to a flood giving audiences greater access to world affairs.

---

[636] Western J.S. and Hughes C.A. (1971). *The mass media in Australia - use and evaluation*. St Lucia, University of Queensland Press. p. 120.

The oil shocks of the 1970s made oil supplies a major international issue and the increasing amounts of satellite footage helped inform Australians of the crisis. The rise in international, followed by domestic, prices made everyday Australians (rather than just exporters such as primary producers) aware of their connection to the world economy. Television, of course, was not the only medium to cover these events but television's increasingly dominant role made it a major source of this information. Television coverage also increases public salience causing audiences to pursue issues such as the oil shocks and their impact and other economic and business news in greater detail in print.

The supply and demand factors for commodities such as oil are well known. Supply and demand factors also act on television news programs and, just as the western world is dependent on oil, economic and business news on television is dependent on politicians and business leaders. The demand for television news material by newsworkers and audiences has been met by politicians and, to a lesser degree, business leaders who have made themselves available and shaped their performances to suit the medium. By making themselves available in a regular, dependable and logistically accessible way politicians increased television's appetite for their performances. Television newsworkers began to cluster around political centres such as parliaments knowing that news content would be available. This trend is further illustrated by centres such as the new Parliament House in Canberra being configured in ways to maximise the access to television by politicians. The politicians also realised that they could be selective in their television appearances for favourable coverage and that print coverage would follow these appearances. The content demands for increasing amounts of television news mean that television newsworkers sometimes now have to accept the demands of key interviewees.

Audiences unconsciously accept the constraints of television including the use of newsworkers on screen when no relevant footage is available or surrogate vision to illustrate hard-to-film issues or concepts. The coverage of economic and business affairs provides a clear example of this. Less-than-dramatic economic/political footage (such as parliament, political press conferences, events such as gatherings of political leaders and generic footage of activities such as home construction) and business footage (such as stock markets, extended talking-head interviews with business leaders and generic footage of industrial processes) have become part of the landscape of news.

Low audience expectations for dramatic visual material on television allowed television news to increase the range of issues and events it presented. The early, and brief, television news programs featured reports of highly visual events such as aircraft fly-pasts and sporting competitions. Reports of this nature are still seen in news and current affairs programs today and attract criticism that television news is dominated by visuals. However, the demand for television news footage has increased as owners seek to maximise revenues with both round-the-clock transmissions and transnational television and newsworkers have been forced to accept a wider range of material. There are two reasons for this acceptance. The first is that news judgements based on visual values fall short of the six commonly accepted news criteria (consequence, proximity, conflict, human interest, novelty and prominence). The second is that the supply of strong visual material is irregular and limited. Taken together this means that newsworkers began to present less than dramatic visual material such as that described in the paragraph above in order to guarantee sufficient and predictable supplies. At the same, time increasing public awareness of the importance of economics and business driven by events such as the oil shocks and government policy changes such as those to superannuation made audiences receptive to this non-dramatic economic and business visual material.

Newsworkers have made the transition from relying on footage of actual events to accepting surrogate footage. This has been a three-part process and the material presented in the early news programs on Channel 9 illustrates the first part of the process. The footage of the Olympic swimming trials signify exactly that; a race between different competitors in a swimming pool. The images are the event and the images and the news content are in close proximity to each other. The images of the jet bombers from Air Force Week are also the event but the content represents something further; national military capabilities and the projection of power. The images of Prime Minister Menzies arriving at the airport are only part of the news content which is the prime minister presenting his views on the Suez crisis. These examples illustrate the distance between the image of the event and the news content. As audiences came to accept this distance and surrogacy of vision the range of material that could be presented on television as news increased. By the mid-1980s this acceptance would help the introduction of more and more economic and business material on television and represents the first part in making economics (and the related politics) and business palatable to television audiences. In Australia this is best represented by Channel 9's *Business Sunday*. By the end of the 1980s this acceptance would also lead to the launch of economic and business specific channels. In the US - and globally - this is best represented by the launch of CNBC. Television was no longer constrained by the tyranny of visuals.

Pseudo-events - press conferences, publicity occasions and the like - are the second part of the process. The images from pseudo-events - such as the champagne toast at the float of a company or a seminar to discuss housing costs - are removed from the act of the float or the issue of housing costs. What these pseudo-events do is to provide the necessary images, however limited, for the overlying issues to be covered on television. Corporate and political image makers have become so adept at devising pseudo-events they have become a staple of television news, prompting few challenges from either newsworkers or audiences, as illustrated by the Council of Australian Governments' (CoAG) water conference between political leaders in Canberra. The positions and options of the different players are established in advance, often by support staff. The actual event of the water conference may be unnecessary in a policy development sense. The event however provides images of the politicians at work that both suits the politicians and provides visual material for television to cover the issue.

The third part of making economics and business acceptable to television audiences is the manner in which the elites - mainly politicians and business leaders - and newsworkers shape messages for the demands of television. This shaping includes the politicians' careful use of locations and backdrops and the building of a communications infrastructure (within for example Parliament House, Canberra) that allows vision and audio to be transmitted to the clustered newsworkers, to television production facilities across the country and around the world. This shaping is also displayed in the advance notice of many events to allow newsworkers to prepare and in the timing of events to fit the news cycle. This shaping is further displayed by the recognition by politicians and business leaders of television as the primary source of communication and the knowledge that the messages presented on television will be followed up by other media. The sources seek to control what programs and interviewers they will grant access to and negotiate what issues they will discuss. The example of a business leader negotiating the scope of his interview is a familiar practice of sources dealing with newsworkers. This is a central part of spin where elites and their staff tell newsworkers which aspects of an issue are important and what should be emphasised or ignored.

Elites have developed communication techniques to meet the requirements of television (and to a lesser degree other media) that include the use of causal narrative (with its emphasis on cause and consequence), conflict and consensus and myth. One example of a battle over causal narratives in the survey material is the dispute between QANTAS and the union movement over basing staff outside Australia. The causal narrative presented by QANTAS CEO Geoff Dixon is that staff need to be based outside Australia to cause cost savings that will bring the consequence of keeping the airline competitive. The counter narrative put by ACTU President Sharan Burrow is that the airline's mistreatment of Australian workers will bring the consequence of lost public support. The example also clearly illustrates the nature of the conflict between the two sides. Consensus between the two in terms of an agreement would also justify a report. An example of myth encountered in the survey material is the banker, St George Bank Chairman Frank Conroy, who, like a hero of long ago, overcomes a weakness (his slowness of action that led to one business failure) to win later success. It is an account easily told on television and readily appreciated by audiences.

These communication techniques mean that television news and current affairs can bring about ideational change. In the QANTAS example the ideas behind long-accepted employment practices are challenged. In the second example the public idea of bankers as inflexible number crunchers is replaced by that of individuals who are willing to admit they make mistakes but are prepared to learn from them and improve. These communication techniques also have implications for the depiction of structure and agency. Television likes to focus on individuals and to create celebrities, however minor. In the above examples the interviewees come to represent their organisations. Dixon becomes QANTAS and Burrow the ACTU and the complex institutional mechanisms for bringing about industrial change are not commented on. On television agents (individuals) are seen to be able to challenge and change structure. Thus television supports a view of the primacy of agency over structure.

The presentation of successful business leaders on television promotes them as celebrities. Their setting and circumstances are usually grand and the newsworkers are respectful. The same often, but not always, applies to politicians. In these cases television newsworkers take advantage of the visuals that are available, emphasising expensive offices, houses and cars. Here television promotes materialism and consumerism. The values of capitalism - of financial success, of hard work and of making the most of opportunities - are reinforced in the narratives presented on television.

Similar values are also presented on transnational television and may influence a different type of change. Networks such as CNBC present US-style values and US business models are reinforced on a daily basis by footage of and discussion about activity by institutions such as the New York Stock Exchange. Reports emphasise the attitudes and approaches of entrepreneurs such as the individuals behind successful organisations. The interplay of regulatory and judicial institutions (for example in the case of Enron) are displayed. In regions such as Asia the sets and presenters are clones of the US originals. Networks such as CNBC represent the media component of soft US imperialism.

Transnational television and other international media such as online news programs and blogs are the result of changing technology influencing how and what information is presented. Audiences are increasingly selecting the specific information they consume instead of trusting to newsworkers to collect, edit and decide what is news. Technological development over the past several decades has helped turn media into a massive commercial global industry. Technological development now allows - for the moment at least - more and more individuals to present and receive diverse information and views. One downside of this is that global media is accused of threatening social, cultural and geographical connections.

Old media in the form of print and television is currently being challenged by new media in the form of the internet and online journalism. There are parallels between the way developments in broadcast technology encouraged television journalism and the way developments in information technology is shaping online journalism. Technological developments in both television and online media have and are reshaping the roles and tasks of newsworkers and are changing the way audiences relate to news. And the nature of news itself is being changed by developing technologies.

Among the parallels between the development of television journalism and of online journalism are the status of newsworkers, how emerging media is viewed by existing media, the speed of the dissemination of news and how elites adapt to emerging media. Print journalists were initially dismissive of television journalism and the Australian Journalists' Association (AJA) was slow to recognise television journalism within the Walkley Awards. This is echoed today by online newsworkers being fearful of being regarded as second class by their mainstream colleagues. Print organisations were initially concerned that television would take away their audiences. Newspapers and television today are witnessing a decline in readers and viewers at the same time as overall internet use and visits to online news sites are increasing. Television's capacity to bring instant images to audiences helped increase the speed and quantity of news and information and the capacity of online journalism to bring almost infinite amounts of information is furthering that trend. Finally, it has been discussed how politicians adapted to television and are choosing to present their messages via that medium rather than print, thus reshaping politics. Some early indications of how the internet might change politics are US presidential candidate Howard Dean's use of the Blog for America site to build support during the 2004 campaign and the role of bloggers in correcting the claims of mainstream media, such as those by Dan Rather on CBS over President George W. Bush's military service.

Economic growth in the west was driven by trade and commodity flows. News and information is following a similar path. Information-rich western nations stand at the centre with information-poor nations on the periphery. The information flowing from the centre provides a model for the periphery to follow. Information flowing to the centre displays the opportunities on the periphery. News production hubs are at the centre with their outstations on the periphery. This production process draws in raw information that is processed into news. The development of CNBC in Europe has outpaced other subject-dedicated networks and illustrates the centrality of economic and business news on transnational television. The sheer volume of information that is being processed means that news has become a commodity with its providers struggling to differentiate their product through brands, personalities and perspectives. Australia's contribution to international media flows is limited while Australia's consumption of international media flows is much greater.

In its fifty-year history, television in Australia has reported on and fed debate on many economic and business issues that have resulted from and contributed to major social and political changes. Television news in general, and economic and business news in particular, has reshaped its values to lessen its reliance on strong visual material. This means that television news has become accepting of weak visual material and newsworkers have become skilled at linking surrogate visual material and the news content of reports in order to ensure a sufficient and regular supply of economic and business content. More and more time has been made available on television for economic and business news. Key players such as politicians and business leaders have also contributed by altering their behaviour to suit the demands of television.

The nature of television has changed and many of those obstacles to television covering economic and business news have been surmounted. Coverage of economics and business on television news and current affairs has overcome the lack of dramatic visuals by lessening the expectation of what visuals are acceptable. The need for brevity has been reduced with more air time available for economic and business material. News workers and political and business elites have made the complex understandable by devising new ways to present material. The personalisation of issues and the personification of a government or a corporation by a single individual is accepted in today's age of celebrity.

The new problems that are apparent, however, are the blurring of news and information and the dependence of news coverage of economic and business issues on what sources provide. The lessening of expectation of visuals means that long interviews with no visual relief are now presented on television yet the news aspect - the identification of the key point - is increasingly left to the audience to decide. The availability of more time for economic and business material and the reliance on political and business elites means television is now hostage to those elites for content regardless of the quality or partially limited nature of that content.

APPENDIX 1

ECONOMIC AND BUSINESS REPORTS

Channel 9 News **June 2004**

1.	15 June	Green power: the federal government announces a multi-million package on spending for the environment.
2.	"	Panthers: inquiry into the business affairs of Penrith Panthers CEO Roger Cowan.
3.	18 June	State property tax: flaws in NSW tax on property sales.
4.	22 June	NSW budget. NSW treasurer hands down his 10th annual budget.
5.	"	Drug backflip: Federal Labor announces it will support price rises in the Pharmaceutical Benefit Scheme (PBS).
6.	"	Rocket plane: SpaceShipOne makes the first private space flight hailed as the dawn of commercial space travel.
7.	23 June	Capital gains: the government rejects a recommendation by the Productivity Commission to review capital gains tax discounts.
8.	24 June	Superannuation debate: the Senate considers superannuation choice legislation.
9.	25 June	Water agreement: agreement between the states and the federal government for a national water plan.
10.	"	Undercoverwear: lingerie company Undercoverwear lists on the stock exchange.

ABC News - **June 2004**

1.	1 June	Apple and pear demonstration: farmers protest against government plans to allow the importation of New Zealand apples.
2.	2 June	Economic slowdown: interest rates on hold for the 6th month in a row.
3.	"	Oil price rise: world wrap-up of oil supplies and prices.
4.	3 June	Howard and US: John Howard visits the US and talks about LNG sales and Guantanamo Bay prisoner David Hicks.
5.	4 June	Reserve Bank houses: Reserve Bank governor Ian MacFarlane says houses are not overpriced.
6.	"	JH asbestos: coverage of the NSW inquiry into compensation for James Hardie asbestos victims.
7.	7 June	Transport funding: new federal government funding for road and rail transport.
8.	8 June	Water cost: Canberra forum to discuss water resources and costs.
9.	9 June	House lending: lending for houses stabilises.

10.	15 June	Energy plan: the federal government announces a multi-million package on spending for the environment.
11.	"	Panthers: inquiry into the business affairs of Penrith Panthers CEO Roger Cowan.
12.	17 June	Trade deal: summary of US-Australia free trade negotiations and election speculation.
13.	18 June	NSW property tax: flaws in NSW tax on property sales.
14.	21 June	Telstra: biggest one-day rise in three years for Telstra shares.
15.	22 June	NSW budget: NSW Treasurer hands down his 10th annual budget.
16.	"	Costly drugs: Federal Labor announces it will support price rises in the Pharmaceutical Benefit Scheme (PBS).
17.	"	QANTAS London base: QANTAS to cut costs by basing staff in London.
18.	24 June	Water debate: states and federal government negotiations ahead of Council of Australian Governments' (COAG) meeting on water.
19.	25 June	Water management: agreement between the states and the federal government for a national water plan.
20.	"	FTA vote: vote on US-Australia FTA causes split among Labor M.P.s.
21.	"	Westfield: shareholders approve Westfield plan to create world's biggest shopping mall owner.
22.	28 June	Workplace reforms: proposals for workplace safety reforms stop short of a crime of industrial manslaughter for employers.
23.	"	Housing affordability: housing summit seeks ways to make renting and buying houses more affordable.
24.	"	Southcorp jobs: winemaker Southcorp cuts 200 jobs to reduce costs.

ABC *The 7:30 Report* - June 2004

1.	8 June	Property and borrowing: disagreement amongst economists about house-price fuelled debt.
2.	"	Latham/industrial relations: Latham plan to dump Australian workplace agreements makes industrial relations an election issue.
3.	14 June	James Hardie: questions about the James Hardie compensation fund for asbestos victims.
4.	15 June	Energy policy: coal and farming industries happy but renewable energy and green groups negative about government energy policy.
5.	"	Kemp interview: David Kemp, environment minister, discusses energy policy.
6.	"	Car dealers: car dealers and independent tuners at odds over new car servicing.
7.	16 June	Taxpayer-funded advertising spending: the difference between public information and political spending in the government's

$120 million advertising blitz.

8.	21 June	Election speculation: election speculation as opinion polls show Coalition clawing back ground from Labor.
9.	23 June	Water - liquid gold: water use in view of continuing drought and possible changes to weather patterns.
10.	"	Pre-election tension: political players under strain with Labor's about-face on drug prices and support for the US-Australia FTA despite doubts.
11.	24 June	Water - part 2: Victoria announces radical new water conservation policy ahead of state and federal summit on water.
12.	"	Singleton interview: businessman John Singleton wants to start an upmarket, Australian-content television network.
12a	"	Bio-diesel: backyard bio-diesel brewers face excise charges.
13.	30 June	Baby bonus: health experts claim arbitrary timing by the government on the $3,000 baby bonus is a risk to mothers and babies.
14.	"	Tasmania waterfronts: mainland migrants to Tasmania seek a quieter, more affordable lifestyle and waterfronts.

Channel 9 *Business Sunday* – 6, 13, 27 June and 4 July 2004

1.	6 June	Tom Gorman: the new president of Ford Australia, Tom Gorman, talks about his goals and the new Ford Territory.
2.	"	Frank Conway: St George Bank chairman Frank Conway reflects on banking and the business world.
3.	"	OPEC: OPEC lifts production as oil futures jump but there is little relief for Australian industry and motorists.
4.	"	Property trusts: merger deals shake up property trusts but rewards and protection from takeovers are uncertain.
5.	"	Greg Clark: Lend Lease CEO Greg Clark makes the case for the merger with GPT.
6.	13 June	Terry Davis: as Coca-Cola Amatil opens a new distribution centre Managing Director Terry Davis discusses new products and modernising the company.
7.	"	Cabcharge: CEO Reginald Kermode discusses expansion plans for the company with 98% of the taxi fare payment business.
8.	"	Trevor O'Hoy: the new CEO of Fosters considers wine oversupply.
9.	"	Leighton safety: the death of a Leighton worker on-site means Leighton's directors will be more responsible for workplace safety with implications for other companies.
10.	"	Lindsay Tanner: Labor's communication spokesman discusses competition in the media.

(Note: no program 20 June due to sport.)

11.   27 June   (Missed item due to technical problems.)

12.   "   Wal-mart legal: a CBS report on a gender discrimination complaint that has turned into a major class action suit.

13.   "   GE Money: CEO Australia Tom Gentile explains expansion and acquisition history and plans for the US-owned group in Australia.

14.   "   Chaney NAB recruitment: NAB"""" Chairman Graham Kraehe discusses the currency scandal, the boardroom fall-out and his replacement Michael Chaney.

15.   "   News Corp. Standard & Poor's: News Corp. removed from key Australian indices after changing domicile to the US.

16.   "   News Corp. panel: a panel of fund mangers and investors discuss the News Corp. change.

17.   4 July   Nudie: niche player in the fruit juice business Nudie does well despite a fire in its factory.

18.   "   E-mail: a CNN report on the negatives and positives of e-mail in the workplace.

19.   "   Craig Emerson: Labor's workplace relations spokesman commits to retaining a decentralised wage fixing system.

20.   "   Pacific Hydro: an Australian green energy group is critical of the federal government's energy policy.

21.   "   Evans&Tate: Franklin Tate, CEO of the West Australian winemaker, discusses acquisitions and a 40% earnings increase.

22.   "   Rugby-Johns: the business of sponsorship behind the Australian Rugby Union's attempt to woo League's Andrew Johns.

ABC *Inside Business* - 6, 13, 20, 27 June 2004

1.   6 June   State against state: premiers vie with each other to attract business investment.

2.   "   McGrath interview: auditor Tony McGrath discusses new US rules for auditing independence.

3.   "   Super cars: Matt Thomas looks for investors to support his dream of the Australian Joss SuperCar.

4.   13 June   News Corp. plan: obstacles to the News Corp. plan to domicile in the US.

5.   "   Coonan interview: Assistant Treasurer Senator Helen Coonan discusses reforms to DIY superannuation.

6.   "   Vaux interview: former investment banker and managing director of DCA David Vaugh discusses the opportunities in aged care.

7.   20 June   Superannuation reform: examination of the new laws on the disclosure of fees and charges levied by superannuation funds.

8.   "   Day interview: Sensis Managing Director Andrew Day explains

why the publisher of the White and Yellow pages has moved into classified advertising.

9.   "   Yvonne Allen: the business of matchmaking with 28-year veteran Yvonne Allen.

10.   27 June   Blitzer interview: S&P's David Blitzer explains why News Corp. was taken out of the Australian indices after moving to the US.

11.   "   Mohl interview: AMP CEO Andrew Mohl explains how he boosted the share price by 50% and his plans for the future.

12.   "   Ritz Cinema: cinema buff George Aleksiunas on the joys and trials of owning an independent cinema.

Appendix 2

Prog:

date:

Coding for television content analysis. June-July 2004 (version 5)

1. Topic - Monetary (   ) Fiscal (   ) Trade (   ) Business (   ) Resources (   ) Other (   )

2. Reason for report - Diary (   ) Non-diary (   )

2a. Market moves (   ) Announcement (   ) Data release (   ) Investigation (   ) Summary (   ) Breaking news ( ) Event( )

3. 1st Actor #app. (   )   2nd (   )   3rd (   )   4th (   )   5th (   )   6th (   )

name:

org:

4. Gender: M (   ) F (   )

5. Institutions: National (   ) Government (   ) Opposition (   ) Business (   ) Finance ( ) Union (   ) Lobby (   ) Academia (   ) Other + non-inst. (   )

6. Role: CEO (   ) Business (   ) Spokesman (   ) Analyst/commentator (   ) Lawyer (   ) Politician ( ) Worker/public (   ) Other (   )

7. Event - Presser (   ) Interview (   ) Studio interview (   ) Set-piece (   ) Dramatic(   ) Vox-pop (   )

8. Vision - File (   ) Handout (   ) New (   ) Satellite (   )

9. Graphics - Static (   ) Moving (   ) No graphic (   )

10. Bennett's rules - Govt. officials (   ) Bus. officials (   ) conflict / consensus (   ) trail of power ( ) rituals and customs (   ) journalists' voice (   )

11. Economic terms Y N   11a. economic terms explained Y N

12. Business terms Y N   12a. business terms explained Y N

13. Causal narrative (   ) 13a. past-past (   ) past-present (   ) present-future (   ) future-future (   )

    crisis implied? (   ) crisis used (   )   player (   ) player (   )

Rpt:
14. Impression - Positive (   ) Negative (   ) No impression (   )

PTC:
15. Item order   16. Total items to sport

Storyline:
17. Duration
                  1st vision:

(Note: some additional analysis performed separately.)

BIBLIOGRAPHY

A.B.C. television station opens. *The Daily Telegraph*, 6 Nov. 1956.

Agardy, Susanna, Bednall, David, Jones, Colin and Fricker, Maria (1978). *Television and the public – the news - Sydney 1978.* (location n/a), Australian Broadcasting Tribunal.

Alhers, Douglas (2006). News consumption and the new electronic media. *Press/Politics* 11(1).

Allan, Stuart (2004). The culture of distance. in (eds.) Allan, Stuart and Zelizer, Barbie. *Reporting war – journalism in wartime.* Abingdon, Routledge.

Alysen, Barbara (2002). *The electronic reporter: broadcast journalism in Australia.* Sydney, UNSW Press in conjunction with Deakin University Press.

Alysen, Barbara (2001). Today's news tomorrow: researching archival television. *Media International Australia incorporating Culture and policy*, No. 99 – May 2001.

Appleton, Gil (1988). How Australia sees itself: the role of commercial television. in Australian Broadcasting Tribunal. *The price of being Australian.* North Sydney, Australian Broadcasting Tribunal.

Arant M.D. and Anderson J. Q. (2001) Newspaper online editors support traditional standards. *Newspaper Research Journal.* 22(4).

Ashbolt, Allan (1974). *An Australian experience – words from the Vietnam years.* Sydney, Australasian Book Society Ltd.

Attack of the Eurogoogle. *The Economist.* 9 March 2006. Downloaded 12 April 2006.
http://www.economist.com/research/articles

Australian Broadcasting Control Board (1956). *Television programme standards. Determined by the Board in pursuance of the Broadcasting and Television Act 1942-45.* Canberra, Commonwealth Government Printer.

Australian Broadcasting Control Board (1957). *Ninth Annual Report.* (1958). *Tenth Annual Report.* (1963). *Fifteenth Annual report* (1964). *Sixteenth Annual Report.* (1965). *Seventeenth Annual Report.* (1968). *Twentieth Annual Report.* (1970). *Twenty Second Annual Report.*
(1973). *Twenty-fifth Annual report.* Canberra. Commonwealth Government Printer.
Australian Broadcasting Control Board. (1959). *Report and recommendations to the Postmaster-General pursuant to the Television Act 1953 and the Television Regulations on applications for commercial television licences for the Sydney and Melbourne area.*
Australian Broadcasting Tribunal (1988). *The price of being Australian.* North Sydney.
Australian Bureau of Statistics (1995). *Australian social trends 1995. Culture and leisure – special feature leisure at home.*
http://www.abs.gov.au/ausstats/abs@.nsf/Previousproducts/A1B5D7636E6719F7CA2570EC00753522?opendocument Downloaded 6 Mar. 2006.

Australian Film and Television School research and survey unit (1978?). *Monograph No. 7. Commercial television licence application hearings Sydney/Melbourne 1955 Brisbane/Adelaide 1958 Perth/Hobart 1958.* AFTRS, Sydney.

Australian Film and Television School research and survey unit (1979). *Monograph No. 8A. Press coverage of the television licence renewal hearings – Sydney 1979.* AFTRS, Sydney.
Bantz, Charles, R. McCorkle, Suzanne, and Baade, Roberta C. (1980). The news factory. *Communication Research.* Vol. 7, No. 1.

Barkin, Steve M. (2003). *American television news: the media marketplace and the public interest.* Armonk, M.E. Sharpe, Inc.

Barnett, David with Goward, Pru (1997). *John Howard: Prime Minister.* Ringwood, Viking.

Barns, Greg (2005). *Selling the Australian government.* Sydney, University of New South Wales Press Ltd.

Barry, Paul (1990). *The rise and fall of Alan Bond.* Sydney. Bantam Books.

Baudrillard, Jean (translated by Sheila Faria Glaser) (1994). *Simulacra and simulation.* Ann Arbor, The University of Michigan Press.

Beck, Ulrich (2002). The cosmopolitan society and its enemies. *Theory, Culture & Society.* Vol. 19(1-2).

Beecher, Eric (2006). Publishers right of reply. *The Australian.* 16 Feb. p. 16. Downloaded 8 March 2006. http://global.factiva.com.ezproxy.library.usyd.edu.au/ha/default.aspx

Behind the TV screen. *Daily Telegraph* 18 Sept. 1956.

Beilby, Peter (1981). *Australian TV – the first 25 years.* Melbourne. Thomas Nelson Australia.

Bell, Glennys. (1981). Quality for the Sunday morning slot. *The Bulletin.* 17 Nov.

Bell, Stephen (2004). *Australia's money mandarins - the Reserve Bank and the politics of money.* Port Melbourne, Cambridge University Press.

Bennett, Andrew and Elman, Colin (2006). Complex causal relations and case study methods: the example of path dependence, *Political Analysis,* 14.

Bennett, W. Lance (2005). *News – the politics of illusion (sixth edition).* New York. Pearson Longman.

— (1997). Cracking the news code, in Iyengar, Shanto, and Reeves, Richard (eds.) *Do the media govern? Politician, voters, and reporters in America.* Thousand Oakes, Sage.

Berman, Sherri (1998). *The social democratic movement: ideas and politics in the making of interwar Europe.* Cambridge, Harvard University Press.

Bernhard, Nancy E. (1999). *U.S. television news and cold war propaganda.* Cambridge, Cambridge University Press.

Bird, S. Elizabeth and Dardenne, Robert W. (1988). Myth, chronicle, and story: exploring the narrative, in Cary, James W. (ed.) (1988). *Media, myth and narratives – television and the press.* Newbury Park, Sage.

Blumenthal, Sidney (1982). *The permanent campaign.* New York, Simon and Schuster.
Blyth, Mark (2002). *Great transformations: the rise and decline of embedded liberalism,* Cambridge, Cambridge University Press.

Block, Stephen (1992). Free trade on television: the triumph of business rhetoric, *Canadian Journal of Communication.* No. 17.

Boczkowski, Pablo J. (2004). *Digitising the news – innovation in online newspapers.* Cambridge, The MIT Press.

Boorstin, Daniel (1961). *The image.* Harmondsworth, Penguin.

Borgmann, Albert (2000). *Holding on to reality – the nature of information at the turn of the millennium.* Chicago, The University of Chicago Press.

Bourdieu, Pierre (1991). *Language and symbolic power.* (edited and introduced by John B. Thompson). Cambridge, Polity Press.

Boyd, Tony (2006). Policies hold Australia back. *The Australian Financial Review.* 15 March.

Boyd, Tony (2004). How the dragon is slaying its rivals. *The Australian Financial Review.* 2 Nov.

Brock, Gerald W. (2002). *The second information revolution.* Cambridge, Harvard University Press.

Brook, Stephen and Brown, Maggie (2006). More people watch the TV than use the net, listen to the radio or read newspapers. *Guardian.* 27 March. http://media.guardian.co.uk/print/ Downloaded 28 March.

Browne, Peter, Thomas, Julian (2005). *A win and a prayer – scenes from the 2004 Australian election.* Sydney, University of New South Wales Press Ltd.

Bruns, Axel (2003). Gatewatching not gatekeeping: collaborative online news. *Media International Australia incorporating Culture and Policy.* No. 107.

Buchanan, Matt (2002). It's the politics, stupid. *The Sydney Morning Herald The Guide.* 20 July.

Budzinski, Oliver (2003). *Pluralism of competition policy paradigms and the call for regulatory diversity.* Paper presented at the New York University. 10June. p. 4. (citing permission needed).

Burge, Glenn and Kitney, Geoff (1995). Lew quits as Coles chief. *The Sydney Morning Herald.* 20 Oct. p. 1. Downloaded 12 June 2006. http://global.factiva.com.ezproxy.library.usyd.edu.au/ha/default.aspx

Burton, Tom (2006). Turn on, tune in, read on. *The Sydney Morning Herald.* 17 Feb. p. 14. Downloaded 9 March. http://global.factiva.com.ezproxy.library.usyd.edu.au/ha/default.aspx

Busse, Jeffrey A. and Green, T. Clifton (2002). Market efficiency in real time. *Journal of Financial Economics.* 65 issue. 3.

Callaghan, Greg (1999). Sultans of spin. *The Australian.* 24 June.

Canning, Simon (2005). Blogs and banners strive to coexist. *The Australian.* 19 May. p. 17. Downloaded 15 March. http://global.factiva.com.ezproxy.library.usyd.edu.au/ha/default.aspx

Carew, Edna (1997). Showdown behind Westpac's boardroom brawl. *The Sydney Morning Herald*, 30 Aug.

Carroll, William K. and Hackett, Robert A (2006). Democratic media activism through a lens of social movement theory. *Media, Culture & Society.* Vol. 28 (1).

Chalaby, Jean K. (2005). *Transnational television worldwide.* London. I.B. Tauris & Co. Ltd.

— (2003). Television for a new global order: transnational television networks and the formation of global systems. *Gazette: the international journal for communication studies.* Vol 65(6).

Chapman, Nigel (2006). BBC's new China website is for language teaching and is not designed to appease Beijing authorities. *Guardian*. 7 Feb. Downloaded 8 Feb. http://media.guardian.co.uk/print/

Chulov, Martin (2002). Hacks or flacks - media economics are blurring the lines between journalism and public relations. *The Australian*. 22 Aug.

Cleaver, Harry M. (1998). The Zapatista effect: the internet and the rise of an alternative political fabric. *Journal of International Affairs*. Spring. 51. no. 2.

Cohen, Elisia L. (2002). Online journalism as market-drive journalism. *Journal of Broadcasting & Electronic Media*. Dec. 46(4).

Cooke, Lynne (2005). A visual convergence of print, television and the internet: charting 40 years of design presentation in news presentation. *New Media & Society*. vol 7(1).

Corner, John (1998). Television news and economic exposition, in Gavin, Neil T. (ed.) *The economy, media and public knowledge*. London, Leicester University Press.

Costar, Brian and Browne, Peter (2005). The aftermath. How Labor lost. in (eds.) Browne, Peter, and Thomas, Julian (2005). *A win and a prayer – scenes from the 2004 Australian election*. Sydney, University of New South Wales Press.

Costa, Gabrielle (2004). Signature takes a belting after juice deal sours. *The Age*. 13 Aug.

Cottle, Simon (2003). News, public relations and power: mapping the field. Cottle, Simon (eds.) *News, public relations and power*. London, Sage.

— (2000). Rethinking news access, *Journalism Studies*, Vol. 1. No. 3. 2000.

Cox, Geoffrey (1995). *Pioneering television news – a first hand report on a revolution in journalism*. London. John Libbey & Company Ltd.

Crisp, Lyndall (2002). Spin specialists. *The Australian Financial Review*. 13 Sept. p. 20. Downloaded 24 June 2005. http://0global.factiva.com.opac.library.usyd.edu.au/en/arch/display.asp

Cummins, Carolyn (2004). Lowy pledges to stay put. *The Sydney Morning Herald*. 26 June.

Cunningham, Stuart and Turner, Graeme (eds.) (1993). *The media in Australia – industries, texts, audiences*. St Leonards, Allen & Unwin.

Curthoys, Ann (1986). The getting of television, dilemmas in ownership, control and culture, 1941-56. in Curthoys, Ann and Merritt, John (eds.). *Better dead than red – Australia's first cold war 1945-1959*. Sydney, Allen & Unwin.

Curthoys, Ann (1991). Television before television. *Continuum: the Australian Journal of Media and Culture*. Vol. 4 No. 2.

Dale, Brian (1985). *Ascent to power*. Sydney, Allen & Unwin.

Davies, Brian (1981). *Those fabulous TV years*. North Ryde, Cassell Australia.

Davis, Aeron (2002). *Public relations democracy - public relations, politics and the mass media in Britain*. Manchester, Manchester University Press.

— (2000). Public relations, news production and changing patterns of source access in the British national media. *Media, Culture & Society*. Vol. 22.

— (2003). Whither mass media and power? Evidence for a critical elite theory alternative. *Media, Culture & Society*, Vol. 25.

Day, Mark (2005). Aunty will keep the Australia Channel credible. *The Australian*. 15 Sept. p. 18. Downloaded 10 March 2006. http://global.factiva.com.ezproxy.library.usyd.edu.au/ha/default.aspx

— (2004). Online players come of age. *The Australian*. p. 20. 21 Oct. Downloaded 15 March. http://global.factiva.com.ezproxy.library.usyd.edu.au/ha/default.aspx

— (2000). Crikey! It's a stuff-up! *The Australian*. Media. 13 July 2000. Downloaded 14 March 2006. http://global.factiva.com.ezproxy.library.usyd.edu.au/ha/default.aspx

Deans, Alan (1986). What the economic gurus say and how they make it happen. *Business Review Weekly*. 7 March.

Derkley, Karin (2003). Banks go with the new flow. *The Sydney Morning Herald*. 5 Aug. p. 5. Downloaded 21 March 2006. http://global.factiva.com.ezproxy.library.usyd.edu.au/ha/default.aspx

Deuze, Mark (2003). The web and its journalisms; considering the consequences of different types of news media online. *New Media & Society*. Vol. 5(2).

Diba, Ahmad and Stein, Nicholas (2000). We came. We clicked. We conquered. *Fortune*. 20 March. Downloaded 21 March 2003. http://money.cnn.com/magazines.fortune.fortune_archive/2000/03/20/276355/index.

Dibble, James (1985). ABC news is dead, *The Australian Financial Review*. 15 March.

Dickie, Mure and Edgecliffe-Johnson, Andrew (2006). BBC tones down news on new China website. *Guardian*. 4 Feb. Downloaded 8 Feb. 2006. http://media.guardian.co.uk/print/

Digital convergence – TV on your phone. *The Economist*. 13 Jan. 2005. Downloaded 5 April 2006. http://www.economist.com/PrinterFriendly.cfm?story_id=3566995.

Disney, Julian and Nethercote J.R. (eds.) (1996). *The house on capital hill – Parliament, politics and power in the national capital*. Leichhardt, The Federation Press.

Domingo, David (2005). *The difficult shift from utopia to realism in the internet era*. Paper from the First European Communication Conference – Amsterdam 2005. Downloaded 30 March 2006. http://racocatala.com/dutopia/docs/domingo_amsterdam2005.pdf

Donovan, Robert J. and Scherer (1992). *Unsilent revolution: television news and American public life*. Cambridge, Cambridge University Press.

Drezner, Daniel W. and Farrell, Harry (2004). *The power and politics of blogs*. paper presented to the August 2004 American Political Science Association. Downloaded 4 April 2006. http://www.henryfarrell.net/blogpaperapsa.pdf

— and — (2004). Web of influence. *Foreign Policy*. Nov./Dec. Downloaded 4 April 2006. http://www.foreignpolicy.com/story/cms.php?story_id=2707

Dreier, Peter (1988), the corporate complaint against the media, in Hiebert, R. and Reuss, C. (eds.) *Impact of mass media*. New York, Longman.

— (1982). Capitalists vs. the media; an analysis of an ideological mobilisation among business leaders. *Media, Culture & Society*. 4.

Elliott, Geoff (2004). Centres of attention. *The Australian,* 24 June.

Elliott, Hugh (1960). The three-way struggle of press, radio and TV in Australia. *Journalism Quarterly,* Spring 1960.

Elster, Jon (1989). *Nuts and bolts for the social sciences.* Cambridge, Cambridge University Press.

Emerson, Scott (2000). Few tears for Kerry outside the golden triangle. *The Australian,* 16 Dec.

Epstein, Edward Jay (1973). *News from nowhere: television and the news.* New York, Random House.

Eriksen, Erik Oddvar, and Weigard, Jarle (2003). *Understanding Habermas: communicative action and deliberative democracy.* London, Continuum.

Federation of Australian Commercial Television Stations submission to the Senate Standing Committee on Education, Science and the Arts, 18 July1972.

Fell, Liz (1985). Impacts of AUSSAT. *Media Information Australia.* No. 38.

Fels, Alan and Brenchley, Fred (2006). Digital TV rules a farce. *The Australian Financial Review.* 7 March. p. 62. Downloaded 9 March 2006.

Fish, Stanley (1980). *Is there a text in this class? The authority of interpretive communities.* Cambridge, Harvard University Press.

Flew, Terry (2002). *New media: an introduction.* South Melbourne, Oxford University Press.
Foisie, Geoffrey (1992). Television and business news: a bull market. *Television Quarterly.* Winter v. 25 n. 4.

Fox, Catherine (1999). PR gets bad press from journalists. *The Australian Financial Review,* 5 Oct.

Freeman, Jane. (1987). The battle for the big spenders. *The Sydney Morning Herald. The Guide.* 11 Aug.

Fishman, Mark (1980). *Manufacturing the news.* Austin. University of Texas Press.

Frey, Bruno, Benesch, Christine and Stutzer (2005). *Does watching TV make us happy? Working Paper No. 2005-15.* Centre for Research in Economics, Management and the Arts. Downloaded 20 Feb 2006. http://www.crema-research.ch/papers/2005-15.pdf

Freudenberg, Graham (1977). *A certain grandeur: Gough Whitlam in politics.* South Melbourne, Macmillan.

Fully equipped Services For News. *The Sydney Morning Herald ATN Supplement.* 3 Dec. 1956.

Gans, Herbert J. (2003). *Democracy and the news.* New York, Oxford University Press.
— (1985). Are U.S. journalists dangerously liberal? *Columbia Journalism Review.* Nov/Dec.

— (1979). *Deciding what's news.* New York, Pantheon Books.

Garcia Aviles, Jose and Leon, Bienvenido (2002). Journalistic practice in digital television newsrooms: the case of Spain's Tele 5 and Antena 3. *Journalism* 3(3).

Gare, Shelley (2000). Independent news keeps us honest. *The Australian.* 12 Feb. Downloaded 14 March 2006. http://global.factiva.com.ezproxy.library.usyd.edu.au/ha/default.aspx

Gavin, Neil T, and Sanders, David (1998). Television, economy and the public's political attitudes. Gavin, Neil T. (ed.). in *The economy, media and public knowledge.* London, Leicester University Press.

— and — (1996). The impact of television news on public perceptions of the economy and government. in Farrell, David et al (eds.) *British parties and elections yearbook 1996*. London, Frank Cass.

Gerdes, Peter and Charlier, Paul (1985). *TV news – that's the way it was*. North Ryde. Australian Film and Television School.

Gibson, Owen (2005). The bloggers have all the best news. *Guardian*. 6 June. Downloaded 7 June 2005.http://media.guardian.co.uk/print/0,3858,5208852-105337,00html

— (2005). We had 50 images within an hour. Blogs. *Guardian*. 11 July. Downloaded 12 July 2005. htt://media.guardian..co.uk/print0,3858,5235536-105337,00.html

Gilchrist, Michelle (2001). Self-monitoring - Budget 2001 - The Aftermath, *The Australian* 26 May.

Gitlin, Todd (1980). *The whole world is watching: mass media in the making and unmaking of the new left*. Berkeley, University of California Press.

Gluyas, Richard (2005). Business whiz ventures afield. *The Age*. 17 March. Downloaded 8 March 2006. http://global.factiva.com.ezproxy.library.usyd.edu.au/ha/default.aspx

Goddard P. Corner, J. Gavin, N. Richardson, K. (1998). Economic news and the dynamics of understanding: the Liverpool project in Gavin, Neil, T. (ed.) *The economy, media and public knowledge*. London, Leicester University Press.

Goggin, Gerard (2004). *Virtual nation - the internet in Australia*. Sydney. University of New South Wales Press Ltd.

Goldberg, Bernard (2001). *Bias - a CBS insider exposes how the media distort the news*. Washington, Regnery Publishing, Inc.

Goldblatt, Henry (1998). People: Sorry guys, she's taken. *Fortune*. 26 October. Vol. 138, Issue: 8.

Goldenberg, Suzanne (2006). A moral minefield for corporate America. *Guardian*. 20 Feb. Downloaded 21 Feb. 2006. http://media.guardian.co.uk/print/

Goldwords £10,000 goes off. *The Sunday Telegraph*. 16 Sept. 1956.

Gorman, Lyn (1998). Menzies and television: a medium he endured. *Media International Australia 87*. May.

Grant, Richard (2004). *Federal government advertising. Research note No. 62*. 21 June. Parliamentary Library.

Gray, Patrick (2005). New media hands power to the people. *The Age*.18 Oct. p. 4. Downloaded 15 March 2006.

Grattan, Michelle (1996). Sharing the same kennel; the press in Parliament House. in (eds.) Disney, Julian and Nethercote, J.R. *The house on Capital Hill - Parliament, politics and power in the national capital*. Leichhardt, The Federation Press.

— (1998) The politics of spin. *Australian Studies in Journalism*. 7:1998:32-45, p. 43.

Gunther, Marc (1999). There's no business like business show business: how CNBC grew from an ugly duckling into a network to make a peacock proud. *Fortune*. 24 May. Downloaded 25 April 2000.

Gurgle - enthusiasm for Google drains away as doubts set in (2006). *The Economist*. 16 Feb. Downloaded 28 Aug. 2006. http://www.economist.com/

Gysen, Joos, Bruyninckx, Hans and Bachus, Kris (2006). The modus narrandi - a methodology for evaluating effects of environmental policy, *Evaluation*. Vol 12 (1).

Halavais, Alexander (2000). National borders on the world wide web. *New Media & Society*. Vol 1(3).

Hall, Peter A. (ed.) (1989). *The political power of economic ideas, Keynesianism across nations*. Princeton, Princeton University Press.

Hall, Sandra (1976). *Supertoy: twenty years of television*. South Melbourne. Sun Books

Hall, Stuart (ed.) (1980). *Culture, media, language : working papers in cultural studies. 1972-79*. London, Hutchinson.

Harrison, Jackie (2000). *Terrestrial TV News in Britain: The Culture of Production*. Manchester, Manchester University Press.

Hartcher, Peter and Wade, Matt (2006). Bank chief's parting shot at PM on rates. *The Sydney Morning Herald*. 19 Aug.

— and Wade, Matt (2005). Reserve feared it was used as election pawn, *The Sydney Morning Herald*. 8 April.

Hay, Colin (2002). *Political analysis*. Houndmills, Palgrave.

Hayward, Mathew L.A. Rindova, Violina P. and Pollock, Timothy G. (2004). Believing one's own press: the causes and consequences of CEO celebrity. *Strategic Management Journal*, 25.

Henderson, Ian (2000). PM passes the buck to RBA. *The Australian*, 24 March.

Hargreaves, Ian and Thomas , James (2002). *New news, old news*. UK Independent Television Commission and the Broadcasting Standards Commission. pp. 76-77.

Henderson, Gerard (1987). The rat pack. *IPA Review*. Aug-Oct.

Henderson, Willie, Dudley-Evans, Tony and Backhouse, Roger (eds.) (1993). *Economics and language*. London, Routledge.

Heywood. Greg (1985). Taking the money and the box. *The Australian Financial Review*. 27 Feb.

Henningham, John (1997). Characteristics and attitudes of Australia's finance journalists. *Economic Analysis & Policy*. Vol. 27 No. 1 March.

— (1995). Political journalists' political and professional values. *Australian Journal of Political Science*. Vol. 30.

— (1988). *Looking at television news*. Melbourne, Longman Cheshire.

Herman, Edward S. and McChesney, Robert W. (1997). *The global media – the new missionaries of corporate capitalism*. London, Continuum.

Himowitz, Michael J. (1995). Cyberspace: the investor's new edge. *Fortune*. 25 Dec. Downloaded 21 March 2006. http://money.cnn.com/magazines.fortune.fortune_archive/1995/12/25/208771index.h

Hofstetter, C. Richard. (1976). *Bias in the news – network television coverage of the 1972 election campaign*. Columbus, Ohio State University Press.

Holland, Ian (2002). *Accountability of ministerial staff? Research paper 19 2001-2*. Parliament of Australia.

Hooks, Barbara (1994). Crusading for better odds in small business. *The Age. Green guide*. 22 Sept.

Horsfall, J.C. (1974). *The Liberal era*. Melbourne. Sun Books.

Household use of Information Technology 2004-5. 8146.0. Australian Bureau of Statistics. Downloaded 7 March 2006. http://www.abs.gov.au/

Hosking, Patrick (1996). Rate fall a cruel cut for some. *The Sydney Morning Herald*. 12 Aug.

Houston, Frank (1999). What I saw in the digital sea. *Columbia Journalism Review*. Downloaded 28 March 2006. http://archives.cjr.org/year/99/4/index.asp

Hubble, Ava (1993). Antenna. *The Sydney Morning Herald The Guide*, 15 March. Downloaded 10 March 2006. http://global.factiva.com.ezproxy.library.usyd.edu.au/ha/default.aspx

Hudson, Phillip (2000). Face music on rates, RBA chief urged, *The Age*. 25 March. Business p.
Hughes, Colin A. and Western, John S. (1966). *The prime minister's policy speech – a case study in televised politics*. Canberra, Australian National University Press.

Hughes, Duncan (2005). GE seeks to work Wizard magic in Asia and the US. *The Australian Financial Review*. 15 July.

Hughes, Tim (2000) Aunty's signals are a lifeline for the bush. *The Australian*, 20 Dec.

Humphries, David (2005). Scrutiny, like nostalgia, has become a thing of the past. *The Sydney Morning Herald*. 1 Oct.

Hungary revolt on TCN. *Daily Telegraph*. 6 Nov. 1956.

Hurst, John (1988). *The Walkley Awards – Australia's best journalism*. Richmond, John Kerr Pty Ltd.

Hywood. Greg (1985). Taking the money and the box. *The Australian Financial Review*. 27 Feb.

Ingham, Bernard (2003). *The wages of spin - a clear case of communications gone wrong*. London, John Murray.

Inglis, K.S. (1983). *This is the ABC*. Melbourne. Melbourne University Press.

Internet Activity. 8153.0. Mar 2005 Australia, Australian Bureau of Statistics. Downloaded 7 March 2006. http://www.abs.gov.au/

It's here, at last! (1956). *Daily Telegraph*. 17 Sept.

Iyengar, Shanto and Kinder, Donald R. (1987). *News that matters - television and American opinion*. Chicago, The University of Chicago Press.

Jacka, Liz (2004). Doing the history of television in Australia: problems and challenges. *Continuum: Journal of Media & Cultural Studies*. Vol. 18, No. 1, March.

— and Johnson, Lesley (1998). Australia. in Smith, Anthony and Paterson, Richard (eds.) *Television - an international history*. Oxford, Oxford University Press.

Jackson, Sally (2004). Business steals the show. *The Australian*. 29 April.

Johnson, Bobbie (2006). Britain turns off – and logs on. *Guardian*. 8 March. Downloaded 9 March. http://media.guardian.co.uk/print/0,,3299429230-105236,00.html

Johnstone, Roger (1986). TV gets taste for business. *Australian Business*. 9 April.

Jones, Colin and Bednall, David (1980). *Television in Australia – its history through the ratings*. (location n/a) Australian Broadcasting Tribunal.

Jordan, Tim (1999). *Cyberpower: the culture and politics of cyberspace and the Internet*. London, Routledge.

Kellner, Douglas (1990). *Television and the crisis of democracy*. Boulder, Westview Press.

Kelly, Hugo (2006). Website jettisons the larrikin 'who put noses out of joint'. *The Australian*. 16 Feb. p. 15. Downloaded 8 March 2006. http://global.factiva.com.ezproxy.library.usyd.edu.au/ha/default.aspx

Kelly, Kevin (2005). Unto us the machine is born. *The Sydney Morning Herald*. 15 Nov. Downloaded 18 Nov. 2005. http://smh.com.au/articles/2005/11/14/1131816858554.html? page=3

Kelly, Paul (1999). The paradox of pessimism, in Waldren, Murray (ed.). *Future tense – Australia beyond election 1998*. St Leonards, Allen & Unwin.

— (1991). Who runs Australia? The press gallery or the parliament? *Gerard Henderson's Media Watch*. June-July 1991.

King,Barrie,*Newsreels*.http://wwwmcc.murdoch.edu.au/ReadingRoom/fillm/image/King.html[1]www.phm.gov.au /hsc/**snowy**/investigating.htm

Kitchener, Jennifer (1999). in Curthoys, A. and Schultz, J. (eds.), *Journalism: print, politics and popular culture*. St Lucia, University of Queensland Press.

Knobloch-Westerwick, Silvia; Sharma, Nikhil; Hansen, Derek L. and Alter, Scott (2005). Impact of popularity indications on readers' selective exposure to online news. *Journal of Broadcasting and Electronic Media*. Sept. 49(3).

Kollmeyer, Christopher J. (2004). Corporate interests: how the news media portray the economy. *Social Problems*. Vol 51, No. 3.

Koutsoukis, Jason (2005). Howard's 'orgy of ads' in lead up to poll, *The Age*. 24 March. p. 3.

Kurtz, Howard (2002). On CNBC, boosters for the boom. *The Washington Post*. 12 Nov. p. AO1. Downloaded 16 March 2006. http://global.factiva.com.ezproxy.library.usyd.edu.au/ha/default.aspx

— (2000). *The fortune tellers: inside Wall Street's game of money, media and manipulation*. New York, The Free Press.

— (1998). *Spin cycle – inside the Clinton propaganda machine*. London, Pan Books.

Kuwabara, Ko (2005). Affective attachment in electronic markets : a sociological study of eBay. in Nee, Victor and Swedberg, Richard (eds.) *The economic sociology of capitalism*. Princeton, Princeton University Press.

Lawrence, Mark (1993). Money – a winner boom or bust. *Green Guide. The Age.*. 26 Aug. p. 1.

Lee, Joo-hee (2005). Internet a key playing field for politicians, but has pitfalls. *The Korea Herald*. 11 Feb. Downloaded 28 March 2006. http://www.asiamedia.ucla.edu/article.asp?parentid=20688.

Lee, Martin A. and Solomon, Norman (1991). *Unreliable sources – a guide to detecting bias in news media.* New York, A Lyle Stuart Book, Carol Publishing Group.

Lee, Tien-Tsung (2005). The liberal media myth revisited: an examination of factors influencing perceptions of media bias. *Journal of Broadcasting and Electronic Media.* March. 49(1).

Lehmann, John (2006). Internet 'threat to pay-TV. *The Australian.* 10 March. Downloaded 7 April. http://global.factiva.com.ezproxy.library.usyd.edu.au/ha/default.aspx

Lehmann, John and Lewis, Steve (2006). Reforms to spark media frenzy. *The Australian.* 15 March.

Leys, Nick (2004). Strewth. *The Australian.* 22 Nov. p. 10. Downloaded 15 March 2006. http://global.factiva.com.ezproxy.library.usyd.edu.au/ha/default.aspx

Lichter, Robert S. and Rothman, Stanley (1988). Media and business elites, in Hiebert, Ray Eldon and Reuss, Carol (eds.), *Impact of mass media: current issues,* New York, Longman.

Lieberman, Trudy (2004). Answer the &%$#* question! *Columbia Journalism Review.* vol. 42 issue 5. 1 Jan.

Lloyd, C.J. (1988). *Parliament and the press – the Federal Parliamentary Press Gallery 1901- 88.* Carlton, Melbourne University Press.

— (1985). *Profession - journalist; a history of the Australian Journalists' Association.* Marrickville, Hale & Iremonger.

Lunn, Stephen (1997) Fischer salutes support for bush. *The Australian.* 25 Jan.

MacDougall, Kent A. (1988). Boring from within the bourgeois press (part 1). *Monthly Review,* Nov. 1988 v40 n6.

Macfarlane, I.J. (2006). Economic news: do we get too much of it? Notes for a talk to *The Australian Financial Review* leader's luncheon. Sydney. 28 April. Downloaded 17 Aug. 2006. http://www.rba.gov.au/Speeches/2006/sp_gov_280406.html.

MacGregor, Brent (1999). Making television news in the satellite age, in MacKay, Hugh and O'Sullivan (eds.) *The media reader – continuity and transformation.* London, Sage.

MacKay, Hugh and O'Sullivan (eds.) (1999) *The media reader – continuity and transformation.* London, Sage.

MacLean, Sheena (2005). Papers deliver at the big end of town. *The Australian.* 24 Nov. Downloaded 7 April. http://global.factiva.com.ezproxy.library.usyd.edu.au/ha/default.aspx

Mah, Sadie (2001). CNBC local drive kicks off with Aussie launch. *Media.* 16 Feb. Downloaded 24 March 2006. http://global.factiva.com.ezproxy.library.usyd.edu.au/ha/default.aspx

Market Watch (2004). *The Australian.* 11 June.

Marr, David (2005). Static from the newsfront, *The Sydney Morning Herald.* 5 March.

Marsh, D. and Stoker, G. (2002). *Theory and methods in political science,* 2nd Edition. Hampshire, Palgrave Macmillan.

Marshall, Ian, and Kingsbury, Damien (1996). *Media realities: the news media and power in Australian society.* South Melbourne, Addison Wesley Longman Australia Pty Limited.

Marshall, Jill, and Werndly, Angela (2002). *The language of television,* London, Routledge.

Martin, A.W. (1993). Robert Menzies: a life Vol. 1, 1894-1943. Carlton, Melbourne University Press, p 399. quoted in Gorman, Lyn (1998). Menzies and television: a medium he 'endured'. *Media International Australia incorporating Culture and Policy*. No. 87 – May 1987.

Martin, Dick (2004). Corporate reputation: reputational mythraking, *The Journal of Business Strategy*. Vol. 25. Iss. 6.

Martin, Louise (1994). ABC does business on Saturday. *The Age. Green Guide*. 9 June.

Martinson, Jane (2005). Television took 30 years to reach a mass market - broadband took three. *The Guardian*. 14 July. 2005.

Masterton, Murray and Patching, Roger (1997). *Now the news in detail; a guide to broadcast journalism in Australia*. 3rd edition. Geelong, Deakin University Press.

McAnulla, Stuart (2002). Structure and agency. in Marsh, David and Stoker, Gerry (eds.) *Theory and methods in political science*, 2nd ed. Basingstoke, Palgrave Macmillan.

McCloskey, Donald (1985). *The rhetoric of economics*. Madison, University of Wisconsin Press.

McClure, Robert D. and Patterson, Thomas E. (1976). Print vs. network news. *Journal of Communication*. April, 26.2.

McElvogue, Louise (1985). Making immediacy the measure. *New Journalist*. No. 46.

Meet the Press sponsored by electrical co. *RTN: Radio Television News*. 31 May 1957.

McGrath, Catherine (2005). PM - Trust my record: Howard's IR guarantee. *ABC Radio PM*, 10 Oct. http://www.abc.net.au/pm/content/2005/s1478936.htm

McKee, Alan (2002). Textual analysis, in Cunningham, Stuart, and Turner, Graeme, (eds.) *The media and communications in Australia*. Crows Nest, Allen and Unwin.

McNicoll, David (1979). *Luck's a fortune*. Sydney, Wildcat Press.

McQuail, Denis (1992). *Mass communication and the public interest*. London, Sage.

Meindl, James R., Ehrlich, Sanford B. and Dukerich, Janet M. (1985). The romance of leadership. *Administrative Science Quarterly*. 30.

Metherell, Mark and Allard, Tom (2004). Labor crumbles on PBS charges. *The Sydney Morning Herald*. 23 June.

Meyer, Philip (2004). *The vanishing newspaper: saving journalism in the information age*. Columbia. University of Missouri Press. eBook.

Miller, Gretchen (1994). Shooting from the hip pocket. *The Sydney Morning Herald The Guide*. 11 July.

Mills, Stephen (1993) *The Hawke years*. Ringwood, Viking.

Mitchell, Sue (2004). Things even better with Coke. *The Australian Financial Review*. 11 June.

Moe, Terry M. (2003). *Power and political institutions*. Paper delivered at the conference Crafting and Operating Institutions, Yale University, April 11-13, 2003. downloaded from http://www.yale.edu/coic/moe.doc

Money (1997). Sectional survey, August 1997, Detailed Findings, Taverner Research.

Murdoch's Asian maze (1994). *The Economist*. 26 March. Downloaded 11 March 2006.
http://global.factiva.com.ezproxy.library.usyd.edu.au/ha/default.aspx

Murdoch, Lindsay (1992). A matter of softly softly for Auntie's Asian invasion. *The Australian*. 1 Dec. p. 17.
Downloaded 10 March 2006. http://global.factiva.com.ezproxy.library.usyd.edu.au/ha/default.aspx

Murphy, Cherelle and Bassanese, David (2005). Costello under fire over rates comments. *The Australian Financial Review*, 19 Aug.

Murphy, Cherelle (2004). Labor promise on housing. *The Australian Financial Review*. 29 June. p. 1
Downloaded 13 June 2006. http://global.factiva.com.ezproxy.library.usyd.edu.au/aa/default.aspx?

Nagy, Joe (1997). *In over our heads*. Pymble, HarperBusiness.

Neuchterlein, Jonathan E. and Weiser, Philip J. (2005). *Digital crossroads – American telecommunications policy in the internet age*. Cambridge, The MIT Press.

Nickelsburg, Michael, and Norpoth, Helmut (2000). Commander-in-chief or chief economist? The president in the eye of the public. *Electoral Studies*. 19 (2-3).

"Nightwatch" van chases the news. *RTN: Radio Television news*. 4 Dec. 1959.

Norris, Pippa (2000). *A virtuous circle – political communications in postindustrial societies*. Cambridge, Cambridge University Press.

— (1998). *Blaming the messenger: television and civic malaise*. Paper for the Public Trust and Democratic Governance in the Trilateral Democracies. Bellagio, Italy, 29 June - 3 July.

— and Sanders, David, (1998). *Does balance matter? Experiments in TV news*, paper presented at the Annual Meeting of the American Political Science Association, Boston 3-6 Sept.

Not contemplating force – Menzies on Suez Canal. *The Sydney Morning Herald*. 19 Sept. 1956.

O'Regan Tom (1993). *Australian television culture*. St Leonards. Allen & Unwin.

Odlyzko, A. (2001). Content is not king. *First Monday*. 2(6).
http://www.firstmonday.dk/issues/issue6_2/odlyzko/index.html

100,000 crowd sets for Aust. television debut. *The Daily Telegraph*. 17 Sept. 1956.

Opening of ATN tonight *The Sun-Herald*. 2 Dec. 1956.

Opening of TV station. *The Sun-Herald*, 28 Oct.1956.

Ornstein, Norman J. and Mann Thomas E. (2000). *The permanent campaign and its future*. Washington, American Enterprise Institute.

Orwell, George (1945). *Politics and the English language*. http://www.k-1.com/Orwell/pol.htm

Packer, Frank (1956). We are proud pioneers in Australian TV. *The Sunday Telegraph*, 16 Sept.

Packer, Steve (1989). Behind Robert Gottliebsen. *The Sydney Morning Herald Good Weekend*. 22 July.

Palmer, Jerry (2000). *Spinning into control – news values and source strategies*. London, Leicester University Press.

2, Derek (1990). *The courtesans – the press gallery in the Hawke era*. North Sydney, Allen & Unwin.
Parsons, Wayne (1990). *The power of the financial press*. New Brunswick, Rutgers University Press.

Pavlik, John V. (1999). New media and news – implications for the future of journalism. *New Media & Society*. 1(1).

Payne, Trish (1999). *The Canberra Press Gallery and the Backbench of the 38ᵗʰ Parliament 1996-98*. Canberra, Department of the Parliamentary library.

Peach, Bill (1992). *This Day Tonight: how Australian current affairs TV came of age*. Sydney. Australian Broadcasting Corporation.

Pearson, Mark and Brand, Jeffrey (2001). *Sources of news and current affairs*, Sydney, Australian Broadcasting Authority.

Petersen, Neville (1999). *Whose news? Organisational conflict in the ABC, 1947-1999*. Australian Journalism Monographs. Department of Journalism. Brisbane. University of Queensland.

— (1993). *News not views - the ABC, the press, & politics 1932 - 1947*. Sydney, Hale & Iremonger.

Philip Meyer (2004). *The vanishing newspaper: saving journalism in the information age*. Columbia. University of Missouri Press.

Phillipps, Richard (2002). *Media advisors: shadow players in political communication*. Unpublished PhD thesis. University of Sydney Fisher Library.

Philo, Greg (1999). *Message received: Glasgow media group research, 1993-1998*. Harlow, Longman.

— and Beharrell, Peter and Hewitt, John (1995). Reasonable mean and responsible citizens. Economic news. in Philo, Greg, (eds.), *Glasgow Media Group Reader, Volume 2*, London, Routledge.

P.M. on Channel 9. *The Daily Telegraph*. 19 Sept. 1956.

Postman, Neil (1985). *Amusing ourselves to death: public discourse in the age of show business*. New York, Viking.

Prensky, Mark (2001). Digital natives, digital immigrants. *On The Horizon*. Vol.9. No. 5. Oct.

Price, Matt (2000). *The 7.30 Report's* sad state of affairs, *The Australian*, 16 June.

Pringle, John Douglas (1973). *Have pen: will travel*. London, Chatto & Windus.

Putnis, Peter (1994). *Displaced, re-cut and recycled: file-tape in television news*. Gold Coast. Centre for Journalism Research & Education, Bond University.

Raboy, Marc (2002). Media policy in the new communications environments, in Raboy, Marc (ed.) *Global media policy in the new millennium*. Luton, University of Luton Press.
Raymond, Robert (1999). *Out of the box - an inside view of the coming of current affairs and documentaries to Australian television*. Henley Beach, Seaview Press.

Reese, Stephen D. (1990). The news paradigm and the ideology of objectivity. *Critical Studies in Mass Communication*, 1990. Vol. 7.

Rehn, Alison (2004). Funding a flow-on to save our waterways. *The Daily Telegraph*, 26 June.

Religious talk and news on TCN Channel 9. *Daily Telegraph*, 18 Aug. 1956.

Report of the Royal Commission on Television (1954). Canberra, Commonwealth Government Printer.

Rheingold, Howard (2000). *The virtual community: homesteading on the electronic frontier*. Cambridge, MIT Press.

Richardson, Graham (1994). *Whatever it takes*. Sydney, Bantam.

Rickard, Maurice (2004). How much will the PBS cost? Projected trends in Commonwealth expenditure. *Department of Parliamentary Services Research Note No. 29*. 10 Feb.

Robins, Kevin and Aksoy, Asu (2005). Whoever looks always finds: transnational viewing and knowledge-experience. in Chalaby, Jean K. (ed.). *Transnational television worldwide – towards a new media order*. London, I.B. Tauris & Co. Ltd.

Robinson, Susan (2006). The mission of the j-blog: recapturing journalistic authority online. *Journalism*. Vol. 7(1).

Rogers, Everett M. with Shoemaker, F. Floyd (1971). *Communication of innovations – a cross-cultural approach*. New York, The Free Press.

Sanders, David and Gavin Neil (2004). Television news, economic perceptions and political preferences in Britain, 1997-2001. *The Journal of Politics*. Vol. 66, No. 4, November.

Seaton, Jean (2003). How the audience is made. in Curran, James and Seaton, Jean. *Power without responsibility: the press, broadcasting and new media in Britain*. London, Routledge.

Satellite broadcasting in Asia - earth-bound (1999). *The Economist*. 16 Oct. Downloaded 10 March 2006. http://global.factiva.com.ezproxy.library.usyd.edu.au/ha/default.aspx

Scannell, Paddy. Schlesinger, Philip. And Sparks, Colin. (eds.) (1992). *Culture and power : a media, culture & society reader*. London, Sage.

Schlesinger, Philip (1978). *Putting 'reality' together: BBC news*. London, Constable.

Scheuer, Jeffrey (2001). *The sound bite society – how television helps the right and hurts the left*. New York, Routledge.

Schultz, Julianne (1992). in (eds.) Horne, Donald. *The trouble with economic rationalism*. Newham, Scribe publications Pty Ltd.

— (1998). *Reviving the fourth estate: democracy, accountability and the media*. Cambridge, Cambridge University Press.

— (ed.) (1994). *Not just another business: journalists, citizens and the media*. Sydney, Pluto Press.

— (ed.) (1993). *Reporting business – a report into the attitudes, values and practice of business, finance and economics journalism in Australia*. Sydney, Australian Centre for Independent Journalism.

— and Matolcsy, Zoltan (1993). Business boosters or impartial critics. in Schultz (ed.) (1993). *Reporting business – a report into the attitudes, values and practice of business, finance and economics journalism in Australia*. Sydney, Australian Centre for Independent Journalism.

— (1992). in (eds.) Horne, Donald. *The trouble with economic rationalism*. Newham, Scribe Publications Pty Ltd.

Seligman, Martin (2002). *Authentic happiness*. Milsons Point, Random House.

Semmler, Clement (1981). *The ABC - aunt Sally and the sacred cow*. Melbourne, Melbourne University Press.

Senate Standing Committee on Education, Science and the Arts. Canberra, Commonwealth Government Printing Office. 4 June 1972.

Seymour-Ure, Colin (2001). *The British press and broadcasting since 1945 (second edition)*. Oxford, Blackwell Publishers Ltd.

Shiller, Robert (2000). *Irrational exuberance*. Princeton, Princeton University Press.

Simons, Margaret (2005). The underground news is a going concern. *The Sydney Morning Herald*. 5 Feb. p. 27. Downloaded 8 March 2006. http://global.factiva.com.ezproxy.library.usyd.edu.au/ha/default.aspx

— (1999). *Fit to print; inside the Canberra press gallery*. Sydney, University of New South Wales Press Ltd.

Simper, Errol (1996) Johns rules out rural quarantine. *The Australian*. 15 Aug.

Singer, Jane B., Tharp, Martha P., and Haruta, Amon (1999). Online staffers: superstars or second-class citizens? *Newspaper Research Journal*. 20(3) . Downloaded 3 April 2006. http://find.galegroup.com.ezproxy.library.usyd.edu.au/itx

Solomon, David (1985). Aunty's new show is promising but it must keep the faithful. *The Australian Financial Review*. 12 March.

Souter, Gavin (1981). *Company of heralds – a century and a half of publishing by John Fairfax Limited and its predecessors 1831-1981*. Melbourne, Melbourne University Press.

Standard & Poor's (May 2004). *Understanding indices*, www2.standardandpoors.com/ spf/pdf/index/A5_CMYK_UIndices.pdf

Starr, Martha A. (2004). Reading *The Economist* on globalisation: knowledge, identity , and power. *Global Society*, vol. 18, no. 4. Oct.

Stone, Gerald (2000). *Compulsive viewing - the inside story of Packer's Nine Network*. Ringwood, Viking.

Street Crowds For Opening Of ATN: Live Show Praised,. *The Sydney Morning Herald*, 3 Dec. 1956.

Street, John (2001). *Mass media, politics and democracy*. Houndmills, Palgrave.

Storm hits new TV. *The Daily Telegraph*, 3 Dec. 1956.

Sweney, Mark (2006). Internet ads close gap on press. *Guardian*. 29 March. Downloaded 30 March. http://media. guardian.co.uk/print/0,,329445144-105235,00.html

Sykes, Trevor (1996). *The bold riders*. St Leonards, Allen & Unwin.

— (2005). What a swell party it was. *The Australian Financial Review Magazine*, May.

Tabakoff, Jenny (2002). 'Testing the market'. *The Sydney Morning Herald The Guide*. 27 May.

Taylor, Lenore (1999). Believe it or not. *The Australian Financial Review*, 6 Nov.

Television Station ATN Channel 7 opened by PMG. *The Sydney Morning Herald*, 3 Dec. 1956.

Tewksbury, David (2005). The seeds of fragmentation: specialisation in the use of online news sites. *Journal of Broadcasting and Electronic Media*. Sept.

— (2003). What do American really want to know? Tracking the behaviour of news readers on the internet. *Journal of Communications*. 53(4).

The global significance of a row over drug prices in Australia (2004). *The Economist*.19 Aug.

Thomas, Sari (1992). Bad business? A re-examination of television's portrayal of businesspersons, *Journal of Communication*. 42(1).

Thornhill, John (2005). Internet study warns politicians on power of blogs. *Financial Times*. 13 July. Downloaded 14 July 2005.

Thousands plan to attend TV parties. *The Daily Telegraph*, 15 Sept. 1956.

Tiffen, Rod (2005). The aftermath. Must Labor Lose? in Browne, Peter, and Thomas, Julian (2005). *A win and a prayer – scenes from the 2004 Australian election*. Sydney, University of New South Wales Press.

— (2004). Under (spin) doctors orders. *The Age*. 21 Oct.

— (1994). in Brett, Judith, Gillespie, James and Goot, Murray (eds.) *Developments in Australian politics*. Melbourne, Macmillan Education Australia.

— (ed.) (1994). *Mayer on the media – issues and arguments*. St Leonards, Allen & Unwin.

— (1989). *News & power*. North Sydney, Allen & Unwin.

Tiger, Lionel (2001). in Collingwood, Harris and Kirby, Julia (eds.) All in a day's work. *Harvard Business Review*. December 2001.

Today's TV. *The Sydney Morning Herald*. 3 Dec. 1956.

Toohey, Brian (1994). *Tumbling Dice*, Port Melbourne, William Heinemann Australia.

— (1993). The entrepreneur as folk hero. Schultz, Julianne (ed.). *Reporting business*. Sydney, Australian Centre for Independent Journalism, University of Technology.

Torpy, Kathryn (2002). ABC gets up to business. *The Courier-Mail*. 10 July.

Tuchman, Gaye (1978). *Making news: a study in the construction of reality*. New York, Free Press.

Tulloch, John (2000). *Watching television audiences; cultural theories and methods*. London, Arnold.

Tumber, Howard (ed.) 2000. *Media power, professionals and policies*, London, Routledge.

— (1993). Selling scandal: business and the media, *Media, Culture & Society*. Vol. 15. Iss. 3.

Tunstall, J (1997). The media are American. London. Constable. in Appleton, Gillian (1988). How Australia sees itself: the role of commercial television. in *The price of being Australian*. North Sydney, Australian Broadcasting Tribunal.

Turner, Graeme (2005). *Ending the affair - the decline of television current affairs in Australia*. Sydney, University of New South Wales Press Ltd.

— (2002). Public relations, in Cunningham, Stuart, and Turner, Graeme, (eds.)*The media and communications in Australia*. Crows Nest, Allen & Unwin.

— (ed.) (1993). *Nation culture text – Australian cultural and media studies*. London, Routledge.

TV "takes to the air" tonight and other reports, *The Sunday Telegraph*, 16 Sept.1956.

TV Day, *The Daily Telegraph*, 16 Sept. 1956.

TVAM Seven means business. *The Bulletin*. 4 June 1988. Advertising supplement.

TViewers (sic) hail news telecasts, *Daily Telegraph*. 18 Sept. 1956.

UCLA Centre for Communication Policy. *Surveying The Digital Future – Year Three*. www.forbes.com/fdc/mediaresourcecentre/UCLA03.pdf

Uren, David and Korporaal, Glenda (2006). Rates drama a hit for RBA. *The Australian*. 17 Aug. p. 1.

van de Donk, Wim, Loader, Brian D., Nixon, Paul G., and Rucht, Dieter (eds.) (2004). *Cyberprotest – new media, citizens and social movements*. London, Routledge.

Van Heekeren, Margaret (2005). *What the web news reader wants*. Paper presented at the Annual Meeting of the Australian and New Zealand Communication Association, Christchurch, New Zealand, 4-7 July 2005. Downloaded 28 March 2006.

Views on the news. *The Sun-Herald television supplement*. 2 Dec. 1956.

Viewers want more TV news. *The Daily Telegraph*, 19 Sept. 1956.

Wade, Matt (2004). Labor means rate rise, PM claims. *The Sydney Morning Herald*. 30 Aug.

Ward, Ian (2003). *An Australian PR state?* Unpublished paper presented at the ANZCA03 conference in Brisbane.

— (1995). *Politics of the media*. South Melbourne, Macmillan.

Warhurst, John and Simms, Marian (eds.) (2002). *2001: The centenary election*. St Lucia, University of Queensland Press.

Waterford, Jack (2005). *The media report, ABC Radio*, 11 Aug.
http://www.abc.net.au/rn/talks/8.30/mediarept/stories/s1435225

Western J.S. and Hughes Colin A. (1971). *The mass media in Australia - use and evaluation*. St Lucia. University of Queensland Press.

Whale, John (1969). *The half-shut eye - television and politics in Britain and America*. London. Macmillan.

Where you can see TV. *The Daily Telegraph*, 15 Sept. 1956.

White, D.M. (1950). The gate keeper: a case study in the selection of news . *Journalism Quarterly*, 27(4), 383-390.

White, James D. (2005). *Global media: the television revolution in Asia*. New York, Routledge.

Whitington, R.S. (1971). *Sir Frank – the Frank Packer story*. North Melbourne, Cassell Australia Ltd.

Wide cover of manhunt. *RTN: Radio Television News*. 20 Nov.1959.

Williams, Graham (1986). The fiscal grind goes on … the ABC will bleed yet again. *The Australian Financial Review*. 17 June.

Williams, Pamela (1997). *The victory*. St Leonards, Allen & Unwin.

Windschuttle, Keith (1984). *The media – a new analysis of the press, television, radio and advertising in Australia*. Ringwood, Penguin Books Australia Ltd.

Women missing in media coverage (2005). Media Tenor Institute for Media Analysis. 28 April. www.mediatenor.com

Wright, Lea (1990). Back in business. *The Sydney Morning Herald The Guide*. 22 Jan.

Yaxley, Louise (2005). Costello says economic figures not 'totally consistent'. *ABC Radio, The World Today*. 2 March. http://www.abc.net.au/worldtoday/content/2005/s1314233.htm

Young, Sally (2004). *The persuaders; inside the hidden machine of political advertising*. North Melbourne, Pluto Press Australia.

Zawawi, Clara (2000). A history of public relations in Australia, in Johnston, Jane, and Zawawi, Clara. *Public relations; theory and practice*. Crows Nest, Allen & Unwin.

INTERVIEWS

Caton, Chris (2000). Chief Economist, BT Funds Management Australia. Former head of the Economic Division of the Department of Prime Minister and Cabinet. Personal interview 21 July.

Combet, Greg (2000). Secretary, ACTU. Personal interview 2 Oct.

Craik, Wendy (2000). Executive Director, National Farmers Federation. Personal interview 3 July.

Dyer, Glen (2000). Executive Producer, *Business Sunday*, Channel 9. Personal interview 27 July.

Edwards, John (2000). Chief Economist, HSBC. Senior Advisor (Economics) to Prime Minister Paul Keating, 1991-94. Personal interview 21 July.

Hook, Ted (2000). Director, Queensland branch, the Australian Shareholder's Association.

Kortlang, Ian (2000). Executive Vice Chairman, Gavin Anderson and Co. Former advisor and chief-of-staff to New South Wales Premier Nick Greiner. Personal interview 23 June.

Lasker, Philip (2000). Finance Reporter, News, ABC Television, Sydney. Personal interview 28 July.

Maher, Peter (2000). Managing Director, Rehame Australia. Personal interview 3 Aug.

Patterson, Mark (2000). Chief Executive, Australian Chamber of Commerce and Industry. Personal interview 16 June.

Roche, Michael (2000). National Manager, Strategic Planning and Review and Chief Economist, Australian Stock Exchange Ltd. Personal interview 16 June.

Ross, James (2000). Media Marketing Director, Bloomberg Asia-Pacific. Personal interview 12 June.

Sykes, Trevor (2000). Senior writer and Pierpont columnist, *The Australian Financial Review*. Personal interview 17 July.

Taylor, Elliot (2000). Editor, *Media*, *The Australian*. Personal interview 3 Aug.

Walsh, Max (2000). Editor-in-Chief, *The Bulletin*. Personal interview 18 July.

www.ingramcontent.com/pod-product-compliance
Lightning Source LLC
LaVergne TN
LVHW022302060326
832902LV00020B/3227